NUCLEAR PROLIFERATION
———— AND ————
THE FUTURE OF CONFLICT

NUCLEAR PROLIFERATION
—— AND ——
THE FUTURE OF CONFLICT

Martin van Creveld

THE FREE PRESS
A Division of Macmillan, Inc.
NEW YORK

Maxwell Macmillan Canada
TORONTO

Maxwell Macmillan International
NEW YORK   OXFORD   SINGAPORE   SYDNEY

The Free Press
A Division of Macmillan, Inc.
866 Third Avenue, New York, N. Y. 10022

Maxwell Macmillan Canada, Inc.
1200 Eglinton Avenue East
Suite 200
Don Mills, Ontario M3C 3N1

Macmillan, Inc. is part of the Maxwell Communication
Group of Companies.

Printed in the United States of America

printing number

1 2 3 4 5 6 7 8 9 10

Library of Congress Cataloging-in-Publication Data

Van Creveld, Martin L.
    Nuclear proliferation and the future of conflict / Martin van
Creveld.
        p.   cm.
    Includes bibliographical references and index.
    ISBN 0–02–933156–0
    1. Nuclear nonproliferation.   2. War (International law)
3. Military policy.   I. Title.
JX1974.73.V36   1993
355.02′17–dc20
                                                    93–212
                                                      CIP

CONTENTS

Introduction

THE LAST PROBLEM

Half a century after Hiroshima and Nagasaki, exhaustion as well as a prevailing sense of the pointlessness of it all has put an end to the nuclear competition among the superpowers. The Cold War has ended and disarmament is well on its way. On one side of the former Iron Curtain, the Russian–Soviet Empire, which took centuries to build, is no more; whatever "Commonwealth of Independent States" has taken its place is so afflicted by economic difficulties—and, in places, incipient civil war—that it has been forced to withdraw from its self-delegated historical mission of constituting "a Third Rome." The Warsaw Pact has ceased to exist, and the mighty "Red" armed forces, which during much of living memory seemed poised to overrun the northwestern European plain, have been (and still are being) cut back very sharply. They have lost many of their most advanced nuclear-weapons delivery vehicles, and much of their older equipment is being sold as scrap. As of the early nineties, they barely managed to maintain even a semblance of their former might.

On the other side of the hill, NATO too has lost its mission in life. American troops, once the mainstay of the Alliance, are being withdrawn from Europe, brought home, and demobilized by the tens of thousands. In every NATO country military men and women are casting a worried eye on their future careers, and with good reason. For example, the armed forces maintained by Germany after unification amount to only half of the combined size of the former Bundeswehr and Volksarmee. By 1994, the British Army will have cut its entire forces by one-quarter, and its combat units by half. From California to the British Midlands, tens of thousands of workers are being discharged, and the defense industries that used to supply the Western world with high-tech weapons dismantled. In the wake of these cataclysmic changes, the most important issues overshadowing strategic thought for decades have suddenly been rendered irrelevant. This applies with particular force to concerns about the "central balance" between the superpowers; and the endless discussions, both "real" and imaginary, of the wars that could break out between them.

Though the easing of West–East tensions in Europe and elsewhere makes the world's continued existence appear more secure than ever, this does not in itself mean that war—even large-scale war—may no longer break out in other parts of the globe. It has even been suggested that the end of bipolarity, and the consequent relaxation of superpower control over their former clients, will lead to an increase in the number of such wars; nor is there any lack of dormant interstate conflicts which only wait to be ignited by some provocative incident. Indeed, there is a potential for armed conflict between Libya and Chad, Ethiopia and Somalia, Hungary and Romania, Turkey and Syria, Turkey and Iraq, and Iran and Saudi Arabia, to name but a few.[1]

Some of these countries, particularly in East and South Asia (as well as the Middle East), have built up fairly strong conventional armed forces, and could fight one other on a considerable scale. Nevertheless, following the collapse of one superpower and the consequent radical shift in the position of the survivor, any wars that might break out between them no longer possess their former potential for intervention, expansion, and escalation on a global scale. In most cases, should the governments of some third-rate military powers still choose to fight each other, then, strategically speaking, there is not much reason for the inhabitants of the First World to worry.

The one exception to this rule, the one factor which may still bring about not just war but Armageddon, is the possession of weapons of mass destruction—in particular, nuclear weapons—by states whose conflicts have been left unresolved. For example, but for the availability to both sides of nuclear weapons, the outbreak of another war between India and Pakistan would scarcely matter to anybody outside the region; however bloody it might be, such a conflict could well be dismissed as a simple clash between two desperately poor local powers over some remote border province that both claim belongs to them. Much the same applies to the Persian Gulf region. The war between Iran and Iraq was the largest since

Korea, whereas Operation Desert Storm was the most modern in history; yet in retrospect all they have proved is that, so long as nuclear weapons were not used, there was not much need for people outside the Middle East to lose their sleep, or even to worry about the price of oil.

Put nuclear weapons into the hands of any of those countries, however, and things change dramatically. Under such circumstances, the prospect of another round of fighting breaking out between them acquires fearsome, even apocalyptic, overtones. Admittedly, escalation would not necessarily be automatic. One or two tactical nuclear devices exploding in the eastern Jordanian desert as part of an Israeli attempt to block the advance of (a presumably nonnuclear) Iraq toward the Jordan would not mean the end of the world; given the nature of the country, there would be hardly any civilian casualties and, assuming that the device was used to block the road rather than destroy the advancing column, few military ones, either. Still, even if it could be contained, and in the absence of a response in kind, the least that such an event would mean probably would be the breaking of an important taboo. As Clausewitz, the Prussian General who is considered the greatest military thinker of all time, says, barriers once pulled down are not easily restored. To this extent, it would represent an ominous step toward global destruction, and one from which others might well follow.

What is true in the case of Israel and Iraq also applies to the use of nuclear weapons in any "eventual" conflict between South and North Korea, China and Taiwan, China and India, India and Pakistan; or any other couple of regional powers, however unimportant, underdeveloped, and poor they might be in other ways. Many of these states either already have nuclear weapons, or else should be capable of acquiring them in the not-too-remote future. Others are currently building the scientific, technological, and industrial infrastructures that will enable their governments to develop them if they should make up their minds to do so. The prospect of any two of them fighting each other *after* having acquired such weapons (even if only one side should have them) is fearsome indeed. Yet, strangely enough, this possibility is not even mentioned in much of the literature purporting to set out the military balance between such countries.[2]

Viewed in this way, the effect of nuclear proliferation from the "old" nuclear powers to other countries does indeed appear as the last critical problem remaining for strategic studies to analyze.[3] Why did those countries decide to acquire nuclear weapons, and how did they go about it? How do their rulers perceive them, and to what extent can their views be considered rational? Do regional powers treat nuclear weapons in the same way as the superpowers, or are they influenced by some ethnic considerations peculiar to their respective cultures? Will possession of nuclear weapons make them more inclined toward adventurism and war, or will it force them to become more cautious in their dealings with each other? Will they follow the superpowers in taking steps in the direction of eventual stabilization and arms control? And, if so, would this mean that large-scale warfare will become extinct between nuclear countries in the developing world in the same way as has already happened in the developed one? Or will the fear of nuclear weapons merely lead to the rise of *new* forms of armed conflict?

In attempting to answer these questions, and particularly the last one, this book will begin by reviewing the essential characteristics of large-scale warfare as it developed *before* the introduction of nuclear weapons. Next, it will examine the things that those weapons did to the largest war-fighting entities (the superpowers), their politico–military strategies, and the relations among them. Further, it will consider the effect of nuclear weapons on the principal developing countries that either possess them or are faced by them: This discussion is arranged geographically, focusing first on East and South Asia and then on the Middle East. Finally, an attempt will be made to assess the impact of nuclear proliferation on the future of war itself.

The sources used in preparing this work can be broadly categorized. First, extensive use has been made of published works on military history, on strategy, and on the Cold War. Second, there are numerous but little-known academic and semiacademic studies of nuclear weapons prepared in countries which own them (mainly India, Pakistan, and Israel). Third, there is a large body of printed discussions in Arabic which, given the shortage of trained Arabists, apparently are not readily available even to intelligence analysts, and which are here presented for the first time. Drawing on these sources, I have tried to present a picture of the effects of nuclear proliferation on war, both present and future. Whether that picture is indeed a reasonable one remains for the reader to decide.

NUCLEAR PROLIFERATION

——— AND ———

THE FUTURE OF CONFLICT

Chapter I

BEFORE NUCLEAR WEAPONS

What has been the impact of nuclear weapons on modern war, and where are they taking us? Did the bombing of Hiroshima on the sixth of August 1945 represent a rung in history's ladder, or is it better understood as a hairpin bend on the road to the future? Are we going forward to larger and more sophisticated war-making entities, or backward to smaller and more primitive ones? An answer to these questions cannot be discovered unless we first of all retrace our steps. It is necessary to find out how the state, the preeminent war-making organization during the period 1648–1945, differed from previous political entities, developed from them, and—fighting off contenders—acquired its monopoly over armed conflict. Next, it is necessary to investigate the nature of the military organization that the state created in order to exercise that monopoly. Finally strategy, the method by which those armed forces wage war, must be discussed.

WAR AND THE STATE

We are accustomed to identifying war with the state. The state, for its part, might be defined as the only organization that, in the modern world, possesses the legal *right* to resort to organized violence or, in other words, war.[1] So firmly established is this right of the modern state that armed conflicts which do not originate as state policy—in point of fact, the great majority—are commonly denied the name of war, properly speaking. Instead an adjective is added, as in *civil* war, *internecine* war, *low-intensity* war, *people's* war, and *revolutionary* war; or else a different, often derogatory, term is used, such as rioting, insurrection, guerrilla activity, terrorism, disturbance, banditry, "troubles" (the British euphemism for bomb-

1

ings and shootings carried out by the Irish Republican Army), or crime.

In fact, whereas armed conflict between organized peoples has existed for all time, the state is a comparatively recent invention. During most of human history, and in many places well into the present century, the predominant form of human social organization was the clan, tribe, or horde. In such societies "politics" in the sense of a field of activity clearly distinct from anything else and concerned solely with government was unknown. The basis of authority consisted either of kinship ties or of magico–religious beliefs. In the first case it rested in the hands of elders, in the second in that of priests; frequently there was some combination of the two. Often these groups had little idea of government, let alone of the state as we now understand that term.

These societies had no man-made law which bound humans alone, but only custom, which they had received from their allegedly supernatural ancestors and which linked them with the physical world around them. They had neither legislative nor executive nor judicial institutions, nor the body of thought or technique of writing on which such could have been based. And yet, for millennia on end, they managed to engage in organized violence against each other.[2] Nor should their war-making abilities be underestimated: From time to time, a great leader would emerge and forge some of these tribes into coalitions, transforming them into formidable fighting machines almost overnight. From the ancient Hyksos' overrunning of Egypt to Attila's campaigns against Rome to Genghis Khan's occupation of China, they proved themselves more than a match for some of the mightiest empires that the world has ever seen.

In contrast to tribal societies, the ancient empires that grew up in such centers as Egypt and Mesopotamia from 3,000 B.C. on did have institutionalized governments, in the sense of bureaucratic structures operating under a king. Yet they, too, were not states: According to the great German sociologist Max Weber, they are best described as "patrimonial" organizations.[3] In them, rulers stood to the ruled as parents to children who have no legal existence separate from that of their elders and who, accordingly, cannot own any property except that which they hold by the King's permission. In the absence of any idea of an abstract entity uniting ruler and ruled, it was not Assyria, or Babylon, or Egypt, which conducted policy, concluded alliances, or made war; rather, this was done by their respective rulers acting in nobody's name but their own.

Since the concept of the state was then in fact unknown, neither the Greek nor the Latin of those times have words corresponding to it. The closest equivalents, *koinon* and *res publica,* are best translated as "the assembly of people" or "that which is common." [4] The organizations that these words described differed from the essential state in that they did not have a legal existence separate from the people who constituted them. For example, Athenian citizens could (and frequently did) bring lawsuits against their magistrates. However, for them to do the same with regard to the *polis* would be not only impossible but meaningless. Nevertheless, it goes without saying that classical city-states and ancient empires alike not only waged war, but often did so with an artistry, and on a scale, which still command our admiration.

In the feudal Middle Ages we encounter a society whose *raison d'être* was based upon—even dedicated to—warfare;[5] yet again we find that the state as a war-making organization was unknown. The Latin term *status,* whose original meaning was simply "situation," was slowly coming to be used to signify "estate" in the sense of the three estates, or classes into which society was divided. In the fifteenth century it could also mean something like "organization" or "welfare."[6] However, it was the essence of feudal society that it did *not* consist of a series of disparate polities, each of them sovereign in regard to its internal affairs and responsible to none above itself. Instead, it conceived of itself as an organic pyramid consisting of reciprocal rights and obligations. Instituted by Heaven, custom, or both, these formed a legal network linking lord to vassal, nobleman to commoner, and baron to serf.[7]

Within this structure, war was conceived as a class prerogative. The upper classes regarded violence employed by the lower classes against them, or *vice versa,* as rebellion or "chastisement" respectively; in case commoners fought each other, it was often treated as burlesque. When members of the upper classes fought each other, as they frequently did, they did so in the name not of "politics" or "interest"—the very terms had yet to be invented—but in that of their respective rights to castles, fiefs, or heiresses. Under such circumstances war was a private matter; or perhaps it would be more correct to say that the distinction between "public" and "private" that underpins our modern concept of the state did not yet exist in the same form.

The centuries between 1450 and 1648 are often described as the formative period of states.[8] However, that fact may be more obvious in retrospect than it was to contemporaries. As might be expected from so fundamental a process, the transition from the medieval political–social–economic–cultural order to the modern one was marked by widespread disorder, confusion, and violence. At the heart of the transformation was the nobility's loss of its former monopoly over *legal* violence. Coming from below, the right to make war was usurped by every kind of nonaristocratic contractor; people who, working either with their own capital or that which they could borrow, raised private armies and used them to turn a profit for themselves and for whoever hired their services. And from the top, rulers such as the Emperor and the Kings of Spain, France, and England, who previously had been merely great nobles themselves, sought to deny their vassals' right to wage war except on their (the monarchs') behalf. Thus the feudal nobility found its military prerogatives squeezed from *both* directions. Thus on several occasions the nobility rose up in armed rebellion—sometimes with success, as in Poland, but usually without.

Adding to the confusion, the old religious unity came to an end. Where before the Reformation there had been a single dominant religion (Catholicism), now there were at least three faiths, all quite prepared to use violence in order to demonstrate that the Son of God's flesh and blood could be turned into bread and wine respectively, or the other way around. These clashes soon became mixed up with the depredations of military entrepreneurs and the rebellions of discontented noblemen, to say nothing of mutinous armies and the efforts of communities everywhere to defend themselves against the excesses committed by all three. The ensuing multicornered conflicts plunged entire countries into civil war; indeed, this was what happened to England during the fifteenth century, and to France, Germany, and the Netherlands in the sixteenth. The process culminated in the confusion of the Thirty Years' War, which lasted from 1618 until 1648. In this pan-European free-for-all, everybody took turns fighting everybody else until one-third of Germany's population is said to have perished.

In the long run, nevertheless, the victors from the struggle were the great monarchs. Either they drew on treasures from the New

World, or they allied themselves with the emerging urban bourgeoisie, or they took advantage of the Reformation in order to confiscate Church property. Using such means, gradually they were able to acquire greater financial resources than anybody else. With these resources, they purchased more cannon and blasted their opponents' levies off the field. The English monarchy asserted its authority under Henry VII (1485–1509). Spain became a united country when Ferdinand V of Aragon married Isabella of Castile in 1479. By the 1620s the French chief minister, Cardinal Armand de Richelieu, was setting the pace. Employing the most varied pretexts, he had the castles of the nobility demolished one by one, thus destroying the basis of its military power and establishing the king's monopoly over the conduct of war once and for all.

The process of centralization was continued by Richelieu's successor, Cardinal Mazarin, and had been substantially completed by the time Louis XIV ascended the throne in 1660. The proud noblemen who, during his youth, had formed the *Fronde* and gone to war to restore their ancient privileges against the King's appointees, were compelled to leave their estates for Versailles. Once there, they were made to wear stockings and wigs, not swords and armor, and found themselves reduced to competing among themselves to see who would hold the King's chamber pot. The example set by the *roi soleil* was not lost abroad—particularly in Germany, where each leading prince sought to increase his powers by similar means.

Its victory over the nobility complete, the state was able to establish its war-making monopoly *vis-à-vis* other organizations remaining from previous periods, such as free city-states and petty principalities. Though they continued to exist until the eighteenth century and beyond, particularly in Germany and Italy, henceforward their principal role in international relations was as pawns in the hands of their more powerful neighbors. The military entrepreneurs, who as late as the Thirty Years' War had often operated almost independent of public authority, disappeared. Either they were destroyed by royal power—as was the fate of the greatest of them all, Albrecht von Wallenstein—or else they were absorbed by it; and so were the armed forces at their command.

Simultaneous with its triumph over particularism, the state fought to head off organizations with pretensions to universal power. The chiefs of those organizations, such as the Emperor and the Pope, had been in almost continuous decline since the second half of the fourteenth century. After 1648 they ceased to exercise politico–military power except insofar as they also presided over territorial states—Austria in the one case, central Italy in the other. Religion disappeared from foreign affairs. Not only was the Treaty of Westphalia the first in which neither God nor the medieval *Respublica Christiana* were so much as mentioned, but it was also the first to be signed exclusively by governments each of which represented a territorial state.

The rise of the great monarchies was accompanied by that of political theory. Separating itself from law for the first time,[9] the purpose of theory was to explain the nature of the new states and, above all, to justify their monopoly over violence. The first great thinker in this context was a Frenchman and a Calvinist, Jean Bodin. His monumental work *Six livres sur la république* (1576) was very much a reflection of the Wars of Religion (fought between the Huguenots and their opponents) through which he lived and under which he suffered. The term "sovereignty" owes its popularity to Bodin; he used it do denote a public authority (i.e., different from that of feudal lord or *paterfamilias*). In contrast to the old feudal lords, that authority—the King—admitted to no superior above itself, and no outside interference in its affairs. The King was to operate under the heading of *politique,* a term by which Bodin meant the opposite of *fanatique.* Employing armed force if necessary, his task was to protect the lives (and, almost as important, the property) of all Frenchmen, regardless of religion, against the depredations of particularist noblemen on the one hand and the universal claims of Pope and Emperor on the other.[10]

Second only to Bodin in formulating the theory of the modern state was a Dutchman, Justus Lipsius, who likewise owed his inspiration to the suffering caused by civil war. Lipsius developed Bodin's thought in that, for the first time since the fall of Rome, right (*ius*) and law (*lex*) came to be clearly separated from each other. Right, in the old medieval sense of a privilege inherent to certain people, or groups, or things, was abolished; henceforward *ius* only existed by virtue of the *lex* specifically enacted to create it. *Lex* itself was defined as a distinct, more-or-less fixed, man-made, explicit, and written body of rules by which the community ought to be governed. Lipsius, who was personally very subservient to authority—in this case that of Philip II of Spain—did not go so far as saying that the ruler was subject to the law, and in any case he agreed with Bodin that it was the ruler who made the law. However, his ideas did lead to the conclusion, subsequently adopted by generations of late seventeenth- and eighteenth-century monarchs who were brought up on his work, that the ruler's most important task was to apply the law; and that, in doing so, it was not he who owned the state, but the other way around.[11]

Finally, the threads of theory were woven together by Thomas Hobbes, another figure who was motivated in large part by his experiences during and after the English Civil War (1640–1648) when his property was confiscated and he was forced into exile. Hobbes' *Leviathan* was perhaps the most important work on politics written in modern times, the first to concern itself with the state as such rather than with the attributes which its government ought to have, or the way in which it ought to exercise its functions. While following Bodin with regard to sovereignty, *Leviathan* took the critical step of establishing the state as an abstract entity with an independent legal personality; in other words, an organization separate from both rulers and ruled, but incorporating both. Thus constituted, its task was to suppress the squabbles of its citizens, monopolize violence in its own hands, and guarantee the kind of law and order under which alone civilization could flourish.[12]

With the publication of Hobbes' work in 1651, the theoretical structure of the modern state as the only organization which, in the modern world, is *entitled* to use violence for its ends was substantially complete. Such eighteenth-century writers as John Locke, Charles de Montesquieu, David Hume, and Jeremy Bentham elaborated on his work. They investigated the sources from which the state drew its authority, gradually moving away from divine sanction and coming to put more and more emphasis on the consent of the governed. They explored its rights and duties with respect to its citizens (and *vice versa*), and disputed the best way in which it ought to be governed. Meanwhile, the remaining premodern, feudal restrictions on state power were removed. Sometimes this was done by a change of government (England's "Glorious Revolution," 1688); or by administrative fiat (Austria under Maria Theresa from 1748 on); or by a slow, imperceptible process culminating in a violent explosion (France, 1789). Without exception the result was a tremendous expansion in the state's powers, including specifically its ability to wage war—to the point that, after about 1750, the large-scale use of troops for internal purposes was seldom necessary any longer.

With the notable exception of Jean Jacques Rousseau, most Enlightenment thinkers had been content to follow Hobbes, in that they started with the individual, passed to society, and ended with the state as the means to regulate that society and those individuals. This, however, was not the case for Georg Friedrich Hegel early in the nineteenth century. His was a period when the Napoleonic Wars were at their height. The reaction against French conquests caused a wave of nationalism to sweep over Europe. Hegel's contribution was to provide a philosophical justification for this nationalism by standing previous thought on its head: According to him, it was not "civil society" and the individuals comprising it that created the state by investing it with sovereignty, but the sovereign state that created "civil society" and, ultimately, the individual. He deliberately set out to transform the state from a mere military and administrative apparatus into an ideal (or, to use his own inimitable language, the "earthly manifestation of the divine idea"). Supposedly, whatever goes beyond the ordinary, day-to-day, commercial existence of society—everything good, wonderful, and sublime it contains—is personified by the state. The state endows the individual's life with meaning, which in turn is why it is entitled to demand his ultimate loyalty, even unto death. War is the most important element in the state's struggle for life—the alternative, according to Hegel, being stagnation and death.[13]

Compared to the original idea, however, even Hegel's grandiose construction was a mere refinement. Regardless of the way they wanted to see its functions regulated, and regardless also of the ethical significance that, increasingly, they came to attach to it, for two centuries after Hobbes no really important author doubted that the state was the principal organization into which civilized humanity was, ought to be, and would continue to be divided; and it was during this period that the concept, originally confined to Western Europe, began to spread beyond the latter's borders to places such as Russia, North America, and Australasia. Only toward the middle of the nineteenth century did there appear a first-class political theorist who objected to the idea of the state as such. Where his predecessors from Montesquieu on had interpreted history as a clash between states, Karl Marx saw it as a struggle between socio-economic classes. Where they had regarded it as a prerequisite for civilized life, he saw it merely as an instrument by which the members of the upper classes sought to oppress their inferiors. Where they had wanted to perfect the state by changing its government, he sought its destruction—considering this a *conditio sine qua non* for man's emancipation from the chains by which, throughout history, he had been bound.[14]

Seen in retrospect, it could be argued that Marx's underestimate of the state's ability to harness people to its ends was the greatest single error he committed. Instead of being forcibly overturned and then withering away, as predicted, states started marching from strength to strength.[15] During the second half of the nineteenth century the living standards of the urban proletariat, while still low, started to rise. Partly for this reason, partly because most West European regimes now incorporated at least a limited form of popular franchise, the revolutionary upheavals that had punctuated the period before 1848 died away. The newly emerging technologies— the railways, the telegraph, and the rotary press—for the first time enabled states to exercise effective control over their entire territories and populations. Efficient, professional police organizations began to be organized from the 1830s on. Thanks in part to the fact that modern capitalist society consists of isolated individuals rather than of groups, clans, or tribes, gradually they were able to impose a degree of internal law and order undreamed of by previous generations. All of this reinforced its ability to wage external war.

The size of the administrative machines at the state's disposal, to say nothing of the share of Gross National Product (GNP) that they commandeered in order to support those machines, grew by leaps and bounds—a process nowhere more evident than in the Communist states that, from 1917 on, claimed to implement "Marxist" doctrines. Partly pushed by military considerations, the state began to expand its functions beyond anything foreseen by the original theorists. A point in case is provided by Otto von Bismarck. Himself an archetypical Junker, Bismarck worried lest the workers now entering the Army in large numbers might refuse to fight for Kaiser and Fatherland. Aiming to steal the Socialists' thunder, his "Revolution from above" instituted such welfare reforms as sickness-and-unemployment insurance, as well as old-age pensions. Shortly after 1900, similar reasoning contributed to the passing of similar measures in Britain and France. Even in the U.S., the idea that government should be as minimalist as possible began to be undermined during the "Imperial" era under Theodore Roosevelt, and was stone dead after 1929. Meanwhile the state, taking over from the Church and all kinds of voluntary organizations, had assumed ultimate responsibility for the population's health, education, and general welfare.

In many ways, the climax of these developments was reached between 1914 and 1945. For fully thirty years, by far the most important purpose to which states used their newly found muscles was to fight one another on an unprecedented scale and with unprecedented ferocity. The state's growing internal strength was used to underpin its ability to mobilize resources and wage war. The more intensive the war effort, the greater the state's ability to interfere with the lives of its subjects, and the greater also those subjects' willingness to tolerate its doing so. Not just men, but women and children, were mobilized. To maximize their war-making potential, the state pronounced laws that regulated their health, income, professional qualifications, consumption of raw materials, and calory intake (and—in Britain—the number of inches of hot water that they might put in a tub while preparing a bath). At peak, as much as 60 percent of GNP was taken away from "civil society" and used to fuel the war effort, leaving the population to live in half-ruined dwellings, wear second-hand clothes, and consume insufficient food that made them vulnerable to disease. The most important states put as many as 10 percent of their populations into uniform, and kept them there for years on end. As they did so, it was discovered—not entirely without surprise—that millions of people who perhaps ought to have known better were willing, often seemingly even eager, to let themselves be killed on their rulers' behalf.[16]

Thus, 1648 marked the beginning of a 300-year period in which the dominant form of organization under whose banners people went to war and were *supposed* to go to war was the state. As defined by Hobbes, the man who in many ways was its true father, the state is a sovereign entity which *creates* the law and, accordingly, admits no legal restrictions except those entered upon by its own free will. Equally important, the modern state is a corporation. The difference between it and all previous political organizations consists precisely in that, unlike them, it is an abstract entity possessing an independent legal personality. It is not identical with either rulers or ruled; instead, it comprises them both and is supposed to benefit them both.

The state's monopoly over the legal use of armed violence, and subsequently its awesome war-making capacities, were the result of a prolonged development. Older contenders—such as the feudal nobility, free cities, religious communities, and international "political" entities—had to be fought and defeated. Next, social and technological developments resulted in an unprecedented degree of internal law and order, making it possible to free resources and mobilize them for external war. Rising hand-in-hand with these changes was political theory which, explicitly starting from the need to monopolize armed violence in the hands of the state, ended up by glorifying it as the highest good and the one most worth dying for. Education, propaganda, and welfare were used to reinforce that idea. Finally, from Europe and the European colonies the state started spreading in all directions. The result has been that, since 1945 at any rate, it has become the highest aspiration of every people on earth to have a state of their own and to see its flag flying alongside those of others like it.

THE ORGANIZATION OF VIOLENCE

The quintessential characteristic of the state is the monopoly it exercises—or claims to exercise—over legal violence (also known as war). Its rise to dominance over other types of organization that either preceded it or existed side by side with it would have been inconceivable without this monopoly. However, the state was defined as a corporation, an abstract legal entity. As such it could not engage in the practical business of waging war, but instead required a concrete instrument to do so on its behalf. From the mid–seventeenth century to the end of World War II and the introduction of nuclear weapons, that instrument was the standing army or, to be precise, the army *tout court*.

Just as the state is an invention of the modern age, so armies in the sense of disparate, permanent, legally established organizations charged with the exercise of organized violence on its behalf represent a historical innovation. True, one may find some parallels in the Hellenistic and Roman Empires;[17] nevertheless, most societies before 1600 or so did not have armies in our sense of the word. Sometimes society itself constituted the army. Such was the case in primitive tribes on every continent, and also in ancient city-states like Athens, Sparta, Republican Rome, and innumerable others. Alternatively the right and duty to make war was reserved for the members of a certain class, as in feudal societies in Europe, Japan, Mamluk Egypt, and elsewhere.

The first type of organization meant that there was no distinction between adult males on the one hand and warriors on the other— even to the point that in many languages the same word was used to describe the two.[18] The second meant that feudal levies did not exist as separate organizations, but rather comprised the members of the upper class, who, receiving their lord's call, abandoned their day-to-day occupations and put themselves on a war footing in order to fulfill their obligations. Since neither type of force consisted of full-time soldiers, they had in common that they came into being only in times of war, and dissolved themselves as soon as it was over. Also, given their social structure, they were incapable of being used as an "instrument" in the hands of anyone except themselves.

By the middle of the fourteenth century, ruling princes in Europe sometimes permitted feudal military service to be commuted for money payment known as *scutagium* (in France, this was the origin of the infamous tax known as *taille*). The sums thus raised could be used to engage mercenaries, or in other words to set up the kind of force that, while still subject to dismissal at the end of the war, would act as an instrument in the hands of him who paid its wages for as long as they were paid. Lacking any loyalty to an abstract entity (such as barely existed in any case), mercenary armies differed from those of the most advanced present-day states in that they could be used, and were designed to be used, for both internal and external purposes. Accordingly, they often included foreigners in their number; and indeed, if the idea was to use them to hold a prince's own subjects in check, foreigners without local ties were considered preferable. In this way the rise of mercenary armies rapidly led to the internationalization of warfare. Serving under their own commanders, entire units consisted of nonnationals, and were liable to switch their allegiance as the fortunes of war and/or their masters' ability to pay, dictated.[19]

Already, in the middle of the fifteenth century, there was a tendency—first manifested in France under Charles VII—to retain at least some of the mercenaries between one war and the next. During the second half of the sixteenth century the most important European armies (those fielded by the Spanish, French, and Imperial monarchies in particular) came to include a standing core, although its relative unimportance can be judged from the fact that Lipsius, in 1598, considered that two "legions" (with a total of 13,200 regulars) were sufficient for the needs of a "large" state, such as France or Spain.[20] As late as the time of the Thirty Years' War, the great majority of the forces of every prince were mercenaries, and indeed the longer any given conflict, the more true this became. These forces were possessed of no particular loyalty toward the population, and fought solely for gain. Their commanders were independent entrepreneurs who, left to their own devices, would cheat their employers by squandering his money as well as engaging in every kind of depredation.

To impose some kind of control over these entrepreneurs, princes such as France's Louis XIII and Prussia's Frederick Wilhelm (the "Great Elector") began to appoint itinerant officials known as inspectors or commissioners. Their task was to regulate, provide for, and review the troops in order to make sure that their masters' money was in fact spent on the army rather than privately pocketed. There was thus created the nucleus of a new type of bureaucracy which, as it grew, assumed some of the rulers' functions, took on a life of its own, and helped contribute to the war-making power of the state that it served.[21]

Though the pace at which mercenary forces were brought under direct royal control varied from one country to the next, by the first quarter of the eighteenth century the process was substantially complete. From Spain to Muscovy, "private war" had become a contradiction in terms. The military nobility was disarmed and drawn into the service of the state. The old medieval militias were either allowed to languish, or else abolished by administrative fiat (in Prussia, the very use of the word for "militia" was prohibited). Every sovereign now had at his disposal a standing army—*militum perpetuum*—of paid professionals whose function was to wage war, and who tended to monopolize its conduct in their own hands. When armor was discarded and uniforms introduced after 1660, the separation between the armed forces and the rest of society was accentuated. Uniforms served less to help combatants distinguish one another, as is commonly supposed, than to mark those who were licensed to engage in legal violence from those who were not.

Uniforms were accompanied by the introduction of a separate military code of law in the form of the articles of war; separate military customs in the form of drill, the salute, and (for officers) the duel; and separate military dormitories in the form of "modern" barracks—which were first built in the 1740s. All of these promoted, as they were intended to promote, the process by which war ceased to be the business of society as a whole but was rather concentrated in the hands of a specialized organization. The process culminated in the establishment of separate domestic police forces, which got underway during the last decades before 1800. Once these forces took over responsibility for maintaining day-to-day law and order, the standing armies were free to focus on their military functions exclusively.[22]

Another aspect of the process whereby the conduct of war was monopolized by state-run armies was the separation of military commanders from rulers and government officials. This, too, was a novel development without precedent in history. Tribal societies were governed—to the extent that they were governed at all—by the same chiefs in both peace *and* war. As their titles prove, in classical Greece and Republican Rome the most important magistrates originally were military commanders; with the result that civil and military authority was known by the same name (in Rome, this was *imperium*) and was wielded by the same people. Hellenistic monarchs, following the precedent set by their Oriental predecessors, commanded their own armies as a matter of course. The same was true of the Roman Emperor, and indeed it should not be forgotten that he was *Imperator,* or victorious commander, before he was anything else. Nor did our present-day separation between military and civilian power exist during the Middle Ages and the Renaissance. From the Emperor down, medieval princes of all ranks were themselves knights, or *milites*. They took to the field as a matter of course, led their own armies on campaign, and unless prevented by incapacity or age (sometimes even if they *were* prevented, as in the case of blind King John of Bohemia) fought in person. Consequently it was quite normal for them to be killed, wounded, or taken prisoner: As late as the first half of the sixteenth century, a ruler who refused to command in battle risked contempt and loss of his authority.[23]

The turning point in this, as in so many other thing pertaining to war and the state, came during the second half of the sixteenth century. Emperor Charles V, who reigned from 1520 until his resignation in 1556, commanded his armies in person. Lacking a permanent capital, he spent much of his life traveling from one campaign to the next: He fought now in Italy and the Low countries against France; now in North Africa against the Ottomans; now in Germany against the Protestant Princes; now in what are today Hungary and Croatia—against the Turks again. So closely associated were he and his Army that on several occasions he challenged Francis I of France to a duel in order "to save the blood of Christian people," as the saying went. Not to be outdone, Francis commanded his own Army at the Battle of Pavia in 1525, was taken prisoner, and had to pay a gigantic ransom to secure his release.

By contrast, Charles' son, Philip II (also known as *el rey prudente*), declined to follow his father's example. Instead he settled in Madrid, near which he had a new palace, the Escorial, built to accommodate himself, his aides, the state papers (which hitherto were hauled from place to place in sealed trunks), and the pictures that he liked to collect. Like a spider in his web—a contemporary description, to be sure—he relied on bureaucratic methods to keep an eye on his commanders in places as far apart as southern and northern Italy, Burgundy, the Netherlands, the New World, and the Philippines.

As the business of government continued to expand during the next two centuries, one by one the monarchs were forced to abandon their old nomadic habits and become sedentary. In most cases they ceased to accompany their armies in the field; alternatively they played a ceremonial role, as did Louis XIV—who liked to make a dramatic appearance at the end of a siege and preside over one of those *belles capitulations* that his ministers, Louvois and Vauban, had prepared for him. By the time of the Seven Years' War (1756–63), Frederick II was the only reigning monarch to command in person. By contrast, his principal opponents (admittedly two of them were women and the third a notorious *bon vivant*) preferred safety to activity, and so remained ensconced in their palaces at Vienna, Saint Petersburg, and Paris, respectively. Though all three Emperors who were present at Austerlitz in 1805 wore uniforms, only one (Napoleon) exercised *de facto* command. The other two (Austria's Francis and Russia's Alexander) contributed to the outcome mainly by placing obstacles in front of their own subordinates. By the time of Waterloo, a mere ten years later, the lesson had been learned: No Allied sovereigns were at hand to interfere with either Wellington or Bluecher. Rulers who operated as both head of state and head of the Army had become an endangered species; after 1870, they were virtually extinct.

Starting with the rulers, the process whereby government and military command were becoming separate expanded downward through the state hierarchy. One of the results of creating standing armies was that functions which, until then, had been carried out intermittently were necessarily put on a permanent basis. By the second half of the seventeenth century, most states were building their commissioners into a rudimentary ministry of war, headed by a Minister of War.[24] The ministry consisted of a body of officials who, though they might wear uniforms, were clearly separate from the Army. Their function was not to fight but to oversee the process of recruiting, clothing, equipping, housing, supplying, and paying the troops. As time went on they also began to look after problems such as officer schools (an early eighteenth-century development), pensions for ex-servicemen, orphanages, institutions to house the invalids, arms procurement, and so forth. Early in the nineteenth century the task of administering occupied territories in the armies' rear was added to their functions.[25] Again, the establishment of these ministries had a double effect. While freeing the armed forces to wage war, at the same time they constituted another step in the process whereby those forces were becoming separate from the institution of government on the one hand, and from the civilian population on the other.

The development of international law, as distinct from the earlier code of chivalry, both reflected these changes and promoted them. Writing during the Thirty Years' War, Hugo Grotius was the first to abandon the "Just War" tradition and to define war simply as a quarrel waged by sovereign princes with the aid of their armies. By the time of Emmerich de Vattel, whose classic work *Law of Nations* dates to the 1750s, the emphasis had changed from princes to states. A sharp distinction was drawn between war—the only legitimate form of organized violence—and all the rest. It was defined as something directed by governments, waged by armies, and paid for by civilians. Each of these three groups had its own rights and obligations in respect to *ius in bello*, being expected to stick to certain rules of behavior and be awarded certain privileges in return. The threefold division applied to all states regardless of regime; Clausewitz in *On War* regarded it as the indispensable foundation on which any theory on the subject must build.[26] Later, during the nineteenth century, the "trinity" of government, army, and civilian population came to be seen as one of the characteristics of progress in general. It had to be adopted by any non-European country aspiring to so-called "civilized" status. Those peoples as did not adopt it were considered fair game for the maxim guns of their European conquerors.[27]

The coming of the French Revolution in 1789 was both to change the methods by which armies were raised, and to widen the social base from which they were recruited. From this point on, wars were supposed to be waged on behalf of the entire people, rather than merely at their expense, thereby permitting a very great expansion of the scale on which they were waged, as well as of the energy with which they were waged. Still, the advent of general conscription did not in itself disturb the way that government, army, and civilians divided the business of war among themselves. Napoleon habitually stripped captured cities of their artistic treasures. His armies lived by requisitioning, and he would sometimes turn a blind eye when his men helped themselves to the civilian populations' possessions. Still, at any rate there was no question of massacring those populations, enslaving them, or driving them from their homes. He could hate with the best, yet with the single exception of the Duke of Enghien (a Bourbon prince whom he had kidnapped and executed) there was no evidence that Napoleon tried either to murder individual opponents, or to wage war *ad hominem*. Both the *Grande Armée* and its enemies usually respected existing international law regarding rights of noncombatants, prisoners, the wounded, flags of truce, and *ruses de guerre*. From 1793 to 1815 the major campaigns (at any rate) remained firmly within the trinitarian tradition of state-run armies fighting each other.

As the French revolutionary armies overran Europe, in one country after another there arose popular resistance movements variously known as *guerrilleros, partisans,* and *Freikorps.* Flouting the orders of their governments on the one hand, and merging into the mass of people on the other, these bodies either continued or resumed the fight even after the regular armies had been defeated. They thereby threatened to upset the established political–military order in their own countries. Nor did the French in combating these "irregulars" follow the ordinary rules of war but, harassed at every turn, engaged in the kind of barbarities so graphically depicted by painters like Goya and others. By 1812–13 Germany, Italy, and even France—to say nothing of Spain—were becoming infested by ill-organized armed bands, some with uniforms and some without. Since they did not consist of regular soldiers, these bands did not enjoy the administrative support of war ministries and treasuries. To survive, they often had to resort to brutal methods similar to those used during the Thirty Years' War. If the Battle of Waterloo had not been as decisive as it was, these bands might well have plunged Europe into chaos. As it was, the first thing that governments did after the final defeat of Napoleon was to suppress the bands and confiscate their arms, thereby returning the power to wage war to the states and their armies alone.

The long-run effect of the Revolutionary and Napoleonic Wars was to reinforce the system whereby war was organized on the principle of a threefold division of labor among the government that conducts war, the army that fights it, and the people who pay for it with their persons and goods. During the period of reaction from 1815 to 1848, most European states feared their own peoples more than they did other nations. Constantly anticipating the recurrence of revolution, the last thing they wanted was putting a rifle on the shoulder of every democratically minded citizen. Professional armies, consisting of long-term regulars and based on some form of selective service (often the well-to-do were allowed to buy themselves out), as opposed to militias or irregulars, reasserted themselves. The separation between the peoples and the armies in some ways became even more strict than it had previously been. In France and elsewhere, the officers as far as possible were again recruited from the aristocracy. The old practice of systematically rotating units from one province to the next to prevent them from forming local ties was revived. As civilian dress tended toward sobriety (these were the years when an early form of the business suit began to take over), uniforms grew more colorful and extravagant than in any period before or since: To accentuate the difference between soldiers and the rest, France's Louis Philippe even ordered soldiers to wear whiskers, and for the whiskers to be black.

The rise of modern firepower during the second half of the nineteenth century caused the reversal of the trend toward sartorial magnificence among the military. At the same time, the introduction of railways and the telegraph permitted the most important military countries to base their armed forces on conscription while also introducing a reserve system of one or another sort. Nevertheless, the threefold division of labor among governments, armies, and peoples not only persisted but became more firmly established than ever. Armies, albeit made up of citizens in uniform, were separate organizations sharply different from society at large; before a citizen was allowed to fight in the state's name, he first had to be mustered, enrolled, disciplined, drilled, instructed in military *mores,* and sworn to obey the military code.

Beginning in the early 1860s, a whole series of international meetings were held whose task was to obtain formal, written approval for this system. The last vestiges of the old tradition, such as the states' right to issue letters of marque to privateers, were swept away. War was formally redefined as something that could only be waged by the state and for the state, a definition which had the effect—perhaps unintended—of putting the majority of non-European societies outside the law in this respect. To allow the regulations to be observed, states undertook to wage war solely by means of their armed forces properly uniformed, properly registered, and properly commanded by their authorized representatives. The use of mercenaries (personnel other than the state's own citizens) was forbidden. So was the participation in hostilities by members of the state who did not form part of the armed forces (civilians). In return, their lives and—"military necessity" permitting—their residences and property were to be spared. Finally, a whole series of conventions regulated the treatment that members of enemy governments, diplomats, emissaries, and the like should receive.[28]

When these arrangements were put to the test during the World Wars of 1914–45, some of them held out better than others. During World War I, in spite of Allied propaganda stories concerning German atrocities in Belgium, the distinction between soldiers and civilians was maintained on the whole; the major exception was the Balkans (after 1918, the Baltic), a backward region where it had been weak to begin with and where both sides freely massacred each other. During World War II the military/civilian distinction broke down to the extent that both sides engaged in large-scale "strategic" bombing of each other's cities, even such as did not contain military targets. Too, terrible atrocities were committed by the German and Japanese occupation forces against the civilian populations under their control. These events foreshadowed the breakdown of the trinitarian tradition.

Still, in the West (at any rate) armies by-and-large did not wage war on civilians, except to the extent that civilians also rose and waged war on them: If the Germans set out to exterminate Jews, this was because they were Jews and not because they were enemy citizens. Though such citizens were interned everywhere, nowhere was an attempt made to use them as hostages. Furthermore, in both World Wars the distinction between armies and governments held up tolerably well. Over the last two decades we have grown accustomed to the fact that scarcely a week passes without an embassy being attacked, or diplomats being taken hostage, or envoys being kidnapped, somewhere in the world. By contrast, in 1914–18 and 1939–45, existing international conventions concerning their privileges were seldom broken. Neither the Germans, nor the Soviets, nor any of the other belligerents, tried to detain each other's diplomats when war broke out between them. Perhaps more surprising, as far as we know there was no attempt by heads of state—though they counted some of the worst scoundrels who ever lived—to wage war *ad hominem*. Unlike Renaissance princes, for example, they did not systematically set out to assassinate one another, members of their families, or their principal assistants; and indeed Hitler is said to have rejected the idea when it was suggested to him.

In sum, nothing is more characteristic of the organization of modern "civilized" warfare prior to the invention of nuclear weapons than the threefold division of functions. Under this system it is the government that directs, the army that fights, and the people who watch, pay, and suffer; so firmly entrenched is this organization, the product of centuries of development, that it is often taken almost for granted. Yet a comparison with earlier periods shows that it dates back no further than the second half of the seventeenth century at the earliest. The system whereby war is a monopoly of state-owned armies, indeed the appearance of armies as such, not only coincides with that of the state but is itself both a product of the state and one of the latter's outstanding characteristics. Since previous societies did not know the state, the kind of armed force by which the latter wages its wars did not exist either. Therefore, should nuclear weapons one day render the state incapable of engaging in its primary function of large-scale warfare, then armies in our sense of the term can be expected to disappear with it.

THE BIRTH OF STRATEGY

The higher conduct of war is usually known as strategy, even to the point where war itself may be—and has been—defined as a "strategic activity."[29] Nevertheless, during most of history the term "strategy" either did not exist at all (in Western Europe, this was the case from the fall of the Roman Empire until the very end of the eighteenth century) or else was used in one out of several completely different meanings.[30] Strategy is a modern phenomenon with a clear beginning in time. As states and their armies rose, so did strategy; what remains to be seen is whether any of these can long survive the introduction of nuclear weapons.

We today are accustomed to thinking of war as conducted on three separate, if interacting, levels. These are the *political,* the *strategic,* and the *tactical* (here I shall ignore "grand strategy," a neologism coined to describe the way in which twentieth-century "total" strategy tended to merge with politics, thereby ceasing to be strategy and turning into something else). Under Clausewitz's classic formulation, the task of politics is to control strategy and use it as an instrument. This in turn presupposes a clear conceptual separation between government (the directing brain) and the armed forces it employs to attain its ends. However, it has already been pointed out that this particular division of labor, so far from being self-evident or eternal, is itself largely the product of the modern state. When the armed forces and/or their commanders themselves *are* the political entity—which happens to have been the case during most of history—political and military operations become indistinguishable. Strategy as a separate field of activity ceases to exist, which eventuality incidentally explains why, beginning already with Clausewitz himself, the most important modern works on the evolution of strategy tend to ignore periods in which there were no states.[31]

To illustrate these relationships, consider the record. As any student of Thucydides, Xenophon, and Demosthenes knows, from at least the fifth century B.C. only a minority of wars among Greek city-states were decided by military means. Cases in which a campaign, a battle, or a siege led to a straightforward victory and were followed by a formal surrender were rare: Instead, the normal way to "decide" a war against this city or that was to bring about a change in its internal regime and, consequently, its allegiance. The role played by *stasis,* or sedition, was as important as that of strategy, a situation which led Philip II, father of Alexander, to comment that where an army could not pass, a donkey laden with gold often could. The methods used in *stasis* were extremely varied, consisting of what can only be called dirty tricks of every kind. They included armed risings by one faction against another; the admission, overt or covert, of foreign troops into the city; and the assassination of opposing leaders, the massacre or expulsion of their followers, and the confiscation of their property (sometimes their wives as well). It is in vain that one looks for such "strategic" expedients in the writings of modern experts such as Jomini, or Schlieffen, or Liddel Hart. Nor would any of this have been conceivable if the armies of these cities had not been identical with their populations and, therefore, both willing and able to take part in politics.[32]

Similarly, during the Middle Ages—in many cases, right down to 1648—our modern distinction between the "private" and "public" domains was almost entirely absent. Hence strategy in its modern, military sense was but one way, and a rather ineffective one at that, of bringing about the type of political–legal change that was the aim of warfare. At the top, subversion, bribery, and hostage-taking directed against a man's family and his principal retainers played as large a part in war as did military operations properly speaking. (One result of this was that, until about 1500, the preferred choice for diplomats and envoys was ecclesiastics who possessed immunity.) At the bottom, by far the most important means by which war was fought consisted of bringing economic pressure to bear in the form of raids—known as *chevauchées* and *guerre guerroyante*—against one's rival's peasantry from whom he derived his income. So long as they did not take place during times of truce, most such activities were regarded as perfectly legitimate. Far from being merely ancillary to the conduct of war, their use could be carried to the point where large-scale military operations all but disappeared. A perfect example is provided by the conflict known to the English-speaking tradition as the Hundred Years' War but that one French historian has called *la guerre peu meurtrière.*[33] The destruction it wrought was immense, yet during its entire course there took place the sum total of four major battles between the opponents' main forces—an average of only one every twenty-five years.

If, on one end of the scale, strategy was almost indistinguishable from politics, on the other the same applied to tactics. The most important reason for this was the nature of logistics. During most of history, military transport consisted of the backs of men, assisted by animals and the vehicles to which they were harnessed. Too, modern methods for conserving and refrigerating foodstuffs had not yet been invented. Hence, except in theaters where waterways happened to be available, armies could not transport their own supplies over any distance, or carry them for any length of time.[34] In order to survive, they had to exploit the surrounding countryside, which in turn was less a question of "strategy" than of persuading or intimidating the population. Indeed, until shortly before 1800, for every day spent in battle perhaps twenty were devoted to foraging.[35] Lines of communication in our sense of that word—routes (forget "zones") linking armies with their bases and utilized to maintain regular series of convoys moving in both directions—simply did not exist.[36] The campaigns of Alexander the Great, Hannibal, Pompeius, Julius Caesar, Gustavus Adolphus, and Marlborough (whose most celebrated battle was fought with an inverted front) illustrate the point. All these commanders had in common that the most "cost efficient" means of transport at their disposal was the oxcart. Had they depended on a regular flow of supplies from the homeland, they would have been utterly unable to operate, if even to exist.

To be capable of feeding large bodies of troops, a country had to be fairly populous. Conversely, demographic considerations pertaining to the density of populations (usually a good indication of a country's prosperity) tended to canalize the operations of armies.[37] In Europe, this was one reason why the majority of campaigns took place in the Low Countries, southern Germany, and northern Italy. So long as the country in which they operated was reasonably prosperous, armies *hardly needed* lines of communication. But for the limits imposed by natural and man-made obstacles, they were almost as free to move about as a navy at sea. Sometimes such armies could be starved out by "devastating" the region from which they drew their supplies, in which case they would eat all there was to eat before proceeding elsewhere and repeating the procedure. However, they were immune to the power of strategy as we have come to understand that term. They could not be outflanked, encircled, or cut off from their bases—insofar as they had bases—except in a narrow tactical sense.

The second reason why strategy was so slow to develop may be found in the nature of communications technology. Whereas battles could be directed by a variety of visual and auditory signals such as flags, standards, bugles, and drums, virtually the sole method by which information could be sent over long distances consisted of messengers. However, messengers (even mounted ones) are comparatively slow. The presence of an enemy tends to make them slower still, to say nothing of the problem of reliability. With rare exceptions, the use of messengers did not permit the co-ordination of large bodies of troops moving at considerable distances from each other against a common enemy; which in turn meant that strategy as it has been understood from Napoleon on was impossible. Since Biblical times most campaigns saw the contingents on each side meeting at some predetermined point and moving slowly forward. Having located each other by means of their scouts, they would halt and set up camp. Next, they would issue challenges, sometimes for weeks or even months on end; and if a battle actually took place, this was usually by a kind of mutual consent between the opposing commanders.[38] As late as the time of Frederick the Great the slowness and unreliability of long-distance communications compelled armies to move about in large, solid blocks.[39] Moving about in this manner, the repertoire of "strategic" maneuvers that they could carry out was extremely limited.

Finally, a third major reason behind the belated separation of strategy from tactics consisted of the weapons technology in use. During most of history, the range even of the most powerful weapons was so short that an enemy more than a few hundred yards or meters away might as well be on the Moon. Under such circumstances, war (properly speaking) began only when the enemy was immediately at hand; battle was a tournament, a distinct event limited in time and space and usually lasting no more than a few hours. Conversely, whatever took place on campaign before and after battle was not war but, as one modern authority put it, an extended walking tour accompanied by large-scale robbery.[40] These realities were reflected in the way commanders operated.[41] The paramount role played by battle in the waging of war helps to explain why, until about 1650, most field commanders did not content themselves with "conducting" campaigns, but themselves donned armor and fought in person. Naturally, while fighting in person they had little time to direct any battle, let alone reflect on its use toward achieving any strategic goal. Many campaigns were in fact decided via *siesta*-length (though considerably more violent) face-to-face encounters between the main forces. To this extent, strategy as understood by Clausewitz, strategy in the sense of maneuvering large forces against each other before and/or after battle, either did not exist at all or was of marginal importance.

Thus, it is no accident that the use of the term "strategy" in anything like its modern sense dates only to Joly de Maizeroy, a French writer active in the last years before the Revolution.[42] By this time the separation between ruler and state had become established in theory and, to a large extent, in fact. By instituting a division of labor which separated command from government and military affairs from political ones, the state acted as the midwife of strategy. As commanders became increasingly professionalized, the first demand made on them was that they stay out of international politics and focus on military affairs exclusively; witness the fate of a French Revolutionary general, Honchard, who failed to read the new realities, opened negotiations with his opposite number on the Allied side in order to arrange the release of prisoners, and was shot for his pains. The equation also worked the other way around. From the sixteenth century on, the rise of modern states and the coalescence of their characteristic institutions is explicable largely in terms of the wars they fought against each other. Thus, our present distinction between political and military power owes its existence partly to strategy. Should strategy disappear, then probably so will this distinction.

If it was the creation of the state that permitted strategy to become separated from the political level above it, the factor that allowed it to become distinguished from tactics below was the development of weapons. So long as troops lived off (and indeed among) the populations by which they were surrounded, the weapons they employed against each other had to be sufficiently simple and discriminating to be used against noncombatants also; this is shown by the fact that even today riot police whose job it is to wade into crowds are issued shields, face masks, nightsticks, and horses in a manner similar to that of Roman legionnaires and medieval knights. Increasingly from about 1648 on, this situation ceased to apply. As artillery developed into the ultimate argument of kings—quoting Louis XIV—it became too powerful, too expensive, and too complex an instrument to be employed by anyone but state-run, regular armies. Conversely, the greater the power of artillery, the less its usefulness in skirmishes, raids, ambushes, foraging, police operations, and so on.

Over time, the result was to draw an increasingly sharp dividing line between the kind of war in which major weapons were useful and that in which they were not. The former was designated war properly speaking, entrusted to regular units, controlled by general headquarters, and subjected to a newly invented system of rules known as strategy. The latter was known as "little war" (*petite guerre, Kleinkrieg, guerrilla*), assigned to irregular troops under their own independent commanders, and governed by minor tactics.[43] Toward the end of the eighteenth century the first staff academies, whose purpose was to teach strategy, opened their doors in France and Prussia. As Tolstoy, speaking through the mouth of the German General Pfuhl, makes clear in *War and Peace,* the new breed of "strategists" turned up their noses on small-scale warfare. This was something they gladly left to half-trained auxiliaries, bandits, and other louts.

Even as the development of crew-operated weapons caused "large" and "small" operations of war to become differentiated in the minds of men, the rise of strategy was favored by the appearance of a new form of organization, the *corps d'armée.* A French innovation subsequently copied by others, the typical "Corps" of Napoleon's day numbered upwards of 30,000 men and possessed a permanent headquarters of its own. In Europe, it was also the first large formation since the Roman "Legions" in which the three arms were combined; a construction which gave it the capability of defending itself, unassisted, for a period of between twenty-four and forty-eight hours, even against superior numbers. A network of *officiers d'ordonnance* moving between them enabled the corps to operate at up to 50 kilometers away from General Headquarters, while at the same time taking part in the execution of a coordinated plan. The limitations hitherto imposed by the primitive means of communication were thereby overcome to a large extent. Once maneuvers on a strategic scale became technically possible, the distinction between them and tactics acquired its modern meaning. As Napoleon wrote when summing up the Ulm campaign, it was with the soldiers' legs, and not with their muskets, that the strategist went to work.[44]

The invention of strategy from the beginning presupposed heavily armed, large, distinct, independent bodies of troops including, besides the "Corps," the "Division," the "Army," and finally the "Army Group." These formations were conceived as capable of coordinating their operations over large spaces, along lines of communication, and among every kind of obstacle, even to the point where the organization of such operations was just what Jomini had in mind when he wrote his famous textbook on the subject.[45] As strategy appeared, so did its characteristic terminology. The first important author to consider the conduct of war in terms of theaters, bases, objectives, angles of approach, lines of communication, diverging and converging lines (corresponding to our distinction between internal and external ones), and so forth was Dietrich von Buelow. His *System der neuere Kriegsfuehrung* was published in 1800 and, in keeping with the spirit of the Enlightenment, read almost as if it were a textbook on geometry complete with definitions, propositions, proofs, and illustrations. Now almost forgotten, at the time it served as the opening shot for a flourishing debate on strategy, in many ways reminiscent of that which accompanied nuclear weapons from 1945 to 1990—and, ultimately, almost as futile.[46]

Toward the middle of the nineteenth century, both the terminology of strategy and the logic on which it rested were greatly favored by the invention of those fraternal-twin instruments, the railway and the telegraph. Whereas previously lines of communication had been somewhat nebulous concepts, now they took concrete shape in the form of steel track and wire, visible to anyone and easily traceable on the new "general staff" maps that were then coming into vogue. Whereas Napoleon had still been forced to ride all over the theater of operations, carrying out his own reconnaissance and occasionally coming under fire, now for the first time it became possible for Commanders-in-Chief to closely supervise operations while sitting in their offices far in the rear. Whereas previously they

had conducted their battles in person, now they displayed a growing tendency to focus on its preparation and its subsequent exploi-
tation, leaving their subordinates to attend to the actual butchery.
As a sign of the changing times, the traditional expression *coup
d'oeil*—which brings to mind a commander, such as Frederick II,
standing on some elevation and overlooking the battlefield—was
abandoned. Its place was taken by our modern "estimate of the
situation" (translated from the German *Lagebeurteilung*), imply-
ing a commander no longer able to see battlefront conditions with
his own eyes.[47]

At the same time, the Industrial Revolution began making its
effect on military logistics felt. Where previously by far the most
important items consumed by armies had consisted of food and
fodder, now advancing technology caused them to be replaced in
importance by ammunition, fuel, and spare parts. Whereas previously armies could move from one district to another while living
on the countryside, the more technology developed, the less feasible
this became. As Liddell Hart wrote, nineteenth-century armies were
becoming tied to an "umbilical cord of supply." In the process, the
old freedom of movement which (as long as they operated in populated districts) they had traditionally enjoyed tended to be lost.
Already during Napoleon's time logistics had developed to the
point where it became possible to defeat entire armies not by engaging them in a pitched battle but by surrounding them and cutting the *etappes,* or rear echelons. From about 1850 on, the
dependence of armies (and of the new steam-driven navies) on
bases, supplies, and lines of communication began to increase by
leaps and bounds.[48] So, consequently, did their vulnerability to
large-scale "strategic" maneuvers aimed at severing those communications—which state of affairs was clearly demonstrated by the
American Civil War and, immediately thereafter, the campaigns of
Moltke, who thereby acquired the reputation of being the world's
foremost strategist.

The twentieth century was to see the intensification of these
trends. The shift from personal weapons heavy crew-operated
(later, motorized and mechanized) ones continued. Telegraphs
were replaced by radio (at first this only applied to major formations), railways by fleets of wheeled and tracked motor vehicles.
Though the details of strategy were modified, its essence was not.
Since the most powerful modern weapons are designed to fight ma-

chines, not men, their effect was to make armies even more specialized for operating against each other. As a result, the time was to
come when one army after another made the discovery that they
had become almost useless for the kind of "war without fronts"
where the principles of strategy do not apply. Specifically, radio
permitted instant communication from any point to any other, regardless of medium, distance, and movement. It acted as an aid to
strategy of the Napoleonic kind, helping the latter to develop into
the rapid-moving armored operations so characteristic of World
War II and of what few large-scale conventional conflicts have been
fought since then.[49] Being more flexible than railways, motor vehicles in some ways increased the armies' mobility. However, by
virtue of their own insatiable demands for fuel, spare parts, and
maintenance, they also increased the dependence of armies on their
bases.[50]

Whatever the advantages and disadvantages of these and other
twentieth-century technological means, on the whole their effect
was to increase range, speed, versatility, and the possibility of coordinating the operations of armed forces. Still, they did not restore
the kind of logistic freedom of movement which those forces had
enjoyed until well into the eighteenth century. Quite to the contrary. Likewise, the rise of air power gave commanders another
means for directing large-scale operations against vulnerable points
deep in the enemy's rear. However, it did not alter the goals of
strategy; in which respect little, if anything, changed between the
time of Marengo in 1800 and the Gulf in 1991.

Modern conventional strategy, far from being self-evident or
eternal, is the product of specific historical circumstances which
could be traced here in outline only. Essentially its growth was the
result of two processes, one working from above and the other
from below. Coming from above, strategy was made possible by a
series of politico–legal developments which tended to concentrate
legal violence in the hands of a special institution, the state-owned
"Regular Army," as opposed to the government on the one hand
and the population on the other. Coming from below, various technological and organizational advances helped establish a relatively
clear dividing line between fighting a battle and conducting a campaign. Even as technological and organizational developments
helped armies to better coordinate their movements across large
spaces, those very developments caused their dependence on lines

of supply to increase. The combination of all these factors laid the foundation for what Jomini called *les grandes opérations de guerre* and what we, following in his footsteps, call strategy.

Finally, the two processes are linked. Just as it was the appearance of the state that led to the modern separation between political and military authority, so the only modern political organization capable of fielding large, regular armies and providing large, continuous spaces for them to maneuver in is the territorial state.

CONCLUSIONS

To understand what nuclear weapons have done, are doing, and will do to armed conflict, it is necessary to begin by comprehending the outstanding characteristics of large-scale, modern warfare before those weapons were introduced. Modern warfare—meaning warfare as it has developed from the time of the Treaty of Westphalia on—has been waged overwhelmingly by the state, an organization so unique in history as to be almost synonymous with the modern age.[51] The instrument that states have developed in order to wage war is the regular army, another post-1648 institution with no precise equivalent in any previous age. The method by which state-run armies wage large-scale war on each other is known as strategy, here understood as a form of warfare which is specific to large, regular armies and is conditioned, if not created, by a particular form of technology. Located between politics on the one hand and tactics on the other, military strategy owes its existence to a particular combination of mobility, control, and logistics. That combination is specific to strategy and, indeed, unique to it. Where no large-scale, regular armed forces exist, neither does strategy.

Though the origins of the first two major constituents of modern war (the state and the army) can already be seen in the century or so before 1648, the third one is clearly an eighteenth-century development starting around 1760. The three combined reached maturity only toward 1800, which explains why the term "strategy"—as well as the most famous works expounding its principles—dates from that period. Originally, "modern" war was limited to those regions that had the state: Europe, its extensions, and its colonies. The twentieth century has seen its expansion to other parts of the world, a process greatly accelerated when large numbers of new states were created after 1945. As non-European societies adopted the state, regular armies and strategy naturally followed, though actually the sequence in which the three elements emerged in each country separately was considerably more complicated. Whether strategy, regular armies, and even the state itself can long survive nuclear weapons remains to be seen. That question will be considered herein first as it pertains to the major powers, and then to regional ones.

Chapter II

ENTER THE ABSOLUTE WEAPON

As World War II approached its climax in 1944, military history appeared to be firmly established on the course set for it during the previous three centuries. By far the most important players were mighty sovereign states, operating either on their own or in coalitions, most of them fairly loose.[1] The armed forces fielded by these states totaled between 40 million and 45 million men, dwarfing anything of their kind in history before or—despite the growth of world population—since. To judge by the number of countries that had been conquered or were in the process of being reconquered, the only organizations even remotely capable of withstanding these forces were others like them. The method by which these nations waged war consisted of strategy (the coordinated movements of huge air, land, and sea forces) directed, as far as possible, against any opponent's exposed rear. By the early summer of 1945 this type of strategy had brought Germany to its knees and was on the point of doing the same to Japan.[2] New power blocks, far larger than their predecessors, had been created, and to judge by all previous history, the day on which they would go to war against each other could not be very far off. Then, coming literally out of the blue, nuclear weapons entered the arena and changed everything, forever.

THE STURDY CHILD OF TERROR

The shape of the postwar global order began to emerge at the Teheran Conference of 1943. It was consolidated during the remaining year and a half of war, and was finally cemented at Yalta and Potsdam.[3] By 1945, at the latest, it was clear that the world would be dominated by two powers, each of which was so unprecedentedly large and strong as to be called by an acronym and have the adjective "super" applied to it. The ideologies to which these two powers subscribed were vociferously, ferociously opposed. As a result, one was explicitly committed to the destruction of its rival, an outcome which it regarded as historically "inevitable." The other, only slightly less radical, talked of "containing" the opponent and "rolling him back" if possible.[4] Though the phrases which they used drew on different political traditions, fundamentally each side called the other "an evil empire" over and over again, and meant what it said. Had mutual hatred and paranoia been the sole causes of war, then few countries in history would have represented more suitable candidates for slaughtering each other than the U.S. and the USSR during much of the Cold War era.

Though each superpower was located in its own hemisphere and possessed all the resources needed for a civilized life, points of friction between them were by no means lacking. One, the USSR, declared itself opposed to the existing international order and was widely perceived as expansionist. At a minimum, its aim was to overthrow "bourgeois imperialism" and extend its social system over as many other countries as possible; if, in the process, it could also gain political influence on, and military bases in, those countries, then so much the better. Following in Lenin's own footsteps,[5] the Communist leaders believed that the best way to achieve this aim was indirect. Instead of going straight for the great strongholds of capitalism, the Soviet Union would attempt to subvert and revolutionize the "world proletariat" as represented by the developing countries from East Asia to Africa and from the Middle East to Cuba—which, in practice, meant stirring up trouble whenever it could.

In its effort to counter this, the U.S., as the leading "free" country, was prepared to go to great lengths. Beginning in the fifties, it often disregarded its own democratic and libertarian principles— the same that had caused it to break with its allies after World War I—in order to offer support to the old, decaying, colonial powers for whose wars it paid and whose struggles it often took over. Provided only that they called themselves anti-Communist, some of the world's worst dictators from Iran to Chile and from Nicaragua to the Philippines were able to draw on American support. Fear of the Soviet Union also led the U.S. to conclude alliances with some of its own recently defeated enemies who happened to be among history's worst scoundrels. From the time of the Korean War on, Germany and Japan were rehabilitated. On condition that they join the anti-Soviet coalition, their past was forgiven them and they were permitted to rebuild themselves.

Another complicating factor was that the two powers were not symmetrical. By virtue of geographical circumstances, the USSR was predominantly a land power, whereas the U.S. made its military might felt primarily at sea. Were it not for the introduction of nuclear weapons, both would have remained secure from destruction at the hands of the other, though few people appeared to have thought so at the time. Some will recall that the U.S. for decades was obsessed with the fear that a Soviet offensive might one day roll over the northwestern European plain, bringing yet another major center of industrial–military power within the Kremlin's orbit, and leading to a fundamental change in the global balance of power. To prevent all this from taking place, the U.S. for the first time in its history entered peacetime alliances by which it committed its forces to the defense of foreign countries. All during the Cold War, American investment in the military vastly exceeded that of its main commercial competitors. Partly as a result thereof, at the beginning of the nineties the mightiest economy the world has ever known was suffering from huge deficits while at the same time undergoing what many saw to be the worst recession in half a century.[6]

Seen through Western eyes at least, since 1945 the USSR appeared to have had less cause for worry: Its land mass was considered unconquerable. It was one of NATO's most prominent commanders, Field Marshal Sir Bernard Montgomery, who pronounced "Don't march on Moscow" to be the first principle of war. However, the Soviets took a different view. Stalin himself on one occasion explained how social backwardness had caused the country to be invaded first by the Tatars, then by the Poles, then by the Swedes, then by the French, and then, in 1914–19, by the Germans followed by the Western Allies. Later, the generation that lost 20 million people to the Nazis in 1941–45 was not likely to forget the way in which, as they saw it, the Western capitalist countries had permitted Hitler to strike in the East;[7] nor were last-minute German attempts to surrender in the West while continuing the struggle against the USSR overlooked. As a result, the USSR was obsessed with the fear that German "revanchists," aided by American "monopoly capitalists," might one day try to destroy the revolutionary Soviet regime, as indeed they *had* attempted to do in 1919–20. Feeling isolated and vulnerable, the Soviet Union did not dismantle its forces after World War II but rather engaged in the largest military buildup in history, the economic consequences being worse even than comparable effects in the U.S.[8]

As if external fears and friction were not enough, the vast armed forces fielded by each superpower had their own momentum. If they did not actually push for war, at any rate they did try hard to create a favorable climate for their political and financial interests by presenting each other in the starkest possible colors.[9] Khrushchev himself owed his victory over his competitors in the Politburo, Malenkov, and Bulganin, partly to the support of the military in the person of Field Marshal Zhukov. Later, if Western analysts may be believed, Khrushchev's attempt to pare down his country's armed forces played a role in his downfall, to the extent that, when the test came, he no longer enjoyed their support. Conversely, from 1965 on, pressure which the armed forces brought to bear acted as one major reason behind the decision of the Soviet Union to embark on the largest and most sustained arms buildup in all history.[10]

In the U.S. fear that the Military–Industrial Complex (MIC) would gain undue influence on both domestic and foreign affairs was sufficiently important for a President (who was himself an ex-General) to draw attention to it in his farewell address.[11] The economic interests of that Complex helped account for the vast rearmament programs initiated by Presidents Kennedy and Reagan; even in the nineties, fear of causing unemployment among its members represented one reason for the continued procurement of some major weapon systems. Whether, historically speaking, such "militarist" pressures have played a large role in bringing about war is moot. All that can really be said is that, if ever armed forces stood to gain by presenting each other in the worst possible light, they were those of the superpowers during the Cold War era.

On the level of personalities, the fact that former President Gorbachev was awarded a Nobel Prize for helping bring about peace between the superpowers should not make us forget that, during at least part of the period since 1945, one of those superpowers was ruled by men whose sense of responsibility and mental stability alike were in doubt. The USSR until 1953 was governed by Joseph Vissarionovich Stalin. His achievements as a mass murderer, even when compared with those of his contemporary, Adolf Hitler, were second to none; and the older he grew, the more paranoid he became.[12] Stalin's successor was Nikita Khrushchev. He had opened his political career by serving as Stalin's henchman in the Ukraine, a region where millions were deliberately starved to death during the thirties. Later, his rise to the top led through a power struggle which probably involved at least one murder (that of NKVD boss Lavrenti Beria). He was a man whom many regarded as an uncouth, missile-rattling buffoon from the provinces who somehow engineered for himself a personality cult second only to that of his predecessor. His own memoirs describe him sitting with Mao at poolside in Beijing, two elderly men of peasant origin discussing nuclear weapons in kindergarten terms.[13]

On the other side of the hill, the effort to present America's presidents as if all of them were reasonable men who would never willingly expose their country to the risk of all-out war against the other superpower[14] is not altogether convincing. At least one, John F. Kennedy, is perhaps best understood as a power-hungry personality who rode to office partly on the strength of his promise to intensify military competition with the USSR. By one account, he was prepared to risk the continued existence of the world during the 1962 Cuban Missile Crisis, merely to prove that he was more than a match for Khrushchev, who after all was the older and more experienced statesman.[15] Much has also been written about President Nixon during the final Watergate days. At that time, such was his state of mind that the members of his own Cabinet were beginning to doubt his ability to govern, and preparations were made to take power away from him if necessary. None of this is to suggest that America's leaders were as bad as some of their Soviet counterparts. It is, however, to say that there is little likelihood, and even less proof, that the statesmen with their fingers on the nuclear trigger on either side of the Iron Curtain were more reasonable than their predecessors at other times and in other places.

Into this explosive mixture of clashing ideologies, conflicting interests, asymmetrical, ever-shifting power relationships, internal pressures, and volatile personalities, nuclear weapons were thrown. They represented incomparably the greatest addition to the means available to strategy, capable of turning war from an instrument of power into certain suicide; hence, it is easy to identify them as perhaps the most important reason why history was confounded and no Third World War took place. However, to say that this was clear from the beginning is to attribute to the previous generation a degree of wisdom which they did not, and reasonably could not, possess.

Before 1945, even the idea that nuclear weapons were technically possible had been limited, in the main, to a handful of physicists and science-fiction writers. Though there had never been a lack of imaginary tales of omnipotent weapons, nothing in history had prepared people for the day these would actually appear upon the scene. This applied to leaders no less than to their followers. It took two years, and a coordinated campaign by some of the world's leading scientists, to convince President Roosevelt to lend his support to the program. As his Vice President, Harry Truman had been aware of the Manhattan Project's existence (which had been brought to his attention during the time that he led the Senate committee investigating the war effort), but did not know what it was all about. When Secretary Stimson informed him of the project, all he could do was mutter "This is the greatest thing in the world".[16]

A few far-sighted individuals, such as Max Born and Bernard Brodie, recognized the full significance of the bomb almost from the beginning.[17] However, most military officers were reluctant to include it in their calculations, even after the first ones had been dropped. After all, if America's defenses were to be built exclusively around nuclear weapons, then a drastic curtailment of the armed force would logically follow. Should deterrence take the place of war-fighting as official doctrine, then in the long run the outcome might be to put the armed forces' *raison d'être,* as the country's ultimate guardians, into question. Accordingly, most of the senior commanders to whom Western politicians turned for advice during the late forties were on the side of caution. They preferred to present "atomic" weapons as unprecedentedly powerful, but not revolutionary, devices.[18] This view was shared by most of the scientific advisers who, increasingly over the years, came to form the other leg of the emerging military–industrial complex. While stressing that atomic warfare was capable of turning entire cities into smoking, radiating ruins, most of them thought that war would still be waged more-or-less as before.[19]

Bureaucratic politics apart, there were reasons for this optimism (if indeed optimism is the right word). Until about 1950, nuclear weapons were unreliable, difficult to store, and relatively few in number. They were considered too precious to be dropped on any but the largest demographic and industrial targets.[20] Owing to their weight (initially between 5 and 10 tons) and size, they could be carried by only the heaviest available bombers, and even these had to have their bomb bays specially modified. Too, these machines were comparatively slow, and thus vulnerable. Given the distances that they would have to travel on their way to targets deep inside the USSR, it was reasonable to assume that attrition rates would be considerable, and that a substantial part of the attacking force would be shot down. As a result, although the U.S. enjoyed a nuclear monopoly, neither side necessarily regarded that monopoly as decisive—and, therefore, as capable of preventing war.

The American planners assumed that, should war break out, then the armored, mechanized forces that constituted the Red Army's main strength would still be able to launch a short, blitzkrieg-style campaign aimed at overrunning Western Europe.[21] The Soviets meanwhile developed the theory of the "five permanently operating factors." According to them, the individual weapons, however powerful, could not decide war—a role that was reserved for long-term political, economic, and social structures coupled with the size and quality of the armed forces. Worked out upon Stalin's personal orders, this doctrine was designed to show that being subjected to nuclear bombardment would not necessarily mean the end of the world; and that, accordingly, the USSR would still be able to win even if subjected to such a bombardment.[22]

Toward the mid-fifties, this situation changed. Both sides now had nuclear weapons—not just of the fission type, but fusion devices as well. On the American side, at any rate, they were becoming plentiful enough and sufficiently miniaturized to be used against targets other than large cities. Though the Soviet strategic arsenal was growing, until 1966–67 American superiority was never in doubt. This was a period when the Strategic Air Command (SAC) was at its peak. From Western Europe through North Africa and South and East Asia all the way to the Pacific Ocean, the Soviet land mass was surrounded by a chain of American bases. At any one time, hundreds upon hundreds of long- and medium-range B-36, B-47, and B-52 bombers far outnumbered a much smaller, technically less sophisticated, and geographically less favorably situated Soviet bomber force. Beginning in 1960, nuclear submarines, each capable of firing sixteen Polaris missiles to a range of 1,500 miles, joined the arsenal. This development took the Soviet Union almost a decade to match. By the time the first submarine-launched Soviet ballistic missiles became operational, Polaris was already on the verge of being replaced by the Poseidon system, capable of carrying three independent reentry vehicles to a considerably greater range.

Admittedly, the Soviets were the first to put an artificial satellite into space. Nevertheless, when President Kennedy entered office in January 1961 the missile gap was already, thanks to high-altitude photography taken from U-2 spy aircraft, recognized as a myth. At that time the Soviets were still limited to a handful of liquid-fueled (hence cumbersome), slow-to-launch, and unreliable first-generation missile. The U.S. by contrast, had already passed this stage and, in addition to its Atlas missiles, was beginning to deploy much more sophisticated, solid-fueled Minutemen into hundreds upon hundreds of fortified silos. In the number of operational ICBMs alone the U.S. led the way by a large margin, peaking in an advantage of perhaps ten to one which it possessed during the early sixties. As a result, this was the time when the USSR was at its most vulnerable to an American first strike.[23]

Such extreme asymmetries notwithstanding, nuclear war did not break out in this period of nuclear plenty any more than it had during the previous one. By the account of McGeorge Bundy, who as chief of the National Security Counsel played a key role in the Cuban Missile Crisis (the most dangerous one by far), it was never even close to breaking out.[24] On the contrary, comfortable superiority led America to adopt a doctrine known as Mutual Assured Destruction, or MAD, which was specifically designed to make sure that nuclear war should *never* break out. The doctrine hinged on the belief—mistaken, in retrospect—that the two sides were roughly equal in power; yet paradoxically, as soon as the Soviet strategic arsenal did begin to draw level with the U.S., the doctrine was abandoned. The change was partly a response to growing Soviet conventional power, partly an outgrowth of such new technological developments as computerized guidance, Multiple Independent Reentry Vehicles (MIRVs), and cruise missiles.[25]

Since none of these highly destabilizing technologies became available to the Kremlin until the second half of the seventies, the U.S. was able to develop a whole series of hair-raising doctrines for employing nuclear weapons in ways which would not bring about the end of the world—at any rate not automatically.[26] From the time of the Nixon administration on there was talk of "surgical strikes" and "limited nuclear options," both of which meant blowing up a military installation here, a minor city there. Small, accurate nuclear weapons might be employed to deliver "warning shots across the bow" or (in another scenario) "decapitate" the Soviet Union by sending a warhead through Mr. Brezhnev's own window at the Kremlin. Again, however, all this remained in the realm of fantasy. Occasional rhetorical flourishes notwithstanding, each side took very good care to make sure that no nuclear warhead was fired at the other. Looking back, it is difficult to imagine circumstances under which any launch might have happened, let alone to think of a cause which would have justified it.

As one form of asymmetry was replaced by another and American nuclear doctrines shifted from second-strike deterrence to limited first strikes, the Soviet Union was anything but quiescent. Its top brass may have been less fertile in inventing "strategies" or, at any rate, publishing those they did invent; however, once nuclear weapons and delivery vehicles became relatively plentiful during the late fifties, the Soviets never tired of emphasizing that, if war broke out, it would immediately become both nuclear and total.[27] Khrushchev himself was capable of extremely provocative behavior, rattling his missiles (which, it later turned out, he did not possess) first in connection with the 1956 Suez Crisis and then, repeatedly, in order to try to force concessions over Berlin.[28] Possibly because they had the Cuban Missile Crisis to think about, his successors were less inclined to make verbal threats. However, no sooner had they come to power than they embarked on a formidable buildup of the Soviet strategic arsenal.[29] By the seventies, that arsenal had reached the point where it first equaled and then overshadowed—by most measures—the one fielded on the other side of the Arctic. Important parts of it, such as the MIRVed SS-18 and SS-20 missiles, appeared as if they had been specifically designed for a first strike against the U.S. and its allies. As a result, many strategic experts began to take the possibility of such a strike seriously for the first time.[30]

These were the years when, following the departure of Henry Kissinger and the subsequent demise of détente, the so-called "Second Cold War" was at its height. Particularly between 1975 and 1979, scarcely six months seemed to pass without the Soviets scoring some significant strategic gain against the hard-pressed West. First came Indochina, which was evacuated by the U.S. and left to the Communists in 1975. This was followed by Angola, where the Red Navy covered a Cuban landing in 1976; Ethiopia, which Soviet forces helped defend against Somalia in 1978; Iran, where America's ally, Shah Reza Pahlavi, was overthrown in 1979 (though this was scarcely the result of Soviet machinations); Afghanistan, which suffered a Soviet invasion in 1979; plus any number of less important incidents. While the Kremlin's apparent Soviet drive for world dominion was gathering momentum, the U.S. led by Jimmy Carter, was caught in a post-Watergate, post-Vietnam depression and seemed unable to resist. There was much loose talk of the decline of the West, attributable to a failure of will, the dear price of oil, or both.

Again, hindsight allows us to say that, even in the face of such supposed asymmetry, there was little if any chance of a nuclear war breaking out. However, *at the time* such a possibility was taken sufficiently serious for the U.S. to embark on its "Star Wars" program, which was designed to render the other side's missiles "impotent and obsolete." Had the program been pushed with anything like the vigor intended by its original proponents, it might well have brought about the bankruptcy of the American economy. However, the coming to power in the Soviet Union of Mikhail Gorbachev revolutionized the entire situation. It is unlikely that the change was brought about mainly by the Soviet inability to follow the U.S. and increase its expenditure for armament.[31] More likely, domestic problems connected with the ossification of the Soviet system caused the USSR to start looking toward reform. First came *glasnost,* then *perestroika.* In 1988 the two sides for the first time reached an agreement which provided for parts of their arsenals to be dismantled. By 1990, the Soviet Union had also abandoned the "first nuclear strike" stance that it claimed to have embraced in the past: It now subscribed to the view that nuclear weapons existed for deterrence only.[32] The arms race ended with a whimper rather than a bang.

The fact that the superpowers have finally reached the peace of exhaustion should not cause us to forget that, for the best part of forty-five years, those same nations were like two express trains set on a collision course. To identify the nuclear balance as the main factor that prevented a collision is not difficult; yet to see that balance as having been symmetrical, let alone assured, at each moment during the Cold War requires a considerable amount of hindsight.

At first, nuclear war itself did not appear particularly horrible or impossible. Later on, scarcely a year passed without some quantitative or qualitative development causing the balance of terror to be called "delicate" or "shifting." The Bomber Gap of 1955–56, the Missile Gap of 1957–61, the Anti-Ballistic Missile Controversy of 1966–69, and so on all the way to the so-called "Window of Vulnerability" of 1978–83, succeeded each other in seeming lock-step. Each time, it was feared that the Soviets were on their way to gaining some terrible advantage. Each time, vast sums of money were spent to ensure that such an advantage would not tempt the Soviet leadership to attack or, at the very least, exploit its "escalation dominance" to extract some far-reaching politico–strategic concessions. Nor did the picture look so different from the Soviet point of view. American economic preponderance apart, from the original bomb to Strategic Defense Initiative (SDI) at any one moment the technological advantage was usually on the side of the U.S. Hence the Soviets found themselves forever condemned to catching up. And even if they did catch up, there was no knowing what their rich, technologically inventive, and—in their view—unstable opponents might come up with next.[33]

To make this built-in instability more dangerous still, during some fifteen years after Hiroshima, procedures for safeguarding nuclear weapons and preventing them from being activated by accident remained primitive, to say the least. Before the advent of Permissive Action Links (PAL), satellite surveillance, over-the-horizon radar, and hot lines, a potential existed for unauthorized or accidental war which appears hair-raising in retrospect.[34] Even after their advent, the fact that only thirty minutes would be available from the time a missile was fired to the moment of impact had horrifying implications for the world's continued existence. All these developments took place against the background of irresponsible, sometimes even terrifying personalities; intense internal pressures; asymmetrical, constantly shifting military capabilities, some of which were incompletely known or understood; numerous conflicting interests spread all over a complicated world; and sharply clashing ideologies. The resulting witches' brew was as explosive as any other in history. International relations seemed like a roller-coaster car out of control, producing local crises without number that were often accompanied by spectacular fireworks. Still, none of these crises led to "central" war or, by some accounts, even got *close* to leading to such a war. While MAD, considered as a doctrine, dates to the Kennedy Administration and the early sixties, as a reality it existed much earlier. Though as a doctrine it could be criticized for its shortcomings and officially abandoned by the Nixon Administration, as a reality it continues to exist, and has survived the countless attempts to upset it. In the end, peace between the superpowers turned out to be the sturdy child of terror.

THE DEATH OF LIMITED WAR

As the advent of nuclear weapons failed to bring about all-out nuclear war between the superpowers (the first time in history, surely, when such powerful weapons were left unused for such a long time), the remaining forms of armed conflict in which they could engage also became more and more restricted. This confining effect was not understood at the outset. By the time it began to be understood, it led to the abrupt dismissal of at least one General (Douglas MacArthur), whom many regarded as among the twentieth century's greatest tacticians but who stubbornly refused to see the new reality. An intellectual crisis ensued. Strategists in government and academia alike engaged in a frantic search for new forms of war which, so it was hoped, could still be fought in a world where nuclear weapons were proliferating. In the end, those hopes were destined to be disappointed. However, by the time they had been disappointed, both superpowers had suffered stinging military defeats and found themselves well on the way to rendering their armed forces impotent, if not altogether obsolete.

We live in a world where Clausewitz's dictum that war is the continuation of policy by other means has become a cliché.[35] This interpretation was not shared by previous generations of strategists; to them, it seemed that his most important message was not that war is an instrument of state policy—which most of them took more-or-less for granted—but rather its natural tendency to use force to the utmost, ruthlessly and without limit.[36] However, by the mid-fifties it had become clear that, in the age of thermonuclear weapons, to allow war to unfold to the maximum limits of force against an equal enemy was tantamount to suicide. To this extent, those weapons altered not just war's basic conduct but indeed its very nature. Most historical experience, including not least the recent experience of two twentieth-century total wars, was thereby rendered irrelevant.[37] In the future, it would be possible to wage war *only* to the extent that it was closely controlled by policy, and *only* to the extent that it was limited.

In the U.S. attempts to make the world safe for nuclear war by surrounding the latter with limits started around 1955. By this time the Soviet Union had exploded a hydrogen bomb and both sides' thermonuclear arsenals were rapidly growing. The doctrine of "massive retaliation"—which proposed to rely on first use of these weapons—appeared less and less credible, given that it implied a willingness to sacrifice Washington and New York in order to save Hamburg, Munich, and perhaps Tokyo. Accordingly, some American strategists proposed that the superpowers sign an agreement not to use bombs with a yield greater than 150, or 500, or whatever, kilotons (quite sufficient to destroy any target, considering that Hiroshima and Nagasaki had been devastated by bombs developing 14 and 20 kilotons respectively). Another idea was that they should agree to use them only against selected targets, such as military forces, bases, or installations.[38] In retrospect, we can see that the attempt to safeguard theater warfare by "decoupling" it from a strategic nuclear exchange was doomed to failure. A prospective agreement to avoid the most important targets and leave the most important weapons unemployed begged the question as to why belligerents who could reach such an agreement should go to war at all, and especially in the case of one that threatened to terminate the existence of both.[39]

During these years, nuclear weapons were becoming plentiful, easy to deliver, and cheap. The slow-flying, difficult-to-maneuver, heavy bombers that initially had been the only vehicles capable of dropping the bombs on their targets were being supplemented by other systems, including fighter-bombers (for example the Air Force's Thunderchief and the Navy's Crusader), medium- and short-range missiles (the Army's Redstone, Corporal, and Honest John), atomic artillery (the 280mm. gun), and even an atomic bazooka (the Davy Crockett).[40] Whereas beforehand delivery vehicles had been comparatively few in number and difficult to hide, now they become mobile and easily concealable. Whereas previously it was thought that nuclear weapons would be used only against large industrial–demographic centers deep in the rear, these technical advances appeared to make their employment in combat possible—for example, in order to destroy the opponent's logistical bases, blast a gap through his defenses or (on the contrary) prevent him from following up a local breakthrough.[41]

Equipped with these devices, the U.S. attempted to find an alternative to full-scale nuclear war in the form of the so-called "pentomic" system.[42] Traditional divisions, consisting of three brigades, were carved up into five smaller—and hopefully more mobile—units. These units were supposed to be linked by the small, transistorized communications that were coming into service just then, permitting them to operate in a decentralized, dispersed mode unlike any before. They were to wage regular warfare at one moment, irregular combat in the next. Leaping from one place to another to avoid the nuclear warheads aimed at them, they would open and close like some huge accordions. To operate in this way they would require novel types of equipment, beginning with giant cross-country land-walking machines and ending with flying jeeps. Some visionaries even painted pictures of tanks whose detachable, rocket-powered turrets jumped into the air and shot at each other.

Since the internal-combustion engine was perceived as too inefficient and demanding to do the job, a substitute simply had to be developed.[43] Since ordinary lines of communication would presumably be blocked, one scenario envisaged supplies being delivered by cargo-carrying guided missiles dropping in from the stratosphere and ending up basically undamaged even though of necessity usually sticking their noses into the earth like enormous darts. The manpower system, too, was to adapt itself to the new environment. As one Army physician wrote, the "bugaboo of radiation" had to be exorcised and the troops indoctrinated to ignore its effects.[44] To facilitate the acclimatization process, they were to be divided into "radiation classes" according to the dose they had received. Depending on the time they could expect to live, each class could then be sent on its appropriate mission. One article appearing in *Military Review* entitled "Atomic Impact on G-1's [Personnel] Functions" proposed that the Army's graves registration service be greatly extended.[45]

To prove that its troops were indeed capable of surviving and further operating on the nuclear battlefield, the U.S. Army carried out a series of field tests. In the most important one, the well-publicized operation Desert Rock VI, a force equal to an armored brigade, minus its "soft" unarmored vehicles, was put into non-combat posture and dispersed at a safe distance from the planned site. The turrets were turned away, the troops inside their buttoned-up vehicles forbidden to watch the blast. Eight minutes after the 30-kiloton explosion had taken place they emerged, drove toward its site, and opened fire—though still carefully avoiding ground zero itself.[46] According to the best available information, the Soviets in 1954 held a similar test in which numerous Red Army troops were killed. This seems to have taught them a lesson, since thereafter such "nuclear" exercises were apparently confined to igniting masses of ordinary fuel and gingerly driving around them.[47] Over thirty years later, the American tests were still being remembered, owing to the increase in the cancer rate among the participating troops. However, such tests did not offer convincing proof that conventional forces could survive, let alone fight, under nuclear conditions; nor, truth to say, is it easy to imagine a way in which such an experiment *could* have been designed.

The dilemma facing the planners was, in retrospect, a simple one: If conventional forces were to survive a nuclear war, they would have to disperse and hide. If hide and disperse they did (discarding much of their heavy equipment in the process), they would then be unable to wage conventional war—or, should things be taken to extremes, any war at all. Thus tactical nuclear weapons, far from offering a relatively safe alternative to full-scale nuclear war, threatened the continued existence of even conventional armed forces, and especially ground ones. It was left to the Kennedy Administration, guided by Secretary of Defense Robert McNamara and Chairman of the Joint Chiefs of Staffs General Maxwell Taylor, to try to square the circle. Their solution, if that is indeed the word to use, consisted of plunging all-out for conventional war, nuclear weapons be damned. A new strategic doctrine, known as "flexible response," articulated this approach and was in fact officially adopted by NATO in 1967. Thenceforward, preparations for conventional war in Europe and elsewhere were to proceed *as if* the threat of nuclear escalation did not exist.[48]

The purpose of flexible response, namely safeguarding the continued existence of conventional forces, was achieved. Year after year, NATO forces stationed in West Germany went on their maneuvers, carefully trying to prevent damaging civilian property whose owners would have to be compensated later on. The catch was that, given the alleged Soviet superiority in conventional forces (and the West Germans' refusal to fortify their borders), most Western analysts believed a determined Soviet attack could be stopped only by using "tactical" nuclear weapons. As early as 1955, a series of war games played on behalf of the Supreme Allied Commander, Europe (SACEUR) had shown that nuclear weapons would cause so much devastation in West Germany that there would be little left to defend.[49] Nevertheless, NATO—and particularly the Americans, who (once again) were preparing to fight across the Atlantic and on other people's soil—forged ahead.

In the end, the successive attempts to restrict war in the "central theater" in such a way as to enable it to be fought never became credible and, fortunately, were never put to the test. Finding this avenue blocked, strategists turned their attention elsewhere, using the Korean War as the starting point for thought. What made Korea so remarkable—if only in retrospect—was the fact that both sides actually managed to observe some limits *vis-à-vis* each other. Neither, though for different reasons, attempted to escalate the war beyond the Korean Peninsula; neither launched air attacks on the other's strategic bases; and the Americans refrained from using their most powerful (i.e., nuclear) weapons.[50] In part because they observed these limits, neither side was able to achieve victory. As a result, the three years' butchery ended in an almost perfect draw. But the lesson was not lost: Given that the shadow of nuclear weapons was nearly always present, it was argued that future wars would have to be carefully circumscribed if they were to be fought at all. To prevent escalation, one or both sides would have to draw certain lines, signal to the opponent willingness to respect those lines, and rest content with something short of total victory.[51]

Korea's suitability as a place where limited war could be safely fought stemmed from the fact that the peninsula was strategically unimportant, a fact which the American Joint Chiefs of Staff recognized even at the time. However, for precisely the same reason the war seemed somewhat pointless. And, once it was over, fear of global escalation caused a phenomenon of downward escalation to set in. To avoid even the slightest risk of a conflict getting out of hand and turning nuclear, each opponent whom the Americans confronted now had to be progressively smaller, less important, and more isolated than the last. Being just that, most of the time the "opponents" in question did not have a modern industrial infrastructure and were, therefore, incapable of waging large-scale conventional war. Worse still (for the argument), the smaller an opponent, the more difficult it became to explain to the American public why it had to be fought at all—particularly if the war lasted for any time, and especially if it involved casualties.

The largest of these wars was staged in Vietnam. It was not fought against a modern army, let alone an organized state in the Western sense of that word. Whatever their official affiliation (whether Viet Cong or North Vietnamese), during most of the time, and to an overwhelming extent, the opponents consisted of antlike guerrillas, clad in black pajamas, who had few heavy weapons and wore pieces of old tires for shoes. By no stretch of the imagination were they capable of endangering vital American interests, much less of attacking the U.S. homeland.[52] Even so, fear of escalation in the form of Chinese intervention hung heavily over the conflict. Johnson and McNamara, assisted by ambassador Taylor in Saigon, well remembered the Korean scare stumbled into when MacArthur, marching to the river Yaloo and ignoring repeated Chinese warnings, had come close to snatching defeat from the jaws of victory. They were going to make very sure that this sort of experience did not repeat itself.[53] The greatest potential for escalation was offered by air power, which was also where America's military advantage was at its most overwhelming. Therefore, it was never put under General Westmoreland's control but rather subjected to the most stringent restrictions. Limits were drawn, and some of the most important targets declared out of bounds—even to the point where Washington insisted on preapproving each raid.[54]

After it was all over, the lesson most people drew from Vietnam was that if victory was to be achieved against even a small and undeveloped opponent in some less-than-strategic place, overwhelming force would have to be used. However, the use of overwhelming force represented exactly the factor most conducive to escalation—possibly even nuclear escalation, given not only Soviet support to the other side but the fact that the number of countries that had such weapons (or were capable of building them) was growing all the time. The outcome of this paradox was to leave fewer and fewer places around the world where large-scale armed force could still be used. The only opponents left being increasingly smaller and weaker, finally the time came when it became difficult to speak of any opponents at all. In places such as Grenada and Panama, so grossly mismatched were the opposing forces that the "wars" they fought took on a comic-opera tone. One result of this situation was that the military could (in the eyes of many) do *nothing* right. As they "fought" the weak they were damned if they did, and damned if they did not, drawing critical fire for being too cautious in the one case, and for using excessive force in another.[55]

As of the early summer of 1990, the Cold War had clearly come to an end. In the absence of a worthwhile opponent, the future of America's conventional armed forces appeared increasingly in doubt, and plans were being drawn up to cut them by one-quarter to one-third. Tens of thousands of American military men and women were already preparing to doff their uniforms and go home. But then Iraq invaded Kuwait. Iraq at the time was a historical fluke. It was practically the only country in the world which, while possessed of large, modern, technologically advanced conventional forces, had not yet got to the point where it could build nuclear weapons. In this way Saddam Hussein presented a target too good to miss, being not merely wicked but weak. Short of resorting to gas warfare, which might have led to awesome retaliation, there was simply no way Saddam could inflict serious damage on the non–Middle Eastern members of the Coalition. (After the Allied deployment was completed this also applied to the Middle Eastern ones.) As the world watched on TV, the United States and its allies mounted a spectacular fireworks display, using the opportunity to rid themselves of surplus military resources that were going to be scrapped anyway. Then, once victory had been achieved and order restored, plans for reducing the armed forces could go ahead as scheduled—and so, in fact, they did.

Though the potential effect of their own nuclear weapons on the Soviet Union's ability to wage war was somewhat different from that of the U.S., the ultimate outcome was just the same. During the early years of the Cold War, the Soviet approach to war was determined by two cardinal factors. First, geographic circumstances dictated that the most important strategic interests should be located in areas contiguous to the Soviet homeland, and indeed close to its borders. Second, the Soviet Union during those years found itself in a position of nuclear inferiority—given that the U.S. had already shown its readiness to employ nuclear weapons, even at a time when no overwhelming need existed (clearly not a position with which the Kremlin could comfortably live). Unable to match American power, the Soviets were compelled to resort to bluster. This already had become evident at Potsdam: To President Truman's great disappointment, Stalin refused to be intimidated by the disclosure of the Bomb's existence. Instead, he merely remarked that he hoped it would soon be used against Japan.[56] For nearly a decade thereafter, Soviet military doctrine continued to downplay the importance of nuclear weapons. To compensate, it emphasized "the five permanently operating factors" supported by the vast conventional forces that Stalin kept at the ready.

After the dictator's death, this posture changed. Though the Soviets now possessed their own nuclear arsenal, apparently the feeling of being only second best was never far away.[57] Insofar as America's nuclear forces for many years exceeded those of the Soviet Union by a large margin, that feeling was justified. Strategic inferiority was one cardinal factor which compelled the Soviet Union to develop a military doctrine directly opposed to American ideas of "limited war." Whereas limited war by definition could be waged only in some faraway theater (the less important, the better), the Soviets built vast land forces and prepared to fight on the borders of their East European empire. Whereas the U.S. was forever looking for ways to make the defense of West Europe credible by "decoupling" it from a "strategic" nuclear exchange, the Soviets never got tired of repeating that *any* war would rely on all available weapons, and that it would quickly escalate.[58] To emphasize the point, they reportedly integrated nuclear weapons into their normal order of battle. Next, they developed a military doctrine which hinged on an all-out "offensive in depth."[59] Only during a brief period in the eighties, when it appeared as if the "central" balance had shifted in their favor, did they display any kind of interest in the possibility that a conventional war in Europe might be fought for some time without turning nuclear almost at once.[60]

For all its occasionally bellicose rhetoric, in the actual use of military force the USSR was even more cautious than the U.S. The Soviets, too, found the central front effectively closed, a situation cemented into the Berlin Wall of 1961 but existing much earlier. Hence, for three decades after 1945 the only countries that felt the direct impact of Soviet military power were its own satellites and supposed allies. East Germany, Hungary, and Czechoslovakia were each in turn "saved" from themselves, and from wicked Western machinations aimed at producing counterrevolution. In the autumn of 1980, it almost looked as if Poland might share a similar fate. These operations apart, the Soviets sent advisers and equipment to many places around the world, including Asia, Africa, and—on a much smaller scale—Central America. Out of several dozen Soviet military adventures of this kind, the largest single one consisted of the sending of 20,000 or so personnel to Egypt. Between 1969 and 1972, they helped train the Egyptian Army, manned the antiair-craft defense system, and flew a few combat sorties (which promptly ended after a clash with the Israeli Air Force brought home the dangers of escalation).[61] If only because they failed to develop an oceangoing navy before the seventies, Soviet armed enterprises were more limited than those of the U.S. Even after this deficiency had been corrected in the seventies, they preferred to employ surrogates, and did little fighting themselves. In 1976 they covered a Cuban landing in Angola without firing a shot, and two years later a small force was sent to assist Ethiopia against Somalia —but again it engaged in little actual fighting.

While American self-confidence reached its nadir during the years following Vietnam, the Soviet Union's military–political power steadily increased. Its conventional forces had always been formidable, outnumbering those of the West by a considerable margin and making a successful invasion of the NATO countries appear like a real possibility. Now, however, the steady deployment of MIRVed missiles (the SS 18 and, in Europe, the SS 20) closed or reversed the gap in strategic forces also. These shifts in the balance of forces seem to have caused the normally cautious, bureaucratically minded men who ruled the Kremlin from 1964 on to feel that they, too, could afford to fight a nice, limited war in order to achieve nice, limited aims. The place they selected was Afghanistan, a country comfortably close to their own borders and regarded by them as part of their own region of influence. As a long-time recipient of Soviet military and economic assistance,[62] Afghanistan had no tight links with any other power. It was a weak state bordered by other weak states (post-Pahlavi Iran and Pakistan) which would not dare to intervene. Finally, the only Afghanistani armed forces worth mentioning were those that the Soviets themselves had helped build—or so they thought. For all these reasons an easy victory seemed assured and the danger of escalation, including in particular nuclear escalation, was exceedingly remote.[63]

As also happened with the American entry into Vietnam, these calculations were vindicated in the early stages of the invasion, which went like clockwork. Driving down the mountain passes, the superbly equipped Red Army divisions overran the country, occupied its capital against little or no opposition, and installed a government of the Kremlin's choice. However, the war soon turned sour. The terrain was mountainous, inhospitable and, during several months each year, virtually impassable. The infrastructure needed to support modern armies—roads, air fields, a telecommunications network—was largely unavailable. The Soviets could hold on to the principal towns, but in the countryside their power was limited to the times when they made an appearance. Even then, it only extended as far as their eyes could see and their weapons could cover. In the face of everything that they could do (including, it was rumored at the time, the use of gas warfare), a nasty guerrilla campaign asserted itself and spread.

For nine years the Red Army floundered about. Allegedly piling victory upon victory in local actions, it was yet unable to defeat its opponents, and in fact took heavy losses in the process. Such heavy weapons as tanks, artillery, fighter-bombers, and the world's best assault helicopters were of little use against an enemy who was difficult to find and, when found, usually able to get away. Even the best troops, the special units or *spetznatz,* were of no avail. Finally, during the Soviets' final retreat through the Khyber Pass, they were jeered by barefoot *mujahideen,* who did not even bother to shoot at them. Though the size of operations never approached that of the Americans in Vietnam (the maximum number of troops used at any one time was about 130,000, against America's 550,000), the impact was not dissimilar. Shortly after they retreated it became clear that the largest military power the world has ever seen was left practically without armed forces capable of waging war and enforcing its will abroad.[64]

First on one side of the Iron Curtain, then on the other, the superpowers' military history during the period since 1945 is very largely the story of attempts to find "limited" ways in which their armed forces might still be used—the alternative being either nuclear war or those forces' eclipse. By virtue of its geography, colonial legacy, and strategic posture, most such attempts were made by the West. The search for ways in which war might be waged without (hopefully) blowing up the world went on for several decades. Looking back, it is possible to divide the attempts into three kinds: First, those that sought to bring about agreement between the superpowers proved totally unrealistic; such agreements ran directly counter to Soviet military doctrine, with the result that no treaty for limiting the size of nuclear warheads to be used in war, or the targets against which they might be used, has even been discussed. Second, the quest for ways to fight a conventional war in the "central" theater also led to failure, ending in the adoption of "flexible response" as a gigantic exercise in make-believe. Third, what limited wars *were* fought outside the "central" theater either led to the conclusion that military power could accomplish nothing, or that the things it could accomplish—against small, nonnuclear powers, needless to say—were scarcely worth having.

The Soviets were even more cautious. Precisely because they felt that any war between the superpowers would at once turn nuclear, they took great care to prevent such a war from breaking out. For many years the principal beneficiaries of their military power were their own protegees in Eastern Europe, whereas others experienced that power mainly in the form of advisers or equipment. Not being put to a serious test, the Soviets were able to disguise the uselessness of their conventional armed forces for somewhat longer than the U.S. However, when they finally did attempt to fight a limited war, they were taught a hard lesson not dissimilar from the one learned by the U.S. a decade and a half earlier, and one whose full political, social, and economic effects are only now beginning to reveal themselves. As compared to the grandiose expansionist designs that were still being attributed to them between 1980 and 1985,[65] the subsequent Soviet withdrawal from world affairs can only be called astonishing. The Kremlin has learned that, in the nuclear age, what could still be achieved by conventional armed forces was not worth fighting for, and what was worth fighting for could no longer be achieved. May thou rest in peace, limited war.

THE TRANSFORMATION OF STRATEGY

From Jomini to Liddell Hart, the original meaning of "strategy" was simply "the body of rules governing large-scale warfare (other than the actual fighting) between large-scale armed forces." Now that nuclear weapons had brought about a situation whereby large-scale warfare between the most important forces by far—those of the superpowers—was no longer practical, that meaning had changed. A splintering process took place: Whereas previous generations had only known strategy *tout court* (except, perhaps, for "naval" strategy), the postwar world saw the blossoming of nuclear strategy, conventional strategy, grand strategy, theater strategy, economic strategy, and other types of strategy too numerous to mention.

As might be expected, the most fundamental split that took place after 1945 was the one between nuclear and conventional strategy. Though this was not immediately realized by most people, nuclear strategy represented an entirely new field. The relationship between the two fields was most problematic and, indeed, itself constituted perhaps *the* most important issue facing "strategic studies." The difficulty consisted in that, as compared with the towering threat presented by nuclear weapons and nuclear war, conventional weapons and conventional war appeared so puny as to be scarcely worth mentioning. Conversely, conventional war could be waged only to the extent that it could be "decoupled" from nuclear weapons, and the threat of escalation avoided. Though rivers of ink have been spilt in an attempt to show how this could be done, to date nobody has been able to *guarantee* that a conventional war between nuclear-armed countries would not quickly run out of hand. Hence, conventional strategy remained possible only to the extent that the nuclear danger was ignored.

Operating within this constraint, conventional strategy remained much as it had always been—namely, a question of large units (from division strength up) using time and space in order to maneuver against each other. Every time a new weapon system appeared, or a war was fought anywhere around the world, the forests paid a heavy price so that one and all could discuss its "strategic" implications. By-and-large, each such weapon was supposed to be more mobile, powerful, accurate, and far-ranging than its predecessor. If only because increases in range, accuracy, power, and mobility were necessary to justify the enormous expenditure involved, most experts agreed that modern operations would progress faster, unfold in greater depth, and be more destructive than their predecessors.[66] Beyond this general consensus, opinion varied. In particular, the 1973 Arab–Israeli War gave questions such as offense versus defense, mobile versus stationary defense, and concentration versus dispersion (which had been the staple of strategy since at least 1918), a new lease on life.[67]

The reason why conventional strategy underwent so little change was, of course, that the forces by which it was supposed to be waged—military land, air, and sea units—all were linear developments of their World War II predecessors. For forty-five years, successive generations of tanks, armored fighting vehicles, artillery tubes, aircraft, helicopters, ships, and submarines replaced each other, with little fundamental development involved, and even less revolutionary change. In particular, the vaunted "missile age" never really got off the ground. Though missiles did supplement aircraft and artillery to some extent, for various reasons their impact was more limited than originally thought probable. Already the Germans during World War II had discovered that surface-to-surface missiles designed for medium-range work (up to 200 miles) were too inaccurate, and too expensive in relation to the size of the warheads they could carry, to bring about any meaningful strategic decision. This proved to be a situation which, as Saddam's use of them during the Gulf War showed, had hardly changed in the succeeding forty-five years. At the other end of the scale, short-range antitank, antiaircraft, and air-to-surface missiles did not so much replace existing weapons as enhance their capabilities.[68]

Missiles apart, the most important technological advances consisted of electronic circuitry incorporated into weapons systems in order to improve target-acquisition, tracking, and aiming capabilities. Particularly after 1970, electronics became almost synonymous with modernity, accounting for an ever-growing proportion of the costs of new systems. The various kinds of platforms, and the munitions from which they were fired, were provided with a vast range of computerized laser rangefinders; active, semiactive, and passive sensors; homing warheads; and incredibly sophisticated communications to link the lot. First in the air, then at sea and on land, there was an attempt to "automate" the battlefield. However, the gadgets fielded by the one side were often neutralized by those of the other. The end result was merely to render war immensely more complicated. When everything was said and done, tanks remained tanks, aircraft aircraft, and ships ships.

A historical survey of post-1945 wars will support this claim. Korea was fought largely with arms left over from World War II; the greatest surprise it brought was that, given suitable terrain, an ill-equipped army of peasants could successfully fight a force many times its superior in terms of equipment and firepower. If the 1967 Arab–Israeli War bore an uncanny resemblance to some early World War II blitzkrieg, this was partly because some of the weapons fielded by both sides *had participated* in the last Soviet and American blitzkriegs of that era.[69] The massive tank battles of the 1973 Arab–Israeli War were almost exact copies of Alamein and Kursk,[70] and the conflict fought by Iran and Iraq in 1980–88 did not even attain that level, being more like World War I. Finally, as far as the operations of armed forces against each other are concerned, the 1991 Gulf War only proved what everybody had known at least since the defeat of Rommel's Africa Korps: The flat, open desert is the worst possible place to operate without air cover.

As successive generations of weapons systems, each much more sophisticated than the last, were introduced, strategic thought froze. Even during the eighties, blitzkrieg—originally conceived fifty to sixty years before by the likes of Guderian, Fuller, and Liddell Hart—was still described as the optimal performance level that a conventional force could achieve; conversely, all NATO could think of was how to defend itself against an eventual Soviet super-blitzkrieg.[71] There was much talk of new operational doctrines with such esoteric names as maneuver warfare, air–land battle, and FOFA (Follow on Forces Attack). Each was presented with great fanfare, as if it constituted some original departure. Still, at bottom each was merely a variation on the fighter-bomber *cum* tank combination first tested by the Germans in Poland in 1939. Given the fact that the 1973 War had revealed a growing threat to the tank, time and time again the concept of "combined arms" was put forward as if it were some great discovery.[72] In fact, however, from 1943 on the German Panzer divisions had been specifically organized for combined-arms warfare, and it was by combined arms that, on both sides, every major campaign was waged since at least that time on.

Meanwhile, the cost of those arms had risen to the point where, even for the largest and richest power that history had ever seen, to continue building them began to appear a prescription for bankruptcy. The more expensive the weapons, the stronger the temptation to stretch development, reduce numbers, skimp on maintenance, and lower readiness.[73] The order of battle had to be pared down. In the U.S. the process got under way during the budget cuts that followed the end of the Vietnam War; a decade or so later, the same kind of budget crunch began to affect the Soviet Union as well.[74] Especially in the case of limited war (in truth, the only kind still possible), even the largest anticipated conventional operations would presumably involve no more than a few divisions, and last no more than a few weeks. Nor, presumably, would they be able to penetrate very deep, or overrun large tracts of inhabited country—since in that case the war might well cease to be limited.

In the end, the outcome of these developments was to make the term "strategy" itself appear less and less appropriate. In the U.S. during the eighties it was replaced by something known as the "operational art of war," invented by the "military reformers" and then adopted as the core subject studied at most military institutes of higher learning. The Reform Movement grew out of the Vietnam experience wherein, it was felt, the U.S. armed forces had failed miserably in that they poured in money, machines, and men without adapting their efforts to the nature of the enemy. Accordingly, it emphasized maneuver at the expense of attrition, mobility at the expense of firepower, and obtaining leverage at the expense of frontal assaults. To the extent that they encouraged awareness of these factors and caused some manuals to be rewritten, the Reformers may have done some good; the Persian Gulf Crisis gave the forces one last opportunity to apply what they had learned. However, to the great majority of the wars fought during the second half of the twentieth century (namely, those "without fronts"), this kind of strategy was simply irrelevant.

The more that conventional strategy was heading toward a dead end, the greater was the tendency to focus attention on nuclear strategy. This, too, fell into two kinds: war-fighting on the one hand, and deterrence on the other. While the term "strategy" has been applied to nuclear war-fighting, this usage should not hide the fact that there exist some critical differences between it and conventional strategy. First, in view of the power of nuclear weapons, presumably there would be no need to attack a target twice—thus more or less giving the lie to Clausewitz's dictum that war does not consist of a single blow.[75] Even more important, in four decades no meaningful defense against nuclear weapons has been found. In the absence of such a defense, a nuclear war between the superpowers would not involve a reciprocal action, or interplay, between the forces—which very interplay represents, to quote Clausewitz again, the essence of strategy.[76]

These facts did not discourage the Dr. Strangeloves of this world from devising countless nuclear strategies over the years; and indeed doing so was transformed into a cottage industry. There was all-out nuclear war, which would be short, and limited nuclear war, which would be more protracted. There were first strikes and second strikes. Significantly, no one seemed inclined to explore the possibility of a third strike, though there was some vague talk of "broken-back warfare" taking place between powers whose main cities had already been reduced to radiating ruins. There were countervalue strategies aimed at the opponent's cities, counterforce strategies aimed at his nuclear forces, and decapitating strategies directed against his government, command centers, and communications system.[77] Some strategies aimed at the opponent's annihilation and sought to quantify the meaning of that term; others were merely designed to make him pause and think.

The remarkable fact about all these strategies was that the more numerous and sophisticated the technical means available for their implementation, the more pointless it all seemed. A quantitative analysis of American war plans drawn up over the years supports this claim: From 1945 to 1950 the Air Force is said to have devised ten different blueprints for a nuclear offensive against the Soviet Union, an average of just under two per year. During the next decade (1951 to 1960) the number dropped by three-quarters, to one every two years. Between 1962 and 1993 there were only three such plans, an average of little more than one every ten years.[78] Presumably this diminution was because the most important targets had already been covered: By the late fifties, several megaton-size warheads were being allocated to *each* Soviet city the size of Hiroshima. More and more, strategy became a question of using magnifying glasses to scan satellite photos for objects somehow overlooked during the previous planning round.

Thus, the growth of nuclear arsenals caused war-fighting to look less attractive with each passing decade. *Faute de mieux,* "strategy" also began to be used in the sense of a method, or methods, designed to *prevent* a nuclear war. And it was out of *this* that deterrence theory grew. Previous works on strategy had scarcely mentioned deterrence (at least the term does not figure in any of the three indexes of Clausewitz that I consulted). Yet, seemingly all at once, perhaps half the literature was devoted to it. The meaning of "deterrence" and the best ways in which it could be achieved were discussed in literally countless publications. Armed with the tools of psychology and cognitive theory,[79] scholars analyzed capability and credibility, reality and perception. Deterrence could achieve its aim either by denial or by punishment. It could be symmetrical, as between the superpowers, or asymmetrical, as between a superpower and some much smaller country.[80] In some situations it was supposed to be stable, in others unstable. Some strategists considered it necessary to lower nuclear thresholds in order to deter; others required that they be raised in order to safeguard the world's continued existence. Deterrence was merged with game theory, and dressed up in mathematical equations. It became an esoteric science comprehensible—if at all—only to a few university professors. Meanwhile, there is no evidence that decision-makers took much notice. As one authority aptly wrote, *c'est magnifique mais ce n'est pas la strategie.*[81]

Whereas traditional strategy had been associated with war, much of nuclear strategy operated only in peace and, indeed, was specifically designed to preserve it. This turned strategy into a continuous exercise: As much as peace penetrated war, war also penetrated peace. Strategy had been the jealously guarded province of the military. Now that war itself came to be seen mainly as something to be prevented or deterred, increasingly it was dominated by civilians and (in the U.S.) the so-called "defense community." Whereas previously it dealt with the deployment of armed forces and their operations against each other, now it was extended until it came to include every aspect of national defense. It became possible to talk of a country's political strategy, economic strategy, technological strategy, and any number of other strategies. Most of these only had the most tenuous connection with strategy as traditionally understood. Since very often it was a question not of waging war but of preparing for it, many of them ran directly counter to Clausewitz's warning that fighting is an art in its own right which should not be confused with anything else.[82] The opponent, who is ordinarily the very factor that makes strategy into a separate field, was often absent; in other cases he was to be found on one's own side, especially when it was a question of distributing scarce resources. "Strategy" became one of the buzzwords of the age, meaning the methodical use of resources to achieve any goal, from selling consumer goods to winning a woman. In the process, it lost most of its connections with the conduct of large-scale war.

More fundamental still, the *objective* of strategy changed. Whereas previously it had been to overthrow and destroy the enemy (the more so the better), now the most it could achieve, or threaten to achieve, was to inflict a certain amount of pain. Instead of attempting to put the opponent in the worst of all possible situations, now it sought to make sure that, for him, life would still be tolerable even after surrendering to our demands. As a result, the practical business of strategy—to the extent that it has any relation to practical business at all—was also transformed beyond all recognition. To quote the greatest of all post-1945 strategists, it consisted of "the diplomacy of violence," "the art of commitment," "the manipulation of risk," and "the dialogue of competitive armament."[83] Falling short of war, and often even if they did form part of war, military moves lost whatever autonomy they may have had. They became part of a complicated game whose purpose was to signal one's intentions, communicate one's claims, make one's threats appear most effective, retreat without losing face, and in general bargain with the enemy—all the while doing one's best to keep the process under control and prevent the world from being blown up.

Understood in this way, history came around full-circle. The birth of strategy had originally taken place at the time when the rise of an abstract entity, the state, enabled military affairs to become separated from politics and commanders from politicians; also, it was the state that had provided the large spaces needed for the forces to operate in. Now that space no longer offered protection, and the overriding goal of strategy was to prevent war or at least limit it, the process went into reverse gear. As the history of countless international crises from 1945 to 1990 demonstrates, in the vast majority of cases it was not soldiers who strategized, but statesmen and politicians; conversely, soldiers entered war academies which supposedly taught them politics as well as military things.

Ninety percent of active "strategy" came to consist of crisis management. As each successive crisis formed, mounted, peaked, and went away, threats were made and forces put on alert. Sometimes units were also moved around, arms sold to clients, and wars fought by proxy. Though there were many tense moments, only once or twice did either superpower get the opportunity to engage in the kind of large-scale war-fighting that traditionally marked the point where politics ended and strategy took over. Nor, in the vast majority of cases, did even the more modest "operational art of war" get a chance to show what it could do.

As "strategy" turned into mere posturing, over time the effectiveness of that posturing declined. With nuclear weapons known to be plentiful, deployed, and capable of almost instantly destroying civilization as we know it, there was no need to rattle them. Both sides learned to play the game of threat, counterthreat, bluff, and brinkmanship equally well. As a result, in virtually no case was either able to gain a positive advantage or change the *status quo* by making nuclear threats; even the greatest "victory" ever won in this way, namely the withdrawal of Soviet missiles from Cuba, was immediately balanced by President Kennedy's deciding to remove American missiles from Turkey on the very next day.[84] From Central Europe to Korea, the most important frontiers were frozen into place and cemented into concrete walls. True, all over the Third World "gains" continued to be made and "losses" suffered; however, as far as the available evidence goes, *none* of the numerous changes that took place was occasioned by, or even connected with, whatever shifts may have taken place in the central nuclear balance. Throughout the period between 1945 and 1985, whenever some Third World country transferred its allegiance from one superpower to the other, this was invariably the result of regional considerations—coupled, not seldom, with a domestic *coup*.[85]

If only because both sides understood the danger inherent in nuclear crises, gradually they tended to become less frequent. To go by one list,[86] there were six crises involving nuclear threats between 1948 and 1958, three between 1959 and 1969, and only two (three, if the war against Iraq is counted) since then. Moreover, time has caused the crises to grow less acute. Probably the last time a serious danger of strategic nuclear war existed was during the 1962 Cuban Missile Crisis. As far as we know, the last occasion when the nuclear forces of a superpower were put on alert was in the aftermath of the 1973 Arab–Israeli War. Even then, scholars familiar with Soviet military–political thinking considered that the crisis existed mainly in President Nixon's imagination.[87] By contrast, when a spokesman for President Carter hinted that nuclear weapons might be used if the USSR tried to move from Afghanistan to the Persian

Gulf, no corresponding military moves took place, and few people even noticed that a crisis existed. Finally, in the eighties the time arrived when both sides started wondering whether the game was worth the candle. As soon as the question "what for" raised itself, the Cold War was all but over, and the Wall (and other walls) started coming down.

The fact that "strategy" is one of the buzzwords of our age should not make us forget the transformation in its nature since World War II. Whereas previously strategy had been the art of waging war, now its overwhelming goal was to preserve peace. Whereas previously it stood for large-scale warfare between large-scale forces, now such warfare remained possible only if and where the most powerful weapons by far were not yet available. Whereas previously the most effective operations were those taking place far behind the enemy's front, now for the most part such operations became too dangerous to contemplate—and, insofar as they involved occupying large inhabited spaces, almost certainly futile in the long run. Though numerous nuclear war-fighting strategies were designed to overcome these defects, they differed from traditional strategy in the absence of any meaningful interplay between the parties. Since there is not, and almost certainly cannot be, any defense, the strategies in question have been limited to exercises in which the opposition has been provided by computers.

The result has been to transform war-fighting (as it applies to the superpowers) into deterrence, and military operations into mere posturing. Increasingly perceived as both useless and dangerous, even that posturing ended up abolishing itself. As of the time of this writing, strategy had retained its effectiveness only when directed against small, nonnuclear powers such as Iraq; and even in that case the final outcome remained to be seen. Fearing escalation, civilians on both sides of the Iron Curtain imposed tighter and tighter control over strategy, taking care that they alone would be able to activate the most powerful weapons by far. This degraded the military until they were compelled to content themselves with the so-called operational art of war, although most of the time they were unable to exercise even that art—either because the opponents were almost ludicrously diminutive or because "operations," as understood from Jomini on, are irrelevant to the most important forms of war in our age: guerrilla, and terrorism.

CONCLUSIONS

As the twentieth century comes to an end, we have reached the point where nuclear war between the superpowers—or what is left of them—seems out of the question. War between one of the main powers and some third country which does not possess nuclear weapons is still possible; however, it is becoming clearer, that, in such a war, the opponent would (strange to say) have to be particularly small, weak, and isolated if to be fought at all.

Though future historians will no doubt be able to point out many reasons why all its attendant fuss and fury have come about, there can be no question concerning the critical role played by the nuclear threat. For the first time in history, nuclear weapons have created a situation whereby one side can win a total victory and still face annihilation. By cutting the link between triumph and survival, they have permitted world peace to survive—and ultimately transcend—acute international rivalries between the superpowers. During much of the past, those rivalries were marked by unrestrained technological competition, some of it highly destablizing; extreme asymmetries in military capabilities, even to the point where one side possessed a nuclear arsenal and the other did not; intense, almost paranoid, internal pressures favoring arms races; command and control arrangements which, in retrospect, can only be called hair-raising; and, in the person of Stalin, one of the most absolute, bloodthirsty dictators in all world history.

Perhaps more remarkable still, deterrence as exercised by the superpowers has survived its own logical contradictions.[88] The lowering of nuclear thresholds to achieve credibility in the fifties did not lead to war any more than raising them did in the sixties and the seventies. A relatively small arsenal of massive weapons did not tempts its owner to strike, but neither did a much larger number of much more powerful and accurate ones. Asymmetrical, ever-shifting capabilities did not affect the balance—at any rate not sufficiently to make an important difference. On the conventional plane, deterrence survived both the tripwire concepts of the fifties and the doctrine of "flexible response" adopted from the sixties on. Though the price of peace consisted of enormous expenditure, constant vigilance, and some tense moments, ultimately that peace held. And as it held, the time came when the question began to be asked whether the tense moments, the constant vigilance, and the enormous expenditure could really be justified. At that moment, the dissolution of one superpower began. From East Asia to Europe, the other has been withdrawing its forces and sending them home by the tens of thousands. In the absence of an external threat, and unless a drastic remedy is found for the deteriorating economic situation, it may yet follow suit.

Chapter III

NUCLEAR WEAPONS IN ASIA

Will the proliferation of nuclear weapons cause other states to follow the superpowers on the road toward stalemate and eventual peace, or will those weapons make them more adventurous in their dealings with each other? How well do Third World leaders understand the nature of nuclear weapons, and to what extent is their understanding different from that which obtains in the West? From the late fifties on, the desire of the principal nuclear powers—the U.S. above all—to retain their oligopoly in the field has led to a vast literature on proliferation, almost all designed to show its nefarious effects. Some of the arguments have not been without a certain irony. For example, during the sixties, entire strategic doctrines were built on the idea that single-warhead Inter-Continental Ballistic Missiles (ICBMs) in the hands of the superpowers had a *stabilizing* effect on relations between them; but twenty years later similar, yet smaller and much less potent, missiles in those of other countries were somehow considered *destabilizing*. Similarly, the sprawling nuclear arsenals in the hands of the superpowers (or at any rate the U.S.) were safe, and only served to deter war—whereas the much smaller and easily controllable ones in the hands of other countries were unsafe, and might increase the risk of either an intended or an unintended clash.

To smooth over such absurdities, it became necessary to pretend that multipolared balances between comparatively small regional powers were more dangerous to world peace than the global bipolar one between the superpowers; or that Third World leaders were less responsible and more adventurous than their great power counterparts; or that Third World leaders and their peoples were governed by some peculiar "ethnic" notions that distorted their political vision, making them incapable of considering nuclear matters in a rational way (rational being defined as Western). The following pages will examine these arguments, beginning with China, which was the first Third World country to acquire nuclear arms. After China will come India and Pakistan, and then—in a separate chapter—the Middle East.

CHINA

To understand the reasons behind China's decisions to build the Bomb, it is necessary to go back a little in history. Seen from the vantage-point of Beijing, the entire century since 1840 had been one of constant humiliation at the hands of stronger, technically more advanced (but morally quite corrupt) Western imperialist powers. Coming from across the sea, those powers had used their superior weaponry in order to impose unequal treaties upon China, particularly in regard to extraterritorial rights for their citizens, trading privileges, and permission to import opium. They tore away choice morsels of its territory, such as Hong Kong. They butchered those Chinese—the Boxers—who dared offer resistance, and went on to set up semisovereign enclaves in China's main cities. The crowning humiliation was inflicted when Japan, traditionally regarded as a kind of "younger sister," joined in the process of dismemberment and occupied Taiwan in 1895. Beginning in 1932, Japan took over as the leading imperialist power, thus revealing (as well as reviling) China in all its helplessness.

Though the victorious outcome of Mao's 1949 civil war put an end to foreign intervention on the Chinese mainland, in some respects the job was left incomplete: On the island of Taiwan there remained a would-be alternative government, guaranteed by a foreign power. Too, the glorious Communist Revolution was only a year old before the Korean War brought an "imperialist" presence back on China's border, putting the People's Liberation Army (PLA) in contact with modern firepower for the first time. Having served the Japanese as the base from which they had set out to invade Manchuria, Korea was considered a sensitive spot. Though the final outcome of the Korean War may have been acceptable to the Chinese,[1] the "human wave" tactics used to offset their technological inferiority necessarily led to horrific casualties. To make Beijing end the war on terms acceptable to the U.S. the Eisenhower administration brandished nuclear weapons in a fairly open manner.[2] What is more, it used secret diplomatic channels to warn the Chinese of the atomic consequences that might follow if they failed to reach a settlement.[3] Since no country has ever admitted to surrendering to nuclear blackmail, the exact role played by these threats in China's decision to bring the war to an end remains unknown; the Chinese themselves maintain that it was the U.S. that had made the critical concession, on matters pertaining to prisoners of war.[4] Still, and at a minimum, the Bomb must have given the Chinese leadership food for thought.

Against this background, China's concern with nuclear matters actually dates to the early fifties. Given the combination of traditional Chinese secrecy plus Communist paranoia, our sources for this period are few, far between, and without exception tendentious. Essentially, they consist of the recently published memoirs of the man in charge, Marshal Nie Rongzen, plus a handful of newspaper interviews (most of them rather general and granted long after the event).[5] As best as can be gleaned from these sources, the actual decision to build the Bomb was taken in January 1955, during the height of the First Taiwan Crisis. With the U.S. once again advertising its nuclear weapons to prevent the Chinese from achieving what were, from the Chinese point of view, perfectly legitimate demands, the leadership in Beijing was convinced that China would never be free of interference so long as she, too, did not possess those weapons. Nie recalls a Politburo meeting in which Mao, toying with a piece of uranium that had been put on display, went into ecstasies and vowed to achieve success. In fact, the concerted drive that followed is best understood less as a purely "strategic" measure than as a national crusade.

As was to become the case in every developing country wanting its own Bomb, the organization responsible for the Chinese nuclear program was highly centralized and completely under political control. Overall supervision was exercised by the Politburo by way of Prime Minister Zhou Enlai. Directly under him came Marshal Nie Rognzen, originally of the artillery corps. His position as program manager was similar to that of Gen. Leslie Groves, who had run the Manhattan Project; however, he was also made Vice Premier. The role of chief scientist, which in the U.S. had been filled by Robert Oppenheimer, was played by Qian Sanqiang. He and his wife, He Zehui, had studied with the Joliot-Curies—well-known for their Communist sympathies—in Paris; now they found themselves at the head of a scientific cadre numbering perhaps a thousand. Another prominent member of the team was Pen Huanwu, who had studied with Max Born at Edinburgh. Apparently the most important missile expert was Qian Weichang, who had spent the war years working at the California Institute of Technology's Jet Propulsion Laboratory. The entire organization seems to have been in place by the end of 1955, and serious prospecting for uranium began in the same year. The construction of a gaseous-diffusion plant for the separation of uranium-235 got under way in 1958, as did building a reactor for plutonium production.

Meanwhile, events surrounding the Hungarian Uprising (October 1956) and its suppression pushed China and the Soviet Union into each other's arms. Prototypes of delivery vehicles—aircraft and ballistic missiles—as well as technical data and the contents of entire factories started reaching China. So, in the first half of 1958, did Soviet nuclear specialists, two of whom were nuclear-weapons designers. The Chinese claim that the Soviets at one point promised them an "educational" bomb to copy; however, Soviet–Chinese cooperation, in nuclear matters as well as others, was never entirely smooth. During a summit meeting held at Beijing, for example, the Chinese leader horrified his Soviet counterpart with facile talk about the need to destroy world "Imperialism"—even at the risk of a nuclear war, and even if it should cost hundreds of millions of casualties (which at least *China* was capable of replacing within a few generations).[6] It is not necessary to take Khrushchev's account literally. He was writing long after the event, in an attempt to justify the role he played in bringing about the Sino–Soviet split; furthermore, he himself put on record that he never liked or trusted Mao. Even if Mao *did* say something of the sort, there is in fact no need to regard him as mentally disturbed. When everything is said and done, China, thanks to its enormous rural population, always has been, and remains, more capable of surviving nuclear war than any other country. This is a fact which the leadership clearly understands,[7] and would be foolish not to exploit—at least for the purpose of political rhetoric.

Though an exact date is not given, the meeting at the poolside in Beijing cannot have taken place too long before or after the Second Taiwan Crisis of 1958. Whether Mao really hoped to reconquer the island for China, or was merely testing the ground, we cannot know.[8] In any case, the result was fierce air and sea battles between

Communist and Nationalist forces, as well as an American threat to use the Seventh Fleet to prevent a possible landing on the island. The two episodes together—as well as the entire "adventurous" Chinese policy during those years—seem to have caused the Soviets to entertain second thoughts concerning the wisdom of helping Beijing. Using various excuses to postpone delivery of the "educational" bomb, in 1959 they started withdrawing their experts. Finally they pulled out altogether, leaving the Chinese with little more than a jumble of pipes for their half-completed gaseous-diffusion plant.

These interesting times were the years of the "Great Leap Forward." Mao's attempt to move industry from the cities to the countryside caused production to plummet. So widespread was economic distress that it led to hunger, even among the scientists involved in the nuclear project—a privileged group though they presumably were.[9] Construction of the reactor in the Gobi Desert was apparently delayed. This holdup led to some internal debate concerning the viability of the entire program, and compelled Nie Rongzen to switch from the plutonium to the enriched uranium road toward the Bomb. In the end, construction of the gaseous-diffusion plant was completed in mid-1963, reportedly coinciding with the delivery of the first ten tons of uranium hexafluoride for processing. It was typical of the entire Chinese "leapfrogging" approach that, instead of building a primitive gun design first, they went straight for the relatively sophisticated, implosion-type Bomb that was finally exploded on October 16, 1964. Within three years China also detonated a hydrogen bomb, thus requiring less time between Bomb prototypes than any other country before or—as far as we know—since.

Amid widespread concern about the military–political consequences that might follow from the nuclear status of a country avowedly committed to upsetting the *status quo* by revolutionary means, the Chinese took another unique step. They issued an official declaration that under no circumstances would China be the first to use nuclear weapons, and that under no circumstances would she subject nonnuclear countries to a nuclear threat.[10] Now it is true that covenants without swords are but words. The first pledge can be violated without notice during a crisis. As to the second, a nuclear threat to neighboring countries exists whether Beijing wants it or not, and will have to be taken into account by them in all their politico–military considerations. Still, it is worth noting that, as far as it goes, the promise contained in the declaration *has* been kept. As compared to the other two superpowers, Chinese references to, and displays of, nuclear weapons and their delivery vehicles have always been few and extremely low-key; and this continues to be the case.

Just as the Soviets assisted China in the early steps toward the Bomb, so they also provided help in the matter of delivery vehicles. First came the Hong-6, a copy of the Tu-16 bomber. This was followed by the DF-2 missile, a copy of the Soviet SS-3, two of which had been given to China in 1958. Reportedly possessing a range of 1,450 kilometers (900 miles),[11] the missiles were deployed along the northwestern Chinese coast, from where they were capable of reaching Japanese cities as well as American bases in that country. After 1966, the DF-2 was supplemented by the DF-3. Like its predecessor, it was liquid-propelled but, with a range of perhaps 2,800 kilometers (1,800 miles), could reach targets as far away as the U.S. bases in the Philippines. It was the DF-3, used as a booster, that allowed the Chinese to put their first satellite into orbit in 1970; by that time, approximately 100 missiles of both types had been deployed.[12] Unlike the superpowers, however, the Chinese did not choose to invest heavily in expensive, hardened silos. Instead, a modest but apparently quite sufficient[13] second-strike capability was achieved by hiding the launchers in the extensive, complicated terrain presented by the mountains in the center of the country. Presumably some of the sites have been located by satellite reconnaissance. Whether it is possible to find all of them, however, remains highly uncertain.[14]

In the meantime, the international situation was transformed. As the strongest regional power by far, China never required nuclear weapons to deal with her immediate neighbors, and whatever doubts existed on that score were conclusively removed by the victory that the PLA won over India in 1962. Building the Bomb was part of a wider drive toward national independence, self-assertion, and scientific progress, all of which reasons figured in a Communist Party Bulletin on nuclear matters that was published in July 1958.[15] Beyond that, the specific enemy against which it was directed was the U.S. As the American involvement in Vietnam deepened, Chinese concerns on this account peaked during the mid-sixties. Beijing responded by extending military and economic aid to the Viet Cong and North Vietnam, and also deployed 35,000 antiaircraft troops inside the latter's territory. Though neither side cared to give too much publicity to the fact, these forces are said to have brought down several American aircraft.[16] Having quarreled with Washington *and* Moscow (in 1963, the aftermath of the Indo–Chinese War witnessed the rare spectacle of *both* superpowers rushing aid to New Delhi), Beijing had good reason to feel isolated. These facts, plus the Cultural Revolution of those years, may account for the particularly strident character of no fewer than twenty-nine nuclear tests. Violating the 1963 Test Ban Treaty (which China went out of its way to denounce), they were conducted in the atmosphere, culminating in the firing of a live warhead from atop a ballistic missile to a site inside national territory—another feat equaled by no other state before or since.

As the sixties drew to an end, the situation changed once again. In Vietnam, the Americans had become bogged down in an unwinnable guerrilla war, making their presence in Indochina appear as less of a threat. Tension with the USSR mounted, fueled partly by Chinese claims on territory taken away by the Tsars during the previous century and perhaps partly—we do not really know—by the Soviet–Indian *rapprochement* initiated in 1964. Things came to a head during the summer of 1969 when the Chinese, by their aggressive patrolling, provoked a series of border clashes that were the largest ever between two nuclear powers. The Soviets may have contemplated a preemptive strike against China's nuclear installations, and may even have sounded out the U.S. as to the stance it would take in such an eventuality.[17] However, the U.S. reportedly refused to countenance the move. Whatever the exact sequence of events that followed, in the end both countries showed their awareness of nuclear realities by drawing back from the kind of escalation that might have led to nuclear war. In September 1969, Zhou Enlai traveled to Hanoi for Ho Chi Min's funeral, taking the opportunity to meet Soviet Prime Minister Alexei Kosygin. Thereafter, the border incidents came to an end—though the tension between the two countries did not disappear, and both sides engaged in a formidable buildup of their armed forces in the region.

Meanwhile, the Chinese continued to take steps toward force modernization, albeit slowly and on a scale that did not even begin to match that of either superpower. Development of yet another missile, the DF-4, which was capable of lifting a megaton warhead to a maximum range of 4,800 kilometers (3,000 miles), began in

1965; deployment took place from 1971 on, enabling China to (circumstances providing) reach most Soviet targets east of the Ural Mountains.[18] The Chinese also built and deployed a handful of powerful two-stage, liquid-fueled ICBMs, known as the DF-5. In many ways this missile resembled the American Titan: Provided with a stabilized-platform inertial-guidance system, gimballed thrust chambers, vernier engines, and swiveling main engines for altitude thrust/vector control, it was a remarkable technological achievement for a developing country and brought targets in the American homeland within range for the first time. A missile with multiple-reentry vehicles (MRVs) was tested in 1982, and a submarine carrying twelve ballistic missiles was launched in 1985.

Organizationally, speaking, the Chinese system for commanding and controlling nuclear weapons follows the Soviet model from which it was originally copied. While the Chinese Air Force and Navy both have nuclear weapons, their number is relatively small and their delivery vehicles for the most part antiquated. The land-missile-based force which (as in the former USSR) represents by far the most important component of the Chinese "Triad" is in the hands of the so-called Second Artillery Arm. Ostensibly this is just a service arm like all the rest. In practice, it seems to be closely controlled by the Politburo.[19]

Whether the Chinese have gone ahead and developed tactical nuclear weapons in addition to strategic ones remains uncertain. Zhou Enlai many years ago said this would not be done,[20] and to date no conclusive evidence to the contrary has been published.[21] On the other hand, over thirty years of nuclear research and development will certainly have given the Chinese the scientific and technical capability necessary for the purpose. Delivery vehicles in the form of fighter-bombers, short-range surface-to-surface missiles, and heavy artillery are also known to be available. China itself has been targeted by tactical nuclear weapons for over three decades—in fact, ever since the U.S. was reported to have deployed them on Taiwan during the Quemoy Crisis.[22] For these three reasons, it would be most surprising if its military–political leadership had taken no appropriate countermeasures.

Throughout the period since the Chinese first turned their attention to nuclear matters, remarkably little could be divined of their nuclear doctrine, if any. One reason for this was that Mao—so long as he lived—did not permit the development of open-ended strategic studies;[23] nor was such reticence unsuited to the requirements of a country whose nuclear forces were (and are) small, comparatively primitive, and completely outclassed by those of the U.S. on the one hand and Russia on the other. Chinese references to nuclear weapons tend to be few, far between, and vague. Though they do not display the fascination with technical detail that is such a characteristic feature of Western strategic thought, on the whole they are as rational as those of anybody else.[24] After all, many of China's early nuclear scientists were Western-trained and in full command of Western languages. Later, hundreds of technical, military, and political cadres were sent out to attend Soviet academies. China's top leadership naturally followed, and commented on the ideas raised by their Soviet allies concerning nuclear weapons.[25] They are also known to have read Western literature on the subject, from the early fifties on.[26]

At the time it first set out to build nuclear weapons, China's main concerns seem to have been national self-assertion, would revolution, and (above all) deterring any invasion—a possibility which, at the time when memories of the Sino–Japanese and Korean Wars were still fresh, did not seem as remote or as absurd as—thanks in part to China's possession of the Bomb—it does today. At first, the threat seemed to come from the direction of U.S.-assisted Taiwanese forces. Looking for popular support inside China itself, they might try to reverse the Communist victory of 1949; in 1958, this fear led to the distribution of a new Tactical Training Guide said to emphasize "modern military skills ... under the conditions of atomic, and chemical weapons, and ballistic missiles."[27] When the American threat receded during the sixties, Beijing (which for reasons unknown had chosen to raise tension along the Soviet border) began to fear a Red Army advance in support of a preemptive strike directed against China's nuclear installations. Fear of a Soviet invasion apparently reached its height in 1969–71, prompting Mao to say that since China was a huge country that could not be easily conquered, he personally was in favor of surrendering some territory.[28]

In response to these fears, China did not imitate the doctrine of either superpower; in other words, she neither planned on the offensive first use of nuclear forces in case of war—which was the Soviet approach—nor followed the U.S. in its attempt to deter war by a show of overwhelming (later, merely "sufficient") strength.

Nor did the Chinese develop an explicit nuclear doctrine, such as the one governing France's nuclear deterrent. Having given their word never to be the first to use nuclear weapons and never to threaten others with them, presumably they could hardly discuss whatever plans they entertained to use them nevertheless. To the extent that Western concepts are applicable at all, the Chinese "strategic" stance is perhaps best described as minimum deterrence: In 1965, Mao is supposed to have told visiting French author Andre Malraux "All I want are six atom bombs—and then I know that nobody will attack me."[29] Such a train of thought fits well with the Chinese approach to war, which has always been regarded not so much as an instrument of policy as an unavoidable evil. Hence the emphasis on a low profile, secrecy, and—also in view of the country's very limited resources—economy.[30]

Following the events of 1969, the Soviet forces in the Far East embarked upon a sustained process of reinforcement and modernization until they were turned into a formidable military instrument facing China. The buildup, which consisted of several dozen armored and mechanized divisions, culminated during the late Brezhnev years, approximately between 1977 and 1982. Across the border in China, it led to a lively debate concerning the appropriateness of "People's War"—the method by which the Communists had come to power—under "modern conditions."[31] It was feared that, as part of a possible invasion of northwest China, the Soviets might resort to tactical nuclear weapons in order to effect a breakthrough. Conversely, there was some vague talk of the PLA itself employing nuclear weapons during the second phase of the war, when the Red Army divisions would be halted and a counterattack mounted. Some large-scale exercises were held to test the various scenarios, leading to some strange notions concerning the ability of those forces to operate under nuclear bombardment and in a radioactive environment.

As late as 1987, PLA training manuals continued to proclaim the merits of antiradiation protection, allegedly provided by smoke screens. They also emphasized the utility of foxholes, specially designed antinuclear suits, goggles, and masks.[32] They developed a doctrine (at least on paper) for fighting a tactical nuclear war, one which emphasized such traditional PLA *fortes* as close-range fighting, night fighting, trench and tunnel warfare, and dispersion into small, mobile teams living off the countryside. How they could hope to reconcile such doctrines with the construction of modern, conventional, mechanized forces initiated by Deng Xiaoping after 1982 is hard to see. How they could hope to avoid escalation from the tactical to the strategic level—given that the territories of China and the USSR are adjacent, without any natural border to separate them—is even harder to understand.[33] Still, what little we do know of Chinese notions does not seem more absurd than did similar ideas incorporated into American military doctrine during the "Pentomic Era." Nor, to its credit, did the People's Liberation Army ever follow the example of the superpowers by putting their ideas to an actual nuclear "test."

While it may be true that Beijing retained its "revolutionary" stance longer than other Communist powers, and still engages in occasional anti-imperialist and antihegemonist rhetoric, in practice the last time China mobilized its armed forces, went to war, and practiced any kind of military strategy was in 1962. Even then, less than one-tenth of the forces available to the PLA were involved in the fighting. Since then, relations with India have become more-or-less normal, though not cordial,[34] enabling China's Prime Minister to visit New Delhi in December 1991. Beijing may not have displayed great international responsibility in staging the 1969 border incidents with the USSR, but at any rate the situation was never allowed to get out of hand and develop into major clashes between the two sides' main forces. Relations between the two countries have in fact been slowly improving since the middle of the eighties, and in April 1991 it was announced that they had reached agreement concerning the border between them. A handful of Chinese divisions did mount a "punitive expedition" against neighboring Vietnam in 1979, but only to a depth of fifteen miles, and only to withdraw almost immediately. Since then, their most adventurous foreign-policy operation has been to offer support to the rebels in Afghanistan and Cambodia. Even so, the scale on which they operated did not come close to matching the efforts mounted by the U.S. and the U.S.S.R. respectively.

Even the problem of Taiwan, which at one point formed the burning focus of China's relations with the rest of the world, has long since become dormant. The last time the armed forces of the two countries exchanged a shot was in 1958. While China's Navy and Air Force are large, for the most part they consist of small coastal craft, antiquated Soviet submarines, and 1960-vintage aircraft. Whether these forces give Beijing the capability for carrying out a complicated amphibious landing on the island is moot.[35] On the other hand, using nuclear weapons for the purpose might wreak such destruction on what China insists is one of its own provinces as to be counterproductive. Furthermore, the Nationalist Republic itself has a large and well-developed, if peaceful, nuclear program. It should be capable of producing both nuclear weapons and some delivery vehicles for them and may, indeed, have gone as far along that road as the need to maintain friendly relations with the United States permits.[36] Should the island feel desperate, then an invasion fleet launched from the mainland would present an ideal target for tactical nuclear weapons, particularly if they were carried atop missiles rather than by aircraft. Possibly as a result of knowing all this, the Chinese some years ago announced that the problem would have to be solved by peaceful means. Then, in April 1991, the first official delegations in forty years were exchanged. Meanwhile, commercial ties between the two countries have been expanding, to the point that Taiwan has become China's largest source of foreign investment, well ahead of both the U.S. and Japan.

Thus, on the whole, there is no evidence that Chinese ideas on nuclear weapons are less realistic, or their policy with regard to them less responsible, than that of the U.S. or the former USSR. If Mao at one time described the U.S. with its nuclear weapons as a "paper tiger," this was long before China acquired the Bomb. He himself later described that phrase as no more than a "figure of speech,"[37] and none of his successors has cared to repeat anything of the sort. Far from being culturally blinkered, China's top political leadership is as well-qualified to understand nuclear realities as anyone else. Indeed, it may be better qualified, given the centralization of the nuclear program in the hands of the government, as demonstrated by the fact that Prime Minister Li Peng previously was in charge of it. If we are somewhat in the dark as to how they *do* understand it, this is in part because they have neither put their nuclear technology on show, nor developed an explicit doctrine for its use, nor made any explicit nuclear threats. To date, they remain the only country that has publicly vowed never to be the first to use nuclear weapons.

Much like the remaining main nuclear powers, China during the late eighties came around to the point where it signed the Non-Proliferation Treaty in March 1992. Also much like them, China's adherence does not prevent it from extending limited nuclear aid to its friends and allies when this is perceived as suiting its interests. Again much like them, though at a slower pace, China has steadily cut the size of its conventional armed forces even while pursuing military modernization. And finally, much like them, it has not made use of those forces against a first-rate opponent for several decades—which is not surprising, given that any such use would entail the risk of escalation. For China, as for other countries, *peace* has been the sturdy child of nuclear terror.

INDIA

To the southwest of China, the other Asian country with pretensions to being a leading regional power is India. However great the differences between them, the two countries still have some things in common. Both regard themselves as the homes of ancient, highly developed civilizations. Both fell into internal decay, after which they became the prey of technologically advanced Western powers from which they gained their freedom only following a prolonged, difficult, and costly struggle. Once free, both were concerned to establish their independence symbolically as well as in fact—and that concern played a critical role in their decision to establish a nuclear program.

India's concern with nuclear matters is actually older than China's, dating from the late forties when Prime Minister Jawaharlal Nehru organized an Indian Atomic Energy Committee with himself at its head.[38] The man in charge was his protégé, Homi Bhaba, another of those Westernized scientists (while studying at Cambridge, he had become the youngest-ever member of the British Royal Society) who did so much to establish the nuclear programs in several developing countries.[39] The Indian effort differed from the Chinese one in two important ways. First, except for one brief period from 1975 to 1977, the country had always been democratic, and discussion quite free. Accordingly, a considerable amount of information is available about the program, which was (and continues to be) the subject of frequent debate in the Indian Lok Sabha (Parliament), official and semiofficial literature, and the press. Second, it involved the construction of a far broader scientific, technical, and industrial infrastructure than exists in China. Much of this is said to have had (and still have) no military impli cations whatsoever; that instead, it operates, according to design, to exploit the country's abundant reserves of thorium—a fissile material which, though it is unsuitable for the production of bombs, could be used for purely civilian purposes.[40]

As Nehru and his successors saw the problem, India had missed the early modern Industrial Revolution, and suffered conquest by Britain as a result. It was not about to miss the Nuclear Revolution, which in the fifties was being widely flaunted as one way for developing countries to catch up. India, however, was determined not to be dependent on foreigners for this crucial aspect of her development; hence the rejection of international controls, and the insistence on indigenous development of every stage in the nuclear-fuel cycle.[41] The nuclear-energy program also had the advantage of cutting through the country's complicated federal structure. As the Central Government's special preserve, it was one high-prestige field of endeavor by means of which the latter's competence could be put on show.[42] The Indians undoubtedly realized that a successful program would give them the Bomb if desired—even though there is no proof that this was their main goal from the beginning: In spite of occasional queries in Parliament,[43] during the early 1960s there were still no indications that India was planning to build a weapon.

Throughout the fifties, one of Nehru's principal concerns in foreign policy was building a "neutralist" block consisting of Third World countries that would resist attempts by the superpowers to impose their hegemony. This approach led him to seek good relations with Communist China, perceived as another neutralist country; and in 1957–58 he even orchestrated a popular "Hindi–Chin Bhai Bhai" ("Hindus and Chinese Are Friends") campaign. How, in spite of numerous warnings from Beijing, he allowed himself to become entangled in a military conflict with China remains unclear.[44] It is certain that the 1962 war, in which his forces were defeated and driven back across the Himalayas, came as a shock to him;[45] in fact, within two years of it he was dead. The Indians have never given up their claim to the territories lost in 1962 but, looking back, they tend to see their clash with China as a fairly marginal affair.[46] For one thing, it did not touch upon fundamental issues pertaining to the country's best security, the more so because the post-1962 border line turned out to be much easier to defend.[47]

India's relationship with Pakistan was a different matter altogether. Each country in a different way posed, as it continues to pose, a challenge to the other's very existence. Pakistanis cannot be persuaded that the Indian leadership has reconciled itself to their country's becoming a separate entity; and in fact, given India's much greater size, population, resources, and strategic potential, it is difficult to see how New Delhi could cease to present at least a latent threat to its neighbor, even if it wanted to.[48] Conversely, Pakistan's self-proclaimed mission as a home for the subcontinent's Muslims represents a permanent challenge to India, threatening her with dismemberment.[49]

The two countries had scarcely been born when they engaged in bloody conflict over Kashmir, an issue which has continued to be bone of contention ever since. Then as now, neither side could afford to give in: India because allowing secession to take place (a possibility apparently contemplated by Nehru during the early years) might well prove the first step toward disintegration; Pakistan because of intense popular pressures. Being much the largest power in South Asia, India has *always* sought to exclude external players, seeking to create instead a series of bilateral agreements with each of its neighbors separately.[50] Conversely, Pakistan—as the weaker party—accused India of "hegemonism" and, by way of a counterweight, sought and received outside assistance by becoming a founding member of the U.S.-led Central Treaty Organization (CENTO) in 1955. During the next decade, this gave her access to American military assistance, including F-86 and F-104 fighters as well as M-48 tanks. Supposedly their purpose was to defend against a Soviet invasion of the subcontinent. In actuality, it was to push an irredentist claim against India.

In 1965 the Pakistanis, then under the military government of Mohammed Ayub Khan, thought that their hour had struck. India was only beginning to recover from her humiliation at China's hands. Nehru was dead and his successor—known as "Little [Lal Bahadur] Shastri"—did not inspire confidence. It is also possible that the Pakistanis were already thinking of the day when India would acquire nuclear weapons, and an attack on her would become too dangerous to contemplate. They must have taken notice of Homi Bhaba's 1964 statement—delivered in answer to questions in Parliament concerning the implications of the first Chinese explosion—that India was capable of producing the Bomb within eighteen months.[51] Apparently feeling that time was running out for them, they took the initiative in staging a number of border incidents in the Ran of Kush during the spring of 1965. That summer Pakistan went to war, launching a full-scale blitzkrieg with the aim of occupying Kashmir. The attack was successful at first, but later it stalled as the Indians counterattacked and outflanked their opponents from the southwest. Ultimately Soviet influence was brought to bear, and the Tashkent Agreement signed, restoring the *status quo ante*. As a result, both national leaders found themselves violently denounced for defeatism, each in his own country.

Throughout the late sixties, and in the teeth of American objections, India's nuclear infrastructure continued its steady expansion. Power stations came on line, and various capabilities involving the fuel cycle were acquired. Each time the Chinese tested another device, there was a storm of queries in Parliament concerning the state of India's nuclear program and the need to come up with an appropriate response; each time the government patiently responded that, although the country's scientists were capable of producing nuclear weapons on comparatively short notice, there was no *need* of doing so.[52] Insofar as the 1965 War had proved that India, with her much superior size and resources, had nothing to fear of Pakistan, there was logic behind this position. A real, "existential" threat to India—a country of 800 million, most of whom live on their farms—could develop only in case China and Pakistan united against it. This was a possibility, but one which (though it could never been entirely ignored) did not materialize, either in 1965 or later during the 1960s.

Meanwhile, India's international position was transformed. Without officially abandoning nonalignment, New Delhi took advantage of the Sino–Soviet split to draw much closer to Moscow. Beginning in the mid-sixties, it became the recipient of large-scale technical and military assistance.[53] India's armed forces were rebuilt with Soviet aid, and in August 1972 the two countries, in a move obviously designed to counter the growing American–Chinese *rapprochement,* signed a Friendship Treaty. With China thus held in check from the north, an opportunity for taking revenge on Pakistan for the 1965 War was eagerly awaited—and one finally presented itself toward the end of 1971. The two parts of Pakistan, separated from each other by hundreds of miles of Indian territory, had long been at loggerheads concerning the allocation of national resources, and also as to who, Islamabad or Dacca, should control the affairs of East Pakistan.[54] Large-scale disturbances broke out in the autumn and, not without some Indian encouragement, expanded into civil war. Terrible atrocities were committed by the Pakistani Army, causing large numbers of refugees (the Indians claim 10 million) to cross the border into India. Here was an opportunity too good to be missed. Prime Minister Indira Ghandi ordered her forces to "liberate" East Pakistan and, responding to Pakistani moves in the Punjab, mount an invasion of West Pakistan as well. Both of these objectives were accomplished in short order.

Looking back, the year 1971 proved to be the watershed in the subcontinent's slow drift toward what is now almost certainly a stable (if undeclared) nuclear balance of terror among China, India, and Pakistan. While each side in the Indo–Pak conflict is eager to blame the other for initiating the proliferation process, apparently the single most critical move was made by the U.S. Just as the war between India and Pakistan was at its height (Mrs. Gandhi's forces were actually occupying several thousand square miles of West Pakistani territory), President Nixon sent the aircraft carrier *Enterprise* into the Bay of Bengal. The move was intended as a warning to India not to go too far,[55] although, like every other country which has ever been in a similar situation, the Indians subsequently claimed that they were not impressed, and that the attempt to blackmail them had miscarried.[56] Still, it must have given them cause to reassess their position with respect to nuclear weapons.

The Indians also claim that, immediately after the war, their intelligence service got wind of a cabinet meeting called by Pakistan's new Prime Minister, Zulfikar Ali Bhutto. Like his rival Indira Ghandi, Bhutto belonged to the Indian aristocracy and had received an excellent Western education. Having been one of the millions who moved to Pakistan for religious reasons in 1947–48, in the mid-sixties he served as Minister of Atomic Energy and laid the foundations for his country's nuclear program by contracting with Canada for a civilian power reactor.[57] As Foreign Minister under General Yahya Khan, Bhutto was regarded in New Delhi as the latter's evil genius. In January 1972, Bhutto found himself called to salvage what was left of his country. According to Indian sources, one of the first things he did was to hold a cabinet meeting in which he vowed that his countrymen would "eat grass," if necessary, to obtain the Bomb.[58] As best as anyone can make out, it was these two incidents, coming within a month of each other, that finally pushed India into testing its so-called peaceful nuclear bomb in 1974. This, of course, does not prove that the device that actually exploded was the only one in the Indian arsenal, let alone that nuclear weapons had not been available to the Indians several years previously.

Since 1974, the government of India has continued to claim that it neither possesses nuclear weapons nor intends to develop them.[59] Though no further bombs were exploded, the nuclear infrastructure continued to expand, the most notable step being the inauguration in 1985 of an advanced breeder-type reactor which gave the country unlimited access to plutonium.[60] In 1990, the Indian nuclear arsenal was estimated to include at least forty to sixty warheads,[61] besides which great progress was also made with regard to delivery vehicles. India has acquired modern Soviet fighter-bombers, some of which it manufactures under license. It has given proof of technological prowess by launching weather- and communications satellites. Along its road to modernity, New Delhi has purchased an old aircraft carrier from Britain, contracted to lease a missile-launching submarine from the USSR (the agreement was later cancelled), and almost certainly developed and deployed an Intermediate Range Ballistics Missile (IRBM) array capable of reaching most, if not all, cities in China.[62] As part of their modernization, India's land forces have also acquired late-model nuclear-capable artillery weapons. (While the Indians should be capable of developing the necessary tactical warheads for them, whether they have done so is uncertain.)[63] All this and more—the Indian armed forces are now the fourth largest in the world, parts of them, as we have seen, at least reasonably modern—was achieved without the defense budget ever exceeding 4 percent of GNP. Although this figure probably excludes most of the expenditure for the nuclear infrastructure, which is divided among other ministries, still it is far less than in the U.S. and compares roughly with that of such medium-sized European states as Germany or France.

As their armed forces have expanded, the Indians have also developed a remarkable "strategic" literature. By-and-large, the quality of that literature will stand comparison with any in the world. This is not surprising, given that much of it is meant for foreign consumption and that close ties exist between India's "defense community" and its counterparts in other developed countries. Though the community includes senior officers, usually their contribution is limited to the occasional brief lecture. The most articulate members are government officials and academics, who are sometimes interchangeable as they move in and out of power. The occasional turban apart (many members of the Indian defense community are Sikhs), a meeting at the semiofficial Institute for Defense Studies and Analyses (IDSA) in New Delhi even *looks* like one at Britain's International Institute of Strategic Studies. This again is not surprising, however, considering that it was modeled on the latter.

As far as nuclear weapons and nuclear doctrine are concerned, an analysis of India's "defense literature" points to several intertwined lines of thought. The Indians depend on foreign aid for some of their internal development programs. Hence, one of their main concerns is to explain the reasons behind their persistent refusal to restrict their nuclear program to purely civilian purposes and to submit it to international controls. Throughout the eighties, their argument went roughly as follows:[64] In a world characterized by "vertical proliferation" (the continuous expansion and modernization of the superpowers' already enormous nuclear forces), India cannot afford to relax her guard. The Indians wish to present themselves as a regional power surrounded by nuclear weapons on all sides—including the south, where the Indian Ocean (*their* ocean) became the scene of a growing American naval presence from 1973 on. They constantly emphasize that India cannot match the superpowers' nuclear arsenals, and has no intention of trying. On the other hand, and given the refusal of other countries to disarm to anything like Indian levels, the nonproliferation regime is perceived as unfair, discriminatory, and totally unacceptable. The government of India would be sadly negligent of its duties if it did not keep the country's scientific, technological, and industrial infrastructure ready, up-to-date, and independent of foreign controls. In this way, India claims to contribute to world peace—or, at the very least, to do no more than anybody else to disturb it.

Apart from these broad geopolitical considerations, the most intense threat to India is perceived to originate in two quarters: China and Pakistan. The past has proven that each separately may be adequately handled, but an alliance between them would constitute a real nightmare. If only because Bangladesh's "gratitude" proved to be short-lived, the successful 1971 War that resulted in the dismemberment of Pakistan did not really change the strategic calculus; in fact, 1971 also marked the year when China replaced the

United States as the most important source from which Islamabad acquired its military hardware.[65] China, the IDSA strategists are fond of reminding us, has never recognized India's sovereignty over several of India's northern and northeastern provinces. It has assisted the Pakistanis in their nuclear-weapons program, and may even have allowed them to test a nuclear device on its territory.[66] The Chinese nuclear arsenal is the third largest in the world, and missiles capable of reaching all of India are stationed in Tibet. In view of this, a single Peaceful Nuclear Explosion (PNE; the Indians are fond of demonstrating their mastery of strategic terminology by coining their own terms) that took place in 1974 hardy represents an exaggerated precaution. If anything, the need for keeping India's nuclear option intact and free from foreign control has been strengthened by the disintegration of the USSR that took place in the early nineties. Now that China is no longer threatened from the north, the shadow that it casts over India has lengthened considerably. This in turn has led New Delhi to depart from its traditional "neutralist" policy and seek closer relations with the USA.

Finally, there is always the Pakistani problem *per se*. The wars of 1965 and 1971 have shown that, conventionally speaking, Islamabad is no match for the much stronger Indian armed forces. However, given the country's failure to achieve democracy, and its inherently unstable political process, a cautious attitude does not seem out of place. This is all the more the case because the Pakistanis have been working very hard to acquire a nuclear arsenal of their own, and to all appearances have succeeded in doing so. Following the Soviet invasion of Afghanistan, the U.S. violated its own laws and waived the Symington Amendment forbidding military assistance to any country suspected of building nuclear weapons. Thanks to this, Pakistan also possesses a modern force of F-16 fighter-bombers capable of delivering the Bomb to targets all over northern India.[67] The Indians are well aware of their vulnerability due to the question of Kashmir, the majority of whose inhabitants are Moslems and have repeatedly demonstrated their wish to join Pakistan. Hence they never tire of painting scenarios in which the Pakistanis would use their nuclear arsenal to cut off the province from the rest of India and occupy it.[68]

As they voice these fears and make these accusations, the Indians are aware—and know that the Pakistanis are aware—of the potential for catastrophic escalation, including the danger of nuclear pollution and contamination along the common border which, along some of its length, cuts through one of the most densely inhabited regions in the world.[69] In view of this it might be argued that, just as has long been the case between the superpowers, the entire question really is an exercise in mutual posturing and make-believe. True, neither India's nuclear forces nor those of Pakistan are comparable with those of Russia or the U.S. in terms of size or sophistication. As far as is known, neither of them possesses missiles with accurate multiple-reentry vehicles (though the Indians are probably working in that direction), or cruise missiles, or nuclear submarines, or extensive satellite-based surveillance, reconnaissance, and command-and-control capabilities. However, backwardness does not always translate into instability. On the contrary, it is precisely the inability of each side to take out the other's delivery vehicles (or even to locate the majority of them at any given moment) that gives them a second-strike capability virtually secure against a preemptive attack.

No doubt partly as a result, the last major Indo–Pakistani War was, early in the 1990s, over twenty years in the past. In recent years the most important expressions of the continuing enmity involved have been rhetoric, covert Pakistani support to the rebels in Kashmir, and the occasional shell that—weather permitting—they lobbed at each other across a remote Himalayan glacier that both sides admit remains of no objective value to either.[70] At long last, in January 1989 the two countries gave a striking confirmation of their understanding of the nuclear danger by signing an agreement not to bomb each other's nuclear installations. Thus, they tacitly admitted that the time for the kind of preemptive strike that the Indians were alleged to be planning[71] had passed. During the past few years, there have also been other signs that the conventional-arms race between them has slowed down, if not in fact halted— and indeed the probability that this would be the ultimate outcome has long been recognized by the Indian military.[72]

PAKISTAN

Both China and India owe their nuclear arsenals at least partly to their great expectations, the former as the self-appointed leader of world revolution, the latter as a self-styled regional power with interests in the Indian Ocean. Pakistan, by contrast, has no such visions of grandeur: Despite occasional talk about an "Islamic" leadership role, the only real foreign-policy problem it has ever faced is India. The clash between the two countries is elemental. Though for different reasons, each by its very existence cannot help but pose a threat to the integrity of the other. As Zulfikar Ali Bhutto found out when he tried to make some slight steps toward defusing the issue in the mid-seventies, this situation exists almost independent of the leaders' wishes. It led to three major wars within twenty-three years of independence, nor is there any reason to think that it is about to change in the foreseeable future.[73]

Pakistan's concern with nuclear matters dates from the mid-fifties.[74] Much like the Indian program, originally the Pakistani one was as much civilian as military, since the atom was seen as a powerful lever which might help developing countries leapfrog their way toward modernity via progress. As in the case of India, too, the construction of a civilian nuclear infrastructure subsequently facilitated, if it did not permit, a greater emphasis on the military side.[75] The most important developments may be summed up as follows: Pakistan's first research reactor was built with the help of the International Atomic Energy Agency. It was activated in 1965 but, being too small to have any military significance, has since been used mainly for training purposes. A Canadian heavy-water–type power-plant reactor (KANUPP) was supplied on a turnkey (ready-for-use) basis and became operational in 1972; however, four years later, suspicions concerning Pakistan's efforts to develop the Bomb caused Canada and the U.S. to cut off the supply of enriched uranium fuel. The efforts of Pakistani engineers to keep the reactor, whose declared purpose is to provide Karachi with electricity, operational have only been partly successful. It has, however, been claimed that success was sufficient to allow the Pakistanis to divert uranium away from it during one six-month period in 1980 when the IAEA controls—in the form of automatic cameras—became temporarily inoperative.[76]

The factor that triggered the decision to stop supplies was the Pakistani bid to purchase a plutonium-separation plant from France. Success would have allowed them to build the Bomb quite rapidly; however, the French refused and the Pakistanis later referred to the attempt as an "inconsistency," as if they had committed some childish error and been caught red-handed.[77] Since then they have admitted to building a small experimental reprocessing laboratory (hot cell), but claim its capacity is much too small to be militarily significant. Instead, efforts to acquire the Bomb—which went into high gear after the defeat of 1971—switched to the uranium route. A key role was played by a Pakistani engineer, Dr. Abdul Qadir Khan. A protege of Bhutto's, Qadir Khan had studied metallurgy at Delft and Louvain between 1963 and 1972. He married a Dutch wife, became thoroughly Westernized, and apparently considered applying for Dutch citizenship. In 1974 he obtained a job at a British–German–Dutch uranium-separation plant at Almelo. Whether he was already working for the Pakistani Intelligence Service at that time is not known—or so the Dutch authorities, seeking to reassure their partners as to their own reliability and competence in security-related matters, claim. At Almelo he is said to have stolen manuals for centrifuge technology, as well as the addresses of German firms which supply it.[78] Returning to Pakistan in 1975, he masterminded the establishment of an enriching plant at Kahuta. In 1984, he was able to announce his country's success in breaking the Western monopoly in this field.[79]

Since KANUPP cannot operate without the uranium that the Pakistanis are unable to buy on the free market, the claim that this is the real purpose behind the Kahuta facility is at any rate not completely nonsensical. On the other hand, Pakistan is known to have tried to obtain other, specifically Bomb-related types of equipment, such as nuclear triggers.[80] Qadir Khan has given several more carefully orchestrated interviews, at least one of them to a major English-language Indian weekly published in New Delhi.[81] Each time he has discussed the remarkable strides his country had made in developing its nuclear infrastructure (without, however, explicitly admitting that it either possessed the Bomb or was planning to acquire it). As in the case of India, foreign estimates (summer 1990) concerning Pakistan's possession of perhaps between five and ten Hiroshima-type bombs are based on guesswork.[82] It is, however, credible guesswork.

Pakistan's most important means for delivering whatever nuclear weapons she may possess consist of the forty F-16s supplied by the Reagan Administration as part of an aid package put together following the Soviet invasion of Afghanistan. Assisted by the Chinese, the Pakistanis are also working on the development of medium-range ballistic missiles capable of reaching targets in northern India.[83] Though few details are available about the program, not much doubt exists concerning their ability to realize this aim.

As usual, the political and strategic background is both more interesting than the technical details, and more complicated to understand. At the very root of Pakistan's insecurity stands its doubtful legitimacy. The country is undeniably an artificial creation without any roots in history; its very name, while also meaning "Land of the Pure" in Urdu, originally represented an acronym. Having been shaped out of one of India's ribs in 1947, Pakistanis from the very highest echelons of government down are forever concerned about the meaning and validity of the special "Islamic" mission that forms their country's *raison d'être*. If only for this reason, they cannot make themselves believe that India has ever given up its objective of reuniting the subcontinent, or ever will.[84]

In Pakistan, to express anti-Indian sentiment is always useful for domestic purposes, since this is one of the few issues that really hold the country together.[85] At the same time, it cannot be denied that its leaders' fears are solidly grounded in geopolitical realities. Even before the 1971 War—which Pakistanis see as at least partly Indian-instigated—reduced their country's population by more than half, India always had several times Pakistan's population, and her resources also are greater in proportion. Under such circumstances, for Pakistan to feel safe (let alone free and equal) is well-nigh impossible; perhaps the only way for New Delhi to reassure its difficult neighbor would be to disarm approximately to the level of Karachi's forces, which idea has in fact been raised many times.[86] The Indians, however, insist that the two countries' situation are *not* symmetrical. The China factor on the one hand, and their own position as a subcontinent jutting out into the Indian ocean on the other, make it imperative to maintain armed forces far in excess of what would have been needed to face Pakistan alone. The cycle of assertions, accusations, and counteraccusations has now been going on for almost two generations. But in fact many of the arguments raised in the early years retain their validity today, thus demonstrating how deeply rooted the problems are.

To convince the external world—and itself—of the justice of its cause, Pakistan has developed a "strategic" literature which, with the exception of India, is without parallel in the developing world. From Mohammad Ayub Khan through the two Bhuttos (father and daughter) down to Qadir Khan himself, many leading Pakistanis

have received at least part of their education abroad. As their ut-
terances and publications prove, they feel themselves at home in
both cultures. This applies with even greater force to the nuclear
community, hundreds of whose members received their training in
such Western countries as Britain, Germany, the Netherlands, and
the U.S. Moreover, Pakistan's officer-training system (and, incidentally, that of India as well) was modeled after that of Britain, and
retains many of its original features.[87] To permit officers access to
worldwide professional literature, much emphasis is put on the
mastery of English, with the result that not even a ruler of humble
social background, such as Zia (who was the son of a noncommis-
sioned officer in the old British-led Indian Army), could have es-
caped Western influence when it came to developing his ideas on
nuclear weapons. While Pakistan has not always been democratic,
the periods of military dictatorship from 1958 to 1971 and from
1977 to 1987 did not do away with all independent publishing
activity. To its credit, the government never tried to make its citizens speak in a single voice, or control discussion in the way that
Communist countries are wont to do.

Like India, Pakistan is partly dependent on foreign assistance for
its development. As in the case of India, therefore, a sizable fraction
of Pakistani publications on matters pertaining to foreign politics,
strategy, and military affairs is intended for foreign consumption.
The fact that periodicals such as *Strategic Studies* are government-
subsidized gives them a semiofficial character and dictates a certain
uniformity in the basic approach; on the other hand, the very attempt to be taken seriously by foreigners implies that the sources
cited and the *type* of argument employed cannot be too notably
different from those that appear, say, in Washington or London.
Zia, who of all the country's rulers was the one to take religion
most seriously, at one point had a book about the "Islamic" art of
war produced and distributed; nevertheless, by-and-large Allah
does not play a larger role in Pakistani discussions of nuclear weapons than Christ does in Western strategic literature. In brief, if Pakistanis (and Indians) entertain any special "ethnic" notions about
nuclear weapons, then this literature is the wrong place to look for
them.

According to the Pakistanis, the decisive turning-point was
formed by the events of 1971, which are seen as an attempt by
India, if not to destroy Pakistan, then at any rate to assert its indis-

putable hegemony in the subcontinent. Pakistanis are not quite certain in their own minds how this evil fate was averted: Angry at the U.S. for refusing to supply Pakistan with (as they see it) sufficient arms for their self-defense, they are yet reluctant to ascribe their salvation to the *Enterprise* episode.[88] The Indians accuse Bhutto of having embarked on an all-out drive toward nuclear weapons at the beginning of 1972. The Pakistanis turned the argument around, claiming that the impetus behind their nuclear-development program was created by India's far more extensive one, culminating in the test of its so-called Peaceful Nuclear Bomb in 1974.[89] Insofar as neither country admits to possessing a nuclear arsenal, each may justifiably point to its own measures as purely precautionary. In other words, Pakistan as well as India has mastered the intricacies of nuclear ambiguity.

Beyond the need to deter India, which they see as self-evident, Pakistanis sometimes engage in loose talk concerning the "Islamic" character of the Bomb they do not have. The phrase was first used by Zulfikar Ali Bhutto in his death-cell testament;[90] just what it means is difficult to say. Pakistanis certainly take their Moslem mission seriously, even to the point of claiming that theirs is the only country founded not merely *by* Islam but *for* it.[91] As a result, Pakistan finds it easy to identify with the Arabs in their conflict with Israel, and in fact to this day Pakistan is the only country (apart from Britain) that recognized Jordan's annexation of the West Bank back in 1948. Pakistani relations with various Arab regimes have had their ups and downs. During the seventies Bhutto, who had Socialist pretensions, formed close ties—including, it was alleged, nuclear ties—with Libya;[92] however, subsequent Prime Ministers have turned more toward such "moderate" states as Jordan, Egypt, and (above all) Saudi Arabia. The lattermost country in particular is supposed to have provided Islamabad with financial aid for various projects, including the construction of an entire new city. It thus permitted savings which in turn were used to develop the Bomb.[93]

On the other hand, Pakistan is said to have given assurances to Israel, to the effect that the latter had nothing to fear of the "Islamic Bomb." [94] Islamabad is not known to have supplied its Middle Eastern friends with anything like the technology that would help them develop the Bomb independently, let alone extended a nuclear guarantee to any Arab country against Israel.[95] Seen from this latter point of view, Pakistani policy has resembled that of regional states such as India and China more than it has that of the U.S., with its extensive network of foreign commitments. Throughout the years of the Cold War, and in spite of the presence of 300,000 troops in Europe, the U.S. was never able to make its promise of nuclear support entirely credible to its Allies. *A fortiori* in the case of Pakistan in face of the Arab countries, where there is neither a formal alliance nor a physical presence of any size.

Given that they do not admit to possessing the Bomb, the Pakistanis have not developed a known nuclear doctrine for its *potential* use. If they *have* the Bomb, they keep their doctrine well out of the public eye. The Indians, at any rate, can legitimately profess to be worried about what may well seem a rather unlikely scenario, such as a sudden "nuclear-covered" Pakistani attempt to seize Kashmir. The Pakistanis, well aware that the conventional balance between the two countries favors India,[96] apparently find it hard to imagine *any* Bombs being used under *any* circumstances save the extreme case of an Indian threat to their very existence. The situation of the two countries thus is not politically symmetrical. Further, no point in Pakistan is much more than 150 miles away from the Indian border, whereas much of India can only be reached from Pakistan by medium-range missiles which, though in recent times under development, have not seemed to be dangerously close to being operational. However, both parties have been acutely aware of their vulnerability to nuclear war in the densely populated border area between them, especially in case their nuclear installations should be hit and spread radiation around.[97]

As of the early nineties, it would seem that the effect of a developing nuclear arsenal on Pakistani defense and foreign policy has been to make its rulers simultaneously more confident of themselves and less adventurous. More confident because, the disparities in conventional strength notwithstanding, they now possess the wherewithal to resist an all-out Indian attempt to destroy the country; less adventurous because of the potential for escalation that is presented by the nuclear buildup on both sides of the border. Hostile feelings between the two sides remain as strong as ever, and may indeed have intensified owing to the uprising against Indian rule that has been growing in Kashmir. Still, the Pakistanis have taken good care not to go too far. For example, when Moslem extremists tried to mount a demonstrative march into Indian territory, their move was prevented by the Pakistani Army. It may be surmised, then, that in this case, as in that of India and China, large-scale warfare between Indian and Pakistani regular forces is almost certainly a thing of the past.

CONCLUSIONS

The fact that the introduction of nuclear weapons in East and South Asia has almost certainly led to the demise of large-scale interstate war in those regions does not mean the disappearance of war as such. For many developing countries, the problem of "security" has always been determined as much by internal factors as by external ones, even to the point where the use of the term in its ordinary Western meaning may itself be misleading.[98] Now that nuclear weapons prevent the regional states that have them from fighting each other, the social function of employing armed force for political ends will almost certainly be taken over by organizations that are *not* states. As *interstate war* is replaced by various forms of *intrastate conflict,* the implications for the ability of existing political structures to assert their authority and even survive will be far-reaching.

To start with China, the events surrounding Tiananmen Square in 1989 (and the earlier student uprising of 1986) have not been forgotten by the population. A Communist regime, one of the world's oldest and last, is holding on to power by occasional brute force, day-to-date repression, and sheer inertia.[99] However, its leadership is aging, and no viable alternative appears in sight. Whether the clique in Beijing can hold on for very long and pass power over to its chosen successors appears doubtful. Whether a regime which for decades on end has sought to eliminate all opposition and incorporate all groups into the existing power structure can reform itself without causing the country to fall apart is—especially in view of the experience of the Soviet Union—also doubtful.[100] Meanwhile, the very successes registered by capitalist-minded economic reforms since the early eighties have also given rise to new strains. Currently the south, soon to include Hong Kong, is doing so much better than the less-developed north that the two almost constitute separate countries. In addition, the growing wealth of coastal areas is draining the lifeblood out of inland locales.[101] As a result, tensions over the distribution of resources have arisen, both among the regions themselves and between them and the center.[102]

Apart from the political and economic strains under which it labors, China is also the victim of powerful centrifugal forces which threaten to pull it apart in the long run. The country's transportation and communication networks remain inadequate to permit effective central control of its immense population and extensive, complicated terrain. Consequently, provincial leaders often are able to do more or less as they please; some of them have even begun to behave much like the warlords of the twenties and thirties. In recent years these developments have been reflected in the revival of the language that used to be associated with those warlords, and which is now said to be applied to empire-building Communist functionaries.[103] Meanwhile, Tibetan aspirations for independence, though muted for the moment, have not been suppressed, and can be expected to erupt into large-scale violence when the opportunity presents itself. China also contains large numbers of Moslems of non-Chinese stock in the northern and northwestern regions of the country. Encouraged by the success of the Afghanistani Muhajideen, and providing that central control over them weakens, they may one day attempt to reestablish the autonomous (or at least semiautonomous) political communities in which they lived until not so very long ago.[104] In sum, the Soviet Union's eclipse, and its own slowly growing nuclear arsenal, make China's ability to withstand major foreign threats against her appear more assured than at any other time since 1840. On the other hand, over much of the country the potential for disorder, terrorism, and maybe even civil war seems excellent.

In India, such war is effectively under way already. Much more than China, India is a conglomeration of widely different peoples, religions, and languages, of which no fewer than thirty-three are spoken by at least a million people. Some of these peoples have centuries-long traditions of hating each other and fighting each other; in fact, their quarrels constituted one very important factor which twice permitted small groups of outsiders—first the Moguls, then the British—to take over and rule the subcontinent. The potential for intergroup conflict was well understood by the Western-educated elite that surrounded Gandhi and Nehru. Accordingly, they aimed at building independent India as a nondenominational, secular, democratic country whose official language is English.

However, there are signs of strain.[105] Though the leadership's intentions may have been of the best, to non-Hindis the Hindu character of Indian secularism was, and still is, glaringly evident. The limits of that secularism, as well as the political implications of the entire issue, were demonstrated once again in 1990 when attempts to reserve a percentage of civil-service positions for low-caste people met massive resistance and had to be abandoned.[106] Meanwhile, India, though it has become the world's tenth largest industrial power in terms of assets, still maintains a per capita income of only about $300 a year. As often happens during periods of rapid industrialization and liberalization, the result had been to widen the gulf between the two Indias, that of the modern rich and that of the traditional poor; also, to create a vast amount of government corruption.[107]

As if these problems were not bad enough, in Kashmir and the Punjab India is facing minorities which seem determined either to join Pakistan or to assert their own political independence. The failure of the 50,000-strong Indian Peacekeeping Force to quell the civil war in Sri Lanka, and its withdrawal from that country in March 1990, have not gone unnoticed in the rest of the subcontinent; probably it helps account for the dramatic increase in violence that has recently taken place in abovementioned regions.[108] Attempts to solve these problems by political means are obstructed by the fact that both of the principal political parties—Congress on the one hand, Janata on the other—are finding it hard to form a government without the support of right-wing, fundamentalist, Hindu factions. As was the case in October 1990 when a quarter of a million troops had to be used to prevent a Hindu takeover of a Moslem mosque at Ayodhya, some of those parties' leaders seem determined to provoke the country's 140,000,000-strong Moslem minority by reviving century-old issues. Much more than in China, the net result of all these problems have been widespread disturbances, riots, and terrorism, including the assassination of the Prime Minister in May 1991. Entire provinces have become virtually ungovernable. Such is the scale of these events that, had they taken place anywhere else, they would have merited the label "civil war."

Even more than India, Pakistan has been bedeviled by problems of integration and legitimacy, right from the beginning of its history.[109] An artificial creation without firm roots in the consciousness of its inhabitants, Pakistan's original *raison d'être* was to serve as a national home for Indian Moslems who could not resign themselves to living under the dominant Hindu culture. The civil war of 1971 that led to Bangladesh's breaking away was seen as undermining that claim, however—to say nothing of the fact that there are now probably as many Moslems living in India as in Pakistan proper.[110] More paradoxical still, having Islam as one's official state religion poses a problem in itself. Among the intellectual elite, at any rate, it is widely recognized as an obstacle to economic modernization and progress.[111] Basically, Pakistan is a poor country without abundant natural resources. Much of the population remains illiterate, its loyalties going not to state and government but to the traditional tribal institutions. Hence the authorities cannot afford to ignore or circumvent this problem in the way that some other, richer Moslem countries have.

From this background stem many of the coups and countercoups that have dotted Pakistani history and prevented the country from achieving the stable, civilian, democratic (albeit Islamic) regime to which it is officially committed. Time after time the politicians— who, from Bhutto and Zia down, often were not native Pakistanis but émigrés from other parts of India—were perceived as failing to come to grips with the issues. Time after time the Army felt itself called on to intervene, impose discipline, and save the country from disintegration.[112] The situation is further complicated by ethnic rivalry between Punjabis (who fondly regard themselves as the "core" Pakistani people) and Sindis, to say nothing of separatist forces active in the west (Baluchistan) and the northwest (Pakhtoonistan). Pakistan and Iran have long cooperated in keeping down the Baluchis. However, the Pakhtoonistan issue is periodically exploited by whatever passes for the government of Afghanistan, which has never recognized the so-called Durand Line separating it from Pakistan.[113] In the past these problems have led to bloodshed up to, and including, the use of air strikes against rebellious villages in both provinces. They are likely to do so again in the future.

Thus, in the case of all three countries, the fact that nuclear weapons have put an end to their ability to wage meaningful external war against more-or-less equal opponents does *not* mean the end to armed conflict. Quite the contrary: The fading-away of the foreign threat may help increase the violence of ongoing internal clashes, even to the point where it could led to civil war and disintegration. As of the early nineties it still appeared difficult to say which of the two (Pakistan or India) was more likely to reach that point first. China has appeared more stable—but in this case, too, internal disorder seemed much more likely than large-scale foreign adventurism.

Chapter IV

NUCLEAR WEAPONS IN THE MIDDLE EAST

East and South Asia apart, the other region where nuclear weapons have been playing a role over the last quarter-century is the Middle East. Since Israel does not admit to possessing them, virtually nothing is known of her nuclear doctrine, if any. On the other hand, no attempt has been made to exploit Arab sources in order to assess Arab perceptions of the Israeli Bomb and their reactions to it. Thus, little factual basis exists for any attempt to estimate the impact of nuclear weapons on the Arab–Israeli conflict—and, in particular, whether it will follow the course set in other regions. To provide that basis is the task of the present chapter.

ISRAEL

With 1.1 billion and 900 million people respectively, China and India are perhaps the only two countries that *could* survive a full-sale nuclear war. Though Pakistani analysts like to present their country's geostrategic situation as "terrible," there is scant doubt that the vast majority among the 100 million Pakistani individuals would survive military conquest at the hands of India and, *a fortiori*, a limited number of nuclear bombs dropped on them. Neither proposition is necessarily true of Israel, a state of 6,000 square miles (8,000 if the occupied territories are included) situated in the midst of an Arab sea, whose very presence in that region has often been regarded as illegitimate by its enemies. Of all the states considered so far, Israel is the only one facing a true existential threat. Should Israel one day be overrun by its neighbors (acting singly or in combination), doubtless the result would be the mass slaughter of at least part of the population, followed by the expulsion of the survivors.

Israel's concern with nuclear matters dates back to the early fifties, just a short few years after its founding. Sources describe erstwhile Premier David Ben-Gurion—much like Mao and Bhutto, who are presented as making their decisions to build their Bombs under somewhat dramatic circumstances—pacing his office "like a lion in its cage" in front of a map, while contemplating the immense differences in size between Israel and its neighbors.[1] The story of what happened next needs only to be summed up very briefly.[2] An Israeli Atomic Energy Commission was set up in 1952. Its first head was Israel Rokah, another one of those Western-educated (*all* Israeli scientists were Western-educated) scientific administrators who, possessing vision and a direct line to the powers that be, did so much to set up nuclear-energy programs in several developing countries. The first 5-MW (5-megawatt/5 million watts) research reactor was supplied by the U.S. and went into operation in 1960. However, the real breakthrough had come in 1957 when Shimon Peres, at that time serving under Ben-Gurion as Director General of the Defense Ministry, negotiated an agreement with France for the supply of a 26-MW reactor capable of producing plutonium. Construction near the southern desert town of Dimona started in 1958 and proceeded in secret. It was only toward the end of 1960, when the American administration announced that it was in possession of photos taken by U-2 reconnaissance aircraft, that Ben-Gurion was compelled to acknowledge the installation's existence.

Like the Chinese (and, as we shall see, Iraqi) nuclear programs, but *unlike* those of India and Pakistan, the Israeli one—which has always borne an almost exclusively military character—did not branch off into power-generation. Like other developing countries, Israel could not take the nuclear-development program in stride, but rather experienced it as an extremely heavy financial burden. This led to some debate inside the Israeli defense establishment: How much in the way of resources should be devoted to the nuclear infrastructure, and how much to the strengthening of the conventional forces? At one extreme, the possibility was raised that a nuclear Israel would cause some of the supposedly "irrational" Arab states to go nuclear, too, thus increasing the threat rather than diminishing it. The head of the "conventionalist" faction was Yigal Allon, head of the left-wing, activist Achdut Ha'avoda Party. The "nuclear" party was led by Moshe Dayan and Shimon Peres, serving as Minister of Agriculture and Deputy Minister of Defense respectively.[3] Heavy censorship notwithstanding, the debate spilled over into the public domain,[4] and may even have played a role in bringing about the resignation of Ben-Gurion (and Peres) in July 1963.[5]

Levi Eshkol, who took Ben-Gurion's place as Prime Minister, had previously served under him as Minister of the Treasury. In this capacity he had opposed the development of nuclear weapons on financial grounds. Lacking his predecessor's flamboyant style, he was however a consummate political operator famous for his skill in bringing about compromise. He succeeded in pouring water upon the nuclear flames, toning down if not entirely preventing public discussion and lowering the country's profile.[6] Bowing—or pretending to bow—to American pressure, he may also have ordered a temporary slowdown in the development of weapons and of delivery systems in the form of surface-to-surface missiles.[7] In return, the U.S. agreed to depart from its traditional policy and sell Israel such conventional weapons as Hawk antiaircraft missiles, M-48 Patton tanks (provided out of West German stocks), and (later) A-4 Skyhawk light attack aircraft.[8]

Whether there was substance to Eshkol's policies—whether, in other words, they were more than mere whitewash designed to deceive Washington, or help Washington deceive both itself and the Arabs, or placate Israel's own antinuclearists—is not known. True, he agreed to permit American teams to inspect Dimona, and the reactor was in fact subjected to five visits between 1964 and 1968; however, there is evidence that "they were not as seriously and rigorously conducted as they would have to be to get the real story."[9] Be this as it may, when Egypt's Nasser initiated the May 1967 crisis, Israel almost certainly did not yet possess an operational nuclear device.[10] Presumably it was this fact that Ben-Gurion was referring to when he accused the Eshkol government of "a lapse in security matters" during and after the 1965 elections campaign. One may speculate that, faced with what appeared at the time as a threat to the nation's physical existence, a nonnuclear Israel found itself constrained to go to war at an earlier point than might otherwise have been the case. There is also the possibility that, had Israel already been known to be armed with nuclear weapons, the crisis might never have taken place.[11]

The swift, overwhelming victory in the June 1967 War at first seemed to justify those members of the Israeli establishment—including, besides Allon (serving Eshkol as Deputy Prime Minister), Chief of Staff Yitzhak Rabin—who had opposed basing the country's defense on nuclear deterrence.[12] At the same time it brought into the government Moshe Dayan, a supporter of Ben-Gurion and a leading nuclearist. Immediately after the War, many Israelis thought that peace would soon follow, but this period of illusions was short-lived. At the Khartoum Conference of September, the Arab countries reiterated their determination not to treat with Israel, nor to recognize her, nor to make peace with her. The Soviet Union was supporting them to the hilt, and Israel did not perceive the U.S. as forming a suitable counterweight.[13] It must have been sometime between June 1967 and the summer of 1969 that Dayan—whether with or (as has been claimed) *without* the knowledge of the rest of the government—decided that Israel could wait no longer. The plutonium-separation plant that the French had apparently supplied with the reactor[14] was activated, and the first Bombs were assembled.[15] Delivery vehicles in the form of French-built Vautour light bombers had been available for a number of years. Before long, additional bombers were acquired in the form of American A-4 Skyhawk and (above all) the much more powerful F-4 Phantom fighter-bombers. As the War of Attrition (1969–70) drew to its end, Israel almost certainly had at its disposal at least a very small nuclear arsenal consisting of a handful of Bombs. However, at that time the country's growing dependence on the U.S. for both military and other financial support made it convenient for Washington and Jerusalem alike to continue acting as if this was *not* the case.[16]

The period 1970–73 was the one when Israeli military prowess *vis-à-vis* the Arabs appeared at its height, and not to Israelis alone. During the War of Attrition, the Egyptians in particular had been made to suffer one humiliation after another,[17] with the result that the mood inside Israel tended to become extremely self-congratulatory; and when the struggle came to an end, the fact that it had ended in a draw tended to be forgotten. Although the Israeli–American alliance was under some strain during the first half of 1970, in September of that year it reached its highest point ever as the two countries cooperated to stop an attempted Syrian invasion of Jordan, thus allowing King Hussein to defeat the Palestine Liberation Organization (PLO). Israel's reward during the subsequent period was to receive American arms—tanks, armored personnel carriers, self-propelled artillery, attack aircraft, air-to-air missiles, helicopters, communications equipment, and avionics—of a quality and quantity beyond anything previously experienced by the Israeli Defense Force (IDF). Meanwhile, the withdrawal of the Soviet experts from Egypt in the summer of 1972 gave Israelis a false sense of security, since the Arabs on their own were considered impotent. Spurred by intense internal pressures that demanded increased "social" expenditure, 1973 saw the defense budget as part of GNP cut for the first time since the early fifties. Headed by Dayan, Israel's military–political establishment seems to have convinced itself that the Arabs could never launch a war without air superiority. Since that was considered beyond their reach, the immediate threat at any rate had receded.[18]

In the face of all this, the outbreak of war in October 1973 came as a tremendous shock. The Israeli government during the first forty-eight hours hardly understood what was hitting them: At first they (and, it should be added, the National Security Council in Washington, D.C.) thought this was merely another one among the very numerous border incidents that had taken place since 1967, albeit on a larger scale.[19] However, the Syrian successes on the Golan Heights and the defeat of their own first counteroffensive against the Egyptian Second Army on October 8 caused the Israelis to change from overconfidence to near panic. That evening, Defense Minister Dayan approached Prime Minister Golda Meir, saying that he had been "wrong about everything" and offering to resign. Shocked by this sudden display of pessimism on the part of the national idol (apparently Dayan, employing highly charged language, had talked of "the fall of the Third House of Israel"), Mrs. Meir called for a cabinet meeting to be held on the morning of Tuesday, October 9. At that meeting the decision was taken to arm the available Bombs and load them aboard waiting fighter-bombers.[20]

So far, the facts. Concerning what happened next, one may only guess. October 9 was a critical day for the Israelis on the Golan. This was particularly true in the north, where one brigade—commanded by Colonel "Yanosh" Ben Gal—found itself under attack by an elite Syrian division (the 3rd Armored, riding T-62 tanks) and came within a figurative inch of being overrun. The battle reached its climax near noon. Having already lost seventeen out of twenty-four tanks with which it entered the battle, the battalion commanded by Lt. Col. Avigdor Kahalani was down to three or four rounds per tank, and started withdrawing toward the escarpment overlooking the Sea of Galilee: Had the Syrians reached that point, they would have commanded a clear field-of-fire as far as Tiberias. Just how the desperate situation was saved remains unclear to the present day. Israel's semiofficial commentator, Gen. Haim Herzog, originally maintained that the trick was pulled off by an improvised unit consisting of a handful of tanks commanded by an officer identified as Yossi (Y. Ben Hanan, subsequently head of the IDF's training branch) probing into the Syrian rear. Several years later he reversed himself, producing a confused account about a thrust by an Israeli division that came up from the south and threatened to trap the Syrian forces.[21] Alternatively, there may have been a veiled Israeli hint concerning nuclear weapons dropped in Damascus' ears.

Be this as it may, the Syrians never attempted to use their highly efficient heliborne forces to attempt to block the Jordan bridges leading to the Heights, in the same way as they seized the Israeli outpost on Mount Hermon. Moreover, when the Syrian withdrawal got under way, it started from the rear and spread to the front; clearly, it was a planned affair and did not simply reflect developments among the leading units. Minister of Defense Mustafa Tlas later claimed that the failure to press forward toward the Jordan River resulted from a deliberate decision taken in President Assad's presence. Tlas added that the time to discuss the reasons behind it had not yet arrived.[22]

Officially speaking, the October 1973 War did not lead to *any* change in Israel's nuclear policy. Responding to pressure from abroad, the Eshkol government had declared that Israel would not be the first country to introduce nuclear weapons into the Middle East. Just what this statement meant has never been clarified.[23] Though the same well-worn phrase continued to be used by top decision-makers in the subsequent Meir and Rabin governments, one may see a significant development in the timing of the various revelations. Thus it was in December 1974—just as the IDF was concentrating forces in the Beth Sh'an Valley in case the Syrians refused to renew the original UN mandate on the Golan Heights, due to expire in two weeks—that we find president Ephraim Katzir, himself a well-known defense scientist, declaring that Israel *could* build the Bomb.[24] The publication in *Time* of a story concerning the events of October 9, 1973—said to be based on leaks inside the Israeli Government, and printed without comment on the first page of Israel's leading daily—took place just as Minister of Defense Peres ordered partial mobilization in an effort to deter the Syrian Army from entering Lebanon and intervening in the civil war. It was followed by statements by both Peres and Dayan as to the need to maintain Israel's nuclear options.[25] Ten years later, the Vanunu episode came amid Syrian pretensions at achieving "strategic parity" following Israel's withdrawal from Lebanon.[26] Looking back, and assuming that there is more here than mere coincidence, there seems to have taken place a gradual, carefully veiled raising of Israel's nuclear profile.

The October 1973 War also marked a turning point in the public prestige of Israel's military–political establishment, hitherto regarded as almost sacrosanct but now becoming subject to increasing criticism. The outcome was the growth of a sophisticated "strategic" debate in many ways similar to that taking place in Britain and the United States on which, in fact, it was modeled. Just as India founded the Institute for Defense Studies and Analysis in New Delhi, and Pakistan the Strategic Institute in Karachi, so Israel opened the Jaffee Center for Strategic Studies at Tel Aviv University. Like its Indian and Pakistani counterparts, the Israeli institute was headed by a former high-ranking member of the defense establishment (in this case Maj. Gen. Aharon Yariv, who had served as head of military intelligence in 1967). Like them, it is semiofficial in character, and to some extent dependent on the establishment for support, information, and recognition. There is no need to assume that the Center's publications reflect official positions on every point. On the other hand, there does exist a close identity with regard to the principal issues that they confront and, insofar as many investigators are ex-officers (intelligence), in regard to thought processes also.

Whereas the Indian and Pakistani Institutes serve as the centers of the nuclear debate in their respective countries, a survey of the Center's publications brings to light some interesting points. Its principal product, *The Middle East Military Balance* (published annually), goes into very great detail regarding the forces of Israel and its immediate neighbors. From it, one may (for example): learn that Egypt's official name is the United Arab Republic; find data on the length of Iraq's roads, both absolute and relative to its territory;

and read about the number of training aircraft available to the Tunisian Air Force. As against this almost picayunesque detail, no mention at all is made of Israel's Dimona reactor; nor of the fact that the country is widely believed to possess a nuclear arsenal of considerable magnitude; nor of any effects that these factors may have on the Middle East politico–strategic situation.

Among Israeli opinion-makers who are not members of the Jaffee Center, by contrast, the question of nuclear weapons has been discussed quite freely from the mid-seventies on. The debate was sparked by an article in which Robert Tucker of Johns Hopkins University argued that the time had come for Jerusalem to openly declare its possession of nuclear weapons: Such a stance would be good for Israel, good for the United States (which would be able to disengage), and good for world peace.[27] It engendered much controversy as to whether Israel would be able to sustain the conventional arms race, and consequently whether she should or should not put limits on it by openly acknowledging her possession of the Bomb.[28] The visit of President Sadat to Jerusalem in late 1977 signified the apparent willingness of at least *one* Arab government to come to terms with Israel. This caused the focus of the debate to shift, the question now being whether a declared nuclear-deterrent posture, coupled with a withdrawal more or less to the pre-1967 armistice lines, could be relied on to put an effective end to the conventional aspects of the conflict.[29]

A few points in this debate are worth noticing. First, nuclear weapons are clearly regarded as a last resort. Though they see advantages in refusing to discuss the circumstances under which the weapons would be used,[30] *no* Israeli has ever suggested that their use should be lightly undertaken, or that it would carry any but the gravest consequences. Second, although Israelis are acutely aware of their country's extreme vulnerability to nuclear attack, there are those among them who favor a balance-of-terror approach, pointing out that the Arab countries are almost equally vulnerable.[31] Third, and contrary to the opinions of Western experts who worry about the "ethnic" aspects of proliferation, there is no indication of Israeli experts' holding any kind of view, or employing any kind of argument, which would have sounded foreign to Western ears or looked out of place in Western publications—publications which, in any case, have long formed the preferred destination for many of their writings.[32]

As the seventies turned into the eighties, coverage of Israel's nuclear capability with regard to both weapons and delivery vehicles increased in foreign publications. Proceeding on the basis of a missile originally supplied by the French, the Israelis developed the medium-range Jericho I and II missiles. Between 1975 and 1977 they also purchased short-range Lance missiles from the U.S., a move that makes sense solely on the assumption that Israel either already possessed tactical nuclear weapons or was planning to build them. These developments of course made the government's official line appear less and less credible, even as a basis for discussion. Then, in 1986, there came the Vanunu Affair, which drove the last nail into the coffin of ambiguity. Mordechai Vanunu was a technician at Dimona who for personal and ideological reasons had become disillusioned with life in Israel. An incredible lapse of security enabled him to take photographs of parts of the installation—particularly the critical plutonium-separation facility—which he then sold to the London *Sunday Times*. Interviewed by Western experts on nuclear weapons, he also reported that the capacity of the Dimona reactor had been enlarged at least once (from 26 MW to 70 MW) and that lithium deutride was being produced. From this it could be deduced that Israel not only possessed five to ten times as many Bombs as was previously thought possible, but that her arsenal might include hydrogen, tactical, and enhanced-radiation warheads in addition to "crude" Nagasaki-type plutonium devices.[33]

In 1988, Israel gave another convincing demonstration of its technological prowess by launching an artificial satellite. To prevent it from falling into Arab hands in case of a mishap, its orbit ran westward over the Mediterranean and counter to the direction of the Earth's rotation—an unusual choice which in turn indicated a particularly powerful booster. Depending on the size of the payload, it is not hard to calculate that such a booster could put a nuclear warhead on any target within a range of several thousand miles from Tel Aviv. In addition, the installation of a home-built supercomputer at the Technion in Haifa[34] may indicate that the Israelis are trying to develop MIRVs for their missiles.

Since the very existence of nuclear weapons remains unacknowledged (officially, at any rate), there can be no question concerning the development of a doctrine for using them, either for deterrence or for war-fighting—the more so because the right-wing Likud government that ran the country for fifteen years was afraid lest open discussion of the problem would make the electorate question the value of Israel's continued occupation of the territories. Again, this has not prevented many Israeli academics and other opinion-makers from Shimon Peres[35] down from raising the problem quite freely in the academic literature, the general press, and even the government-owned electronic media. Against the background of very great economic difficulties, the most important question seems to be whether Israel can afford to follow other countries, placing greater reliance on nuclear forces for deterrence while cutting back its conventional ones.[36] Both before and during the Gulf Crisis, one sometimes heard speculation concerning the use of tactical nuclear warheads in order to halt an Iraqi invasion of Jordan. After the Gulf War was over, there were reports that Israel had put its missiles on alert, and that the alert had been detected by American intelligence,[37] as perhaps it was designed to be. Again, none of this has been either confirmed or denied by official Israeli sources.

Meanwhile, the effect of nuclear weapons on Israeli foreign and defense policy alike is becoming clear enough, even without any change in the official line. Though the size of the country is small, Israel has been successful in its attempt to keep the whereabouts of its nuclear arsenal a closely guarded secret. Its nuclear-capable Lance and Jericho missiles, high-performance fighter-bombers, and air-to-ground missiles give it what is, in effect, an assured second-strike force capable of surviving anything that the Arabs can throw at it now or in the foreseeable future. This is undoubtedly one reason why, as of the advent of 1993, the last major war between Israel and its immediate neighbors had been relegated to memories from twenty years in the past—and why, after decades in which the Arab states refused to acknowledge Israel's existence, peace talks had begun in earnest. Barring unexpected developments (such as the disintegration of one or more of those states, and the consequent inability thereof to prevent guerrilla attacks, which might then escalate), another war seemed highly unlikely. Indeed, the governments of both Syria and Jordan seemed very much concerned to prevent such an eventuality. Already in 1982 it was probably the existence of a nuclear umbrella, coupled with the Peace Treaty that had just been concluded with Egypt, that gave the Begin government the necessary self-confidence to embark on its Lebanese adventure.

Marching along the path first taken by the U.S. and followed, sooner or later, by every other country that has acquired the Bomb, both Israel's conventional forces and its defense industries have actually been shrinking since the mid-eighties, and are expected to shrink still further. While there are excellent economic reasons behind this process, clearly nuclear deterrence has already to a considerable extent taken the place of those conventional forces in at least one role—namely, that of guaranteeing the state's existence against an all-out Arab attempt to destroy it. Prime Minister Shamir, shortly before the Gulf War, threatened "awesome and terrible retaliation" in case of an Iraqi attempt to use chemical weapons against Israel.[38] If this was a slip of the tongue, then it was utterly uncharacteristic of the man. When the war broke out and Scud missiles were fired at Israel, the government, pressed by the U.S. apparently felt sufficiently confident not to retaliate. Meanwhile, Chief of Staff Dan Shomron was reported as saying that Israel would not be the first to *use* nuclear weapons.

THE ARAB STATES

As might be expected, in December 1960 the public revelations surrounding the existence of the Dimona reactor did not pass without extensive comment from the Arab countries. The Arabs had been following the effect of nuclear weapons on relations among the superpowers, and Lebanese, Jordanian, and Iraqi commentators all voiced the fear that an Israeli Bomb would lead to the "freezing" of the conflict—and thus to the end of any hope for the liberation of Palestine.[39] Beginning in 1965, hardly a week passed without the question being discussed by some Arab newspaper and/or broadcasting station. Among those who took note of the developing "Jewish threat" and discussed possible Arab reactions to it were some of the highest-ranking personalities in the Arab world. They included Egyptian Prime Minister Ali Sabri; the President of Egypt's National Assembly, Anwar Sadat; King Hussein of Jordan; Syrian President Za'in; and Syrian Foreign Minister Ibrahim Mach'us.

Politically, militarily, and ideologically speaking, far and away the most important Arab leader at the time was Egypt's Gamal Abdel Nasser. Many, including not the least the Palestinians, looked to him for leadership with regard to the Israeli problem.[40] For him to adopt the position that nuclear weapons would freeze the *status quo* was politically impossible; instead, he seems to have operated along four courses in parallel. First, he sent his diplomatic representatives—among them his deputy, Field Marshal Abdel Hakim Amar—to talk to de Gaulle in Paris, in order to garner as much information about the Israeli program as possible.[41] Next, he dispatched Anwar Sadat to Washington, in order to persuade the Johnson administration to make Israel either halt or delay the program.[42] Third, speaking in public, Nasser on several occasions put it on record that Egypt would not take the existence of an Israeli Bomb laying down, but rather would launch a "preventive war" against it. This position did no more than reflect resolutions officially passed at the Third Arab Summit Conference held at Casablanca in September 1965 and later endorsed by the Palestinian Revolutionary Council.[44] Fourth, he apparently tried to obtain nuclear weapons from the Soviet Union during his visit to Moscow in January 1966. However, like everybody else before or since, the Egyptian leader was rebuffed. All he could get out of Secretary of Defense Alexander Grechko was a promise that the USSR would take "due care" of Egypt's interests.[45]

Just what role was played by the nuclear issue in the events leading to the June 1967 War is not known,[46] but the closer one looks at the few available facts the more likely it becomes that it *did* play a role. Toward the beginning of 1966, Nasser had apparently reached the conclusion that the Americans were either being deceived by the Israelis, or trying to deceive him; and also that, contrary to Washington's repeated assurances, Israel was about to build the Bomb *and* obtain the delivery vehicles (Skyhawk aircraft) promised by the Johnson administration.[47] By this time, the term "preventive war" had turned into common currency all over the Arab world. Everybody—including the American State Department[48]—knew just what it stood for.[49] From the Egyptian leader's point of view, it was now or never; the Syrian–Israeli clashes over the sources of the Jordan River must have come as a welcome pretext for action. Just as President Kennedy had twisted Khrushchev's arm by blockading Cuba five years earlier, so Nasser's closing of the Straits of Tiran *may* have been meant to force Israel to dismantle the reactor or (which is more likely) put it under international controls to prevent its use for military purposes. Just as the USAF had flown a high-altitude reconnaissance mission over the missiles in Cuba, so the Egyptians on May 17, 1967 flew one over the Dimona reactor, causing anxiety in Israel.[50] It thus seems likely that there was a nuclear dimension to the crisis which both sides, each for its own reasons, chose to ignore in their subsequent public declarations.

The Six-Day War ended in a catastrophic defeat for Egypt. However, its position *vis-à-vis* the rest of the Arab world was not dramatically altered, since any hope of eventually turning the tables on Israel still depended on what only Cairo could and would do. The Egyptian media continued to discuss the question of the Israeli bomb,[51] gradually taking a new line (which was to assume very great importance during the years leading up to the October 1973 War). Before 1967, the Egyptians entertained no doubt that Israel was well on the road to acquiring the Bomb—or so their special envoys claimed in Paris, Washington, Moscow, and anywhere else people would listen. Now that defeat seemed to demand positive action on their part, in order to reverse the war's results, they changed their tune. Egyptian spokesmen like Nasser[52] and Vice President Sadat[53] began to issue statements that Israel *might indeed* be working on the Bomb. However, it was claimed that any reports that she already possessed one—such as those printed in the *New York Times*[54]—were no more than rumors spread by Jerusalem as part of a "psychological campaign" waged against the Arab states.[55]

In pretending that the problem did not exist, the Egyptians were greatly helped by the fact that Israel, desirous of avoiding a hostile American reaction, neither tested its Bomb nor declared itself in possession of surface-to-surface missiles for delivering it. At that time a policy of "nuclear ambiguity"—the term itself had not yet been invented—represented a considerable innovation. After all, from the time of the first detonation in New Mexico, every nuclear power had tested its own Bomb as soon as it got it. The fact that computer simulations might substitute for an actual explosion was only beginning to be understood. Though Israel's policy succeeded in placating the U.S., which continued to supply it with weapons, it suffered from the disadvantage that a *nonexistent* bomb could not have a deterrent effect, either. In this way Israel gave the Egyptians—and, presumably, the Syrians as well—some leeway to behave as if the enemy did *not* yet have the Bomb.

In other words, there exists plentiful evidence that the Arabs, between 1967 and 1973, were perfectly aware both of the devel-

oping Israeli nuclear threat and of the politico–strategic consequences that this might have.[56] After all, their media had discussed
the problem almost continuously from 1961 on. It was also an
Arab—the Lebanese Fuad Jabber, working in London—who published the very first full-length English-language book on the subject in 1971;[57] nor did it take long before his work was translated
into Arabic. The critical factor that permitted the October War to
take place nevertheless was that Israel's government denied the
Bomb's existence and thereby presented the Arabs with a "window
of opportunity," however narrow. Through this window Sadat and
Assad leaped, launching a limited war a few miles into the occupied
territories. The gamble worked, but only by a hair's breadth. So
inclined to panic was Israel's government that even a limited war
almost led to nuclear weapons being put to use on the Golan Front.

It is possible to discern two opposing currents, from November
1973 on, in Egyptian opinion concerning the question of an Israeli
Bomb. At one end of the spectrum stood various high-ranking officials whom Sadat removed from office at one point or another:
Among them were ex–Vice President Muhi a Din; ex–Foreign Minister Isma'il Fahmi (resigned, 1977); ex–Chief of Staff Sa'ad a Din
Shazli (dismissed, 1973); and ex–Minister of Information Mo-
hamed Heikal (dismissed, 1970, and later arrested). All four regarded themselves as Nasser's faithful paladins. The first two
implicitly, and the last two explicitly, were to end up by denouncing
Sadat as part traitor and part buffoon, who had given up the struggle, surrendered to Israel, and abandoned the Arab cause. Denied
access to the Egyptian media, all four tended to expound their
views in the Jordanian, Lebanese, and Western presses. In particular, Heikal—who had been fired from his post as editor of the semiofficial daily *Al Ahram* to head the Egyptian Institute of Strategic
Studies in Cairo—saw Israel's possession of the Bomb and its delivery vehicles as a *fait accompli*.[58] The result was a dangerous
"asymmetry" in the Middle Eastern balance of forces: It would put
Israel in a position to resist returning all the lands occupied in 1967,
and it might even give her the necessary confidence to start another
war against Egypt, with the aim of restoring her lost dominance.
Hence, it was imperative that the Egyptians, for their part, "get,
buy, or steal" the Bomb.

Though Israel did in fact evacuate the Sinai following the Camp
David Agreements, Heikal and his associates—including another

ex–Chief of Staff, Mohammed Sadiq—remained unrepentant.[59] Specifically, the Vanunu revelations concerning the Dimona reactor were noted in Egypt.[60] They caused the question to be taken up once again by Egypt's left-wing, Nasserite, opposition parties. Their conclusion was that the revelations were intended as a warning; whether wittingly or not, Vanunu had been a stalking-horse for Israel's intelligence service, the fearsome Mossad.[61] The Arab world would never be free of the Israeli threat, nor would the consequences of Zionist aggression be finally eliminated, so long as only the latter possessed the Bomb and its delivery vehicles. Thus Egypt should develop them, too—possibly with the aid of other Arab states which would help foot the bill. This expectation was in fact repeated time after time in 1986–87.[62]

The possibility that Egypt might launch its own large-scale nuclear program was, in fact, seriously discussed during the last years of the Sadat presidency (1974–81). Visiting Cairo shortly before his resignation, President Nixon proposed to sell both Israel and Egypt reactors for power generation and water desalination. By that time, though, the optimism that accompanied the "Atoms for Peace" program of the fifties had long since passed. By simply looking at India and Pakistan, Egypt could observe how massive investments in nuclear energy had failed to pull those countries out of poverty and backwardness. Unlike India, Egypt during Sadat's time did not feel the urge to stand up to the U.S., USSR, and China combined. Unlike Pakistan, it has a 7,000-year history, and a corresponding confidence in its own ability, if not to prosper then at any rate to endure and survive. Egypt also differs from both countries in that it has sufficient oil to cover its domestic consumption while leaving something for export. Hence the expansion of the nuclear infrastructure was rejected on both ecological and financial grounds. This position, which was subsequently reinforced by the events surrounding the Chernobyl disaster, continued to be maintained during the eighties.[63]

Against this background, Cairo began to issue warnings (which could also be read as pleas) to Israel, not to flaunt its nuclear deterrent in too provocative a manner lest Egypt be compelled to follow suit.[64] At the same time, and addressing domestic audiences, they came up with all kinds of excuses as to why the Israelis could not have the Bomb—or, if they *did* have it, why this fact should not cause undue alarm, either in Cairo or in other Arab capitals. Under

Sadat, this line of thought was put forward by the Secretary of State for Foreign Affairs, Butrus Ghalli.[65] Later, under Hosni Mubarak, its most prominent advocate was none other than the Minister of Defense, Abdul Halim Abu Azal. In a series of interviews, Azal argued that the Bomb had not been tested—or, if it *had* been tested, that only a small number might be available (this in the teeth of the 1986 Vanunu revelations, which Azal explicitly denied!). At one point, Azal's patience tried by the critics' persistence, he even went on record as saying that when Israel's leaders said their country did not possess nuclear weapons, he believed them.[66]

Mubarak, who had worked with Abu Azal since they were cadets together in the late forties, was finally forced to let him go, after Azal's involvement in an illegal attempt to obtain components for the Egyptian–Iraqi–Argentinian Condor Missile from the U.S. was exposed. However, this did not prevent Cairo from sticking to its guns, in spite of growing difficulties. As late as October 1988 the Egyptian Defense Ministry met a journalist's question concerning Israel's nuclear potential by flatly refusing to look facts in the face; instead it said that the question was irrelevant, since Egypt had never been subjected to an Israeli nuclear threat.[67] In brief, the Egyptian government cannot afford to explicitly admit that the Israeli nuclear threat played a role in limiting their own 1973 offensive, for to do so would be to question the value of the "victory" won by its army.[68] Nor, for fear of appearing defeatist, can it admit that the Bomb influenced the Camp David Peace Agreements to any considerable extent.[69] On the other hand, Egypt long ago—and for reasons that have little to do with Israel—decided it does not want to make the effort involved in going nuclear. Hence, the "ambiguous" line taken by Jerusalem suits Egypt's purpose very well. And it might almost be said that, in gingerly skirting the issue, the two countries are working hand-in-hand.[70]

Whereas Egypt has long been in a position where she *could* develop the Bomb if she decided to (or if Israel compelled her to do so by flaunting its own nuclear deterrent), the same does *not* apply to Syria. Syria is a small, poor, backward country with hardly any nuclear infrastructure to speak of.[71] Accordingly, even before the June 1967 War, spokesmen such as Foreign Minister Ibrahim Mach'us used to take the line that, in the face of Western-supported Israeli technological superiority, the correct method for liquidating the consequences of Zionist aggression and affecting the liberation of Palestine led through a "people's war" of the kind so successfully waged in Algeria, Vietnam, and many other places.[72] The Syrians see the 1967 Israeli attack on the Golan Heights as sheer, unprovoked aggression against them; hence the 1973 War was no more than an attempt to regain lost territory. Even so, the initial losses taken by Israel during the war took the leadership in Tel Aviv by surprise, wrecked their confidence in their own military prowess, and forced them to modify their thinking. In the future, opined a detailed analysis published by a Syrian intelligence officer in a Lebanese periodical soon after the end of hostilities, a desperate Israel might well resort to nuclear, chemical, and biological weapons in order to offset its emerging conventional inferiority.[73]

The Syrian position after 1973 differed from the Egyptian one in that Assad, a cold-blooded politician, did not bury his head in the sand. Instead of imitating the ostrich, Damascus almost immediately, after the October War, decided to look facts in the face. A realistic assessment was made that the Arab world, in spite of its much greater geographical size, population, and potential wealth, was in many ways almost as vulnerable to nuclear bombardment as Israel.[74] Nor, since there is no desert separating Syria from Israel, did the possibility of using a Bomb *against* her appear attractive in Damascus' eyes—given that Israel's small size and the prevailing Western winds might very well lead to numerous casualties among the Arabs themselves.[75]

Since, in any case, an independent Arab nuclear force that could put an end to "Zionist aggression" was nowhere in sight, the only solution Damascus could see was a Soviet nuclear guarantee.[76] Defense Minister Tlas at one time claimed that such a guarantee had, in fact, been given.[77] However, the final draft of the Friendship Treaty signed between the two countries in October 1986 seems to have come as a disappointment to Assad; almost certainly it did not include anything remotely like an explicit guarantee of this sort.[78] And, in fact, when Israeli forces launched a massive invasion of Lebanon in June 1982 and attacked the Syrian forces stationed there, the Soviet Union failed to lift a finger to help them. President Assad was by no means the first Arab statesman who tried to buy the Bomb or ask for nuclear assurances.[79] He was merely the *last* one who *failed* to obtain it.

From late 1982 on, Syrian attempts to deal with the Israeli nuclear threat, if only on the declaratory level, evolved along two separate—and somewhat contradictory—lines. On the one hand, Damascus, supported first by the Soviet Union and then by China and North Korea, tried to achieve "strategic parity" with Israel by strengthening its armed forces. To this end it purchased modern arms including tanks, fighter-bombers, and, by way of a "poor man's deterrent," surface-to-surface missiles carrying chemical warheads.[80] At the same time, there was a return to the old "people's war" line;[81] this became particularly clear after the *détente* in East–West relations that began to take place in 1987 put an end to any hopes for Soviet support. In speech after speech, Assad himself—taking his cue from the Ba'ath Party's chief ideologue, Abd'ala al Akhmar[82]—referred to the "sophisticated new weapons" in the hands of Israel and its allies. Recalling Vietnam "and many other places which I do not wish to mention," he promised his listeners that there was no need to despair, and that the Arab masses would end up by prevailing, even if it took them 200 years—as happened during the Crusades.[83]

In the early nineties the two Syrian strategies—preparing for military confrontation on the one hand, a "people's war" on the other—met diverging fates. Following the collapse of the Soviet Union, the former approach proved no longer credible: Syria on its own does not have the infrastructure for maintaining large, modern, conventional armed forces. In the absence of a restraining superpower hand, the possibility has remained that another round of hostilities might bring the Israeli Defense Forces to Damascus. For Assad to engage in such a round *without* obtaining nuclear weapons first would be folly; to do so *with* nuclear weapons would be greater folly still.

By contrast, the Syrians are continuing to claim that a "people's war" is succeeding—at any rate to the point where Jerusalem finally seems prepared to negotiate seriously with the Palestinians about autonomy which might eventually develop into statehood. These considerations help explain why, after four decades during which Syria's leaders consistently refused to have anything to do with Israel, bilateral peace talks held in Washington, DC have appeared to have the potential to lead to an agreement concerning the Golan Heights and at last to peace. Even were they not to, however, the shadow cast by nuclear weapons still would loom so ominous that the era of large-scale warfare between the two countries would almost certainly be mandatorily over.[84]

Like their Egyptian and Syrian colleagues, Iraqi commentators have been discussing the problem of a nuclear-armed Israel almost continuously from 1961 on. They were among the very first to conclude that the outcome would be to freeze the Arab–Israeli conflict, which from the Arab point of view was entirely unacceptable.[85] However, Iraq's position differs from that of Egypt and Syria in important ways. The country has a traditional and very dangerous enemy, Iran, against which it fought a major war during 1980–88. Too, both before and after the Gulf War the Iranians supported Kurdish and Shi'ite movements, whose aim is to dismember Iraq. As of the summer of 1992 they were reported to be forging ahead on their own nuclear program, and may indeed have obtained parts for one or two Bombs by purchase from the ex–Soviet Republic of Kazachstan.

In addition, Iraq does not have a common border with Israel, from which it is separated by the Kingdom of Jordan. This fact for many years enabled the Iraqi government to avoid any contact with the Zionist state—even in the form of signing an official cease-fire—while at the same time making it possible to take a lukewarm position with regard to the Palestinian problem. In 1970, and again in 1982, Saddam Hussein himself (first as Vice President, then as President) explained that the Palestinian cause was not so dear to the Iraqi people's heart as was to save for the Palestinians the need to look after themselves. This was one element in the developing conflict between himself and Michel Aflaq, the founder of his own Ba'ath Party, who finally decided to leave the country in protest.[86]

Saddam, however, also saw himself and his country as potential leaders of the Arab world. His long-term goal was to avenge the humiliations suffered at the hands of colonialism during the nineteenth and twentieth centuries, and to restore the kind of greatness that the Arabs had known during the early Middle Ages.[87] Harking to the days of Salah-al-Din, and even to those of the Babylonian King Nebuchadnezzar, the Iraqi Ba'ath assumed for itself the role of creating "a new Iraqi man" who, in addition to being pure and brave, would acquire "mastery over modern science."[88] Much as India's nuclear program derived from a mixture of nationalist, global-strategic, and regional considerations, so the Iraqi effort has been driven by several different factors, of which the Israeli prob-

lem remains only one.[89] Still, no Arab country and no Arab statesman can aspire to lead the Arab world without at least claiming to
do something about the Zionist problem. To this extent, Israel *did*
figure in Iraq's nuclear calculations.

Until 1973 inclusive, Iraq had been content to leave leadership in
the Arab–Israeli conflict—also with regard to its nuclear aspect—to
Egypt.[90] Egypt, however, underwent a change of heart in the wake
of the October War, relinquishing the Nasserite dream of pan-Arab
leadership, and all but withdrew from the conflict. Since other Arab
countries were perceived as either unable or unwilling to carry the
torch, the burden was left for Iraq to assume, almost by default.
One can only suppose that, as he took on this role, Saddam's thinking resembled that of Egypt's Heikal. Without nuclear weapons,
the Arab world would never be able to "confront" (a term he used
several times during the eighties) Israel on equal terms; whereas
another full-scale war against her would be tantamount to suicide,
particularly if it threatened to become successful.[91] Based on this
thinking, and aided by the enormous revenues generated by the
rising prices of oil, Iraq's own hitherto fledgling nuclear program
was greatly accelerated. A 70-MW reactor was purchased from
France, uranium from Brazil, and hot cells for plutonium separation from Italy.[92] To judge by the fact that the reactor in question
was fueled by highly enriched (93 percent) uranium, and that the
Iraqis refused to substitute another fuel when this was offered to
them, their principal and perhaps sole purpose was to manufacture
the Bomb. It serves little purpose to speculate on what *might* have
happened during the Iran–Iraq War had the Israelis not struck and
destroyed Osiraq in June of 1981.[93]

Since the destruction of Osiraq, and particularly since the conclusion of the Iran–Iraq War in the summer of 1988, Saddam's
efforts to "confront" Israel have proceeded along different lines.
An attempt was made to rebuild the country's nuclear potential by
negotiating the purchase of a new reactor of the same type as the
one that had been destroyed.[94] When the French balked at this,
Baghdad (though it continued to deny any intention of building a
bomb[95]) took a series of measures which pointed to the uranium
line of development, such as the covert purchase of centrifuges, and
blueprints for them.[96] However, the Iraqis must have known that
progress, if any, would be slow, painful, and very expensive. More-

over, they worried—or claimed to be worried[97]—about a possible repetition of the July 1981 attack. Hence their renewed nuclear effort was carefully dispersed and concealed. They also followed Syria's example and built up a large chemical arsenal, as the poor man's deterrent.

Speaking on the occasion of the Ba'ath Party Day in April 1990, Saddam Hussein addressed this issue by threatening "to burn half of Israel" in case the latter tried to strike at "some industrial metalwork" in Iraq.[98] However, he added that Iraq "knew its limits." Three months later, when interviewed on French television, he made it perfectly clear that he well understood the mismatch between Israel's nuclear capability and his own country's chemical one.[99] And, in fact, Saddam—in spite of all his previous bluster—did not use chemical weapons either against the Coalition forces in the Gulf, or against Israel. Since at the time he was being subjected to an air offensive of unprecedented fury, Saddam's missile attack on Israel, so long as it remained conventional, carried little risk. Even had Israel decided to retaliate, it was too far away from Iraq to add significantly to the overwhelming power already being deployed by the Coalition.

Once the Gulf War was over, international inspection teams were sent to ferret out Iraq's nuclear secrets. Somewhat mysteriously, it was announced that most of the country's extensive nuclear facilities had neither been discovered by the American intelligence services during the five-month Allied buildup period, nor targeted during the war itself. In fact, the effort that was being made in these facilities, while not immediately dangerous, turned out to be both much more sophisticated, and on a much larger scale, than previous information had indicated. Instead of going for a "primitive" Hiroshima-type Bomb, Saddam's experts apparently had already conducted a test of the precision-made plutonium "lenses" needed to explode a more sophisticated device. Also, captured documents showed that, like the Israelis, he was interested in lithium deutride and thus the possibility of building a boosted hydrogen device. All this indicated that, had he been able to continue his efforts for another two or three years, Iraq might have confronted the world with an arsenal consisting of at least several bombs.

In early 1993, in the face of ongoing international sanctions that continued to hurt his people, Saddam remained at some pains to explain why the Iraqi war effort needed to go on endlessly, and the dismantling of its nuclear capacity by the UN inspectors obstructed if not prevented. To this purpose an Iraqi "Staff Colonel" by the name of Hazim Abd Al Rawi was allowed to publish, in the government-controlled Iraqi paper *Al-Jumhuriya*, an analysis of the Israeli arsenal. The analysis, which was quite sophisticated, relied on accepted internationally published sources to make its case. Following traditional lines, it focused on capabilities on the one hand and intentions on the other. The author's conclusion was that since the Soviet Union has ceased to exist, and so is no longer able to make its restraining hand felt, Israel might soon be more willing to risk an adventure employing the Bomb than ever before.[100]

In confronting Israeli nuclear power, the Arab countries have long faced a dilemma: whereas to ignore its existence has been perceived as too dangerous, to admit it would be to surrender any thought of liberating Palestine by force of arms. Depending on their resources and geopolitical position, their reactions to it have varied. So far, the only country to tackle the problem head-on has been Iraq. As part of its drive toward modernization and leadership, but also in connection with the Iranian threat, it has twice tried to "confront" (the term habitually used by Saddam) Israel by developing its own independent nuclear program, and failed. The other principal Arab countries have either pretended that the problem has not existed (which is the line followed by Egypt since the early seventies), or else they have zigzagged between "strategic parity" and "people's war" (Syria).

Each of the three approaches is realistic in its own way. *All* have in common that the power of the Bomb is well understood, the danger of escalation in case of another major war widely recognized, and the difficulty of using the Bomb *against* Israel realized—even to the point that the Iraqi missiles fired in the general direction of the Negev during the Gulf War were later found to have carried concrete warheads.[101] As a result, and in spite of the occasional displays of rhetorical fireworks and brinkmanship, the prospect of war continues to appear less likely than at any other time since 1948. During the past few years the Arab Armies—including even the Syrian one—have been reduced to guarding Israel's borders against their own countries' populations—an outcome which, significantly enough, was predicted by Heikal as early as 1976.[102]

CONCLUSIONS

As in East and South Asia, the introduction of nuclear weapons into the region comprising the Arab–Israeli conflict seems to have brought about the end of large-scale warfare between opposing states utilizing their regular armed forces. As in East and South Asia, the result of this development is likely to be not the disappearance of war but a growing shift toward other forms of armed conflict conducted by political organizations which, being of different kinds, cannot be targeted by nuclear weapons. In this context, two places are particularly relevant: southern Lebanon, and the territories occupied by Israel.

Whereas on the Golan Heights the border between Israel and Syria has been almost perfectly peaceful for many years, southern Lebanon represents a kind of no man's land where there is *plenty* of ongoing military activity. Since 1985, when Israel established its "security zone," virtually none of that activity has pitted the regular armies of both sides against each other; instead, it is a question of small-scale action by, between, and against various militias. The PLO, which used to be the most important organization of its type, has been pushed aside by the Shi'ite-based Amal and the Iranian-sponsored Hizbollah. Both possess their own independent sources of money, men, and arms, but both also receive Syrian assistance in their attempts to cross the security zone and carry out acts of sabotage inside Israel. They are opposed by the Israeli-supported South Lebanese Army, as well as by the Israeli Defense Forces themselves. Complicating the situation are several thousand United Nations troops scattered in outposts all over the country and trying to act as peace-keepers. Since their primary concern is to ensure their own safety in the midst of ongoing skirmishes, their ability to influence events is not large. However, both sides, in planning their operations, must take care not to provoke them too much, and to remain on reasonable terms with them.

The various militias, as well as the IDF, do not act in a vacuum. The countryside is complicated, mountainous, heavily vegetated, and extremely rugged; during the winter it tends to be cold, wet, and foggy. It is also dotted with numerous villages, which in turn are surrounded by terraces, fields, orchards, and stone walls of various heights. Since many of the militiamen wear uniforms only when it suits them, they are often indistinguishable from the villagers. Some villagers are loyal to one side, some to another. Given proper inducements and/or threats, many of them are prepared to assist one side or the other on either a temporary or a permanent basis by providing shelter, intelligence, and lookouts against attack. There are no clear borders, no extensive territorial areas that belong exclusively to one side or another, and no simple ways to distinguish friend from foe, combatant from innocent bystander. Under these circumstances the war consists of an endless series of minor actions: attempts at infiltration, patrols, raids, ambushes, and bombs concealed by the roadside. Though heavy weapons—tanks, artillery, helicopters, and attack aircraft—are employed quite frequently by the Israelis, in the absence of clear targets their effect is limited. The outcome is a draw which could last indefinitely. While the Israelis are very largely successful in preventing the guerrillas from penetrating into Israel itself, there seems little prospect of defeating them and thus putting an end to their operations.

Inside the occupied territories, too, the Arab–Israeli conflict has long assumed the form of a struggle without fronts, without large-scale operations and—on one side—without an army. Since the outbreak of the Palestinian uprising at the end of 1987, rock-throwing, knifing, riding-down, firebombing, and shooting have become common. Apart from the fact that much of the violence (though by no means all) takes place between Jew and Arab, it is essentially random in character, and some of it is suicidal. The line between war and crime is becoming blurred, with the result that the security forces in and out of uniform no longer know what to look for, and have been hard-pressed to cope. The Palestinian uprising is also shaped by the fact that it takes place in a country that has long been at the center of the world's interest and amidst some of the most intense media coverage in the world. Operating against an opponent who is perceived as weak to the point of helplessness, the security forces stand condemned if they take strong measures, and condemned if they don't. Criticized by both doves and hawks, they are showing growing signs of strain. To many on both sides of the ethnic divide, their ability to guarantee life and limb appears increasingly in doubt.[103]

Since virtually the whole male population serves in the reserves, Israel is a country where weapons are widely available. This makes it easy for disaffected groups to set up militias, which then attempt to fill the gap left by the government forces. The clashes between the Israeli security apparatus and Arab terrorist organizations, as well as among those organizations themselves, are regularly a matter of record. However, there have also been numerous attempts to set up Jewish self-defense organizations, most of which have gone unreported. Wherever one looks, militias—official, semiofficial, and unofficial—are springing up as if out of the ground. Arab attempts at self-defense have been successful to the extent that the Israeli military can enter Arab settlements only in force, whereas Israeli civilians can hardly enter them at all. Meanwhile, Jewish settlements in the occupied territories or close to them have set up their own well-armed civil guards. With or without government permission they mount patrols, set up roadblocks, and occasionally send groups of marauders into neighboring Arab villages, in response to some particularly vicious act of terrorism. Against the background of a nuclear-imposed stalemate, a peace of sorts with the neighboring Arab countries appeared, as of early 1993, within reach. Internally, however, Israel's government was losing its monopoly over armed violence, and appeared unable to regain it unless a wall between Jew and Arab could be built.

Postcript

THE FUTURE OF CONFLICT

Ironically, perhaps, at a time when more countries than ever either possess nuclear weapons or are planning to acquire them, it appears that fears of the consequences of nuclear proliferation have been greatly exaggerated all along. The geopolitical circumstances surrounding the stances that such countries as China, India, Pakistan, and Israel have taken toward the Bomb remain very varied. So (as far as they are known) do the roads taken toward the Bomb, and the doctrines developed with respect to it. Nevertheless, there seems to be no factual basis for the claims that regional leaders do not understand the nature and implications of nuclear weapons; or that their attitudes to those weapons are governed by some peculiar cultural biases which make them incapable of rational thought; or that they are more adventurous and less responsible in handling them than anybody else.

Given the fact that the latter countries in question were latecomers to the field, this result is not surprising. All over the developing world, the scientists who built the Bombs, the military personnel responsible for handling the delivery vehicles in case of war, and the political leaders authorized to order their use, originally looked either to the West or to the East for their ideas on nuclear technology and nuclear strategy. Over four decades, thousands of them attended universities and institutes of higher military learning in either the West or the East, where they received formal instruction in these ideas. In other cases the learning process was informal, taking place by way of the international strategic literature, the media, personal interchanges, and the like.

Since they are dependent on foreigners for important aspects of their continuing development as technologically up-to-date nations, much of the strategic literature of countries such as India,

122

Pakistan, and Israel is meant for foreign consumption. Hence, far from representing some esoteric growths, what nuclear doctrines they are known to have developed tend to draw on the same sources, and are often deliberately dressed in the same terms, as those used by Western defense communities. The same applies to countries which, though they do not themselves possess nuclear weapons, are confronted with them. Take for example the Iraqi analysis of the Israeli threat that was published in the summer of 1991: It followed traditional American models, in that it was couched entirely in terms of capability on the one hand, and intentions on the other. Except for its conclusions, it might have originated in the U.S. arms-control community (from which, in fact, its data were probably adapted).

An even more critical reason why regional leaders tend to be at least as careful in handling nuclear weapons as those of the superpowers is the fact that many of the countries in question are quite small, adjacent to each other, and not separated by any clear natural borders; often they share the same local weather systems and draw their water from the same river basin. Hence the question of how escalation, radiation, and contamination may be avoided appears even more baffling in their case than in that of the U.S. and the former USSR, which used to be located on different hemispheres and which for decades prepared to fight each other on terrain belonging to third parties. As agreements concluded between India and Pakistan demonstrate, there can be no doubt that regional leaders are aware of these disincentives to the use of nuclear weapons. This problem can be shown to have preoccupied even some of the more radical among them, such as Syria's Assad. An Arab Bomb dropping on Tel Aviv would almost certainly inflict grievous damage on precisely the Palestinian people whose cause Assad claims to be upholding, whereas exploding such a weapon on the Golan Heights, only 50 kilometers (30 miles) from Damascus and with the prevailing winds blowing from the west, is an even less attractive proposition.

In view of these facts, much of the international (in other words, Western) literature on proliferation appears to be distorted, ethnocentric, and self-serving. It operates on the principle of *beati sunt possedentes* ("blessed are those who are in possession"); like the various international treaties and regimes to which it has given rise, its real objective is to perpetuate the oligopoly of the "old" nuclear powers. To this end, regional powers and their leaders have been described as unstable, culturally biased, irresponsible, and whatnot. To this end, weapons and technologies that used to be presented as stabilizing when they were in the hands of the great powers were suddenly described as destabilizing when they spread to other countries.

In practice, the leaders of medium and small powers alike tend to be extremely cautious with regard to the nuclear weapons they possess or with which they are faced—the proof being that, to date, in *every* region where these weapons have been introduced, large-scale interstate warfare has disappeared. As used to be the case during the Cold War, when the U.S. and USSR were always drawing up worst-case scenarios against each other, there can be no absolute guarantee that this situation will always persist. So far, however, the effect of proliferation has been greater rather than lesser stability in the relations of the states that have them or are confronted with them. This has been true even when the weapons have been few in number; even when delivery vehicles and methods of command and control were comparatively primitive; even when very great asymmetries existed in the forces of both sides; and even when the entire process was covert rather than overt. In some cases, particularly in the Middle East, the fact that proliferation would lead to stalemate was expressly foreseen years (and even decades) in advance. In others (e.g., between China and Taiwan) it has almost certainly contributed to the stifling of revolutionary rhetoric, and to a lessening of tensions.

The virtual disappearance of large-scale interstate warfare from the regions in question does not necessarily mean that they are going to be free of armed conflict. One does not eliminate the causes of war by threatening to blow up cities: In East and South Asia, as well as the Middle East, nuclear proliferation has left socio-economic imbalances, religious tensions, and ethnic animosities much as they used to be. The fact that regional states are now unable to achieve their objectives by fighting each other seems to encourage the rise of violence between organizations that are *not* states yet whose goal, in many cases, is *precisely* to demolish the existing political system.

As of the early nineties, the organizations in question could be numbered by the dozen. Some, such as the PLO, remained large, well-known, and possessed of a considerable measure of international recognition; others stayed small and at times proved ephemeral. A few have been entirely independent, whereas others (such as Hizbollah) operated at least partly as state-sponsored entities. What they have in common—and enables them to go on fighting in spite of the presence of nuclear weapons in their regions—is the fact that, unlike states, they do not possess large, well-defined territories clearly separate from those of their neighbors. Since their operations are semicovert, they can barely be distinguished from each other, and since their members wear a uniform only when (so to speak) it suits them, they can hardly be told apart from the surrounding population. They do not possess permanent capitals, and their nerve centers may be located thousands of miles away, in neutral territory. For all these reasons, they cannot be targeted by nuclear weapons or, for that matter, by most other types of heavy modern weapons. Thus, the rise in these regions of Low-Intensity Conflict represents no more than the sound tactician's response to nuclear proliferation: If one cannot beat one's enemy in a straightforward contest, one should seek to undermine him.

To prevent the operations of these organizations from going to the point where they might compel states to intervene, and nuclear threats to be realized, the armies of the countries surveyed in this study are gradually being transformed into police forces. More and more, their function is less to fight each other than to prevent groups and organizations inside their national territories from carrying out provocative acts which might then escalate and bring about a confrontation between states. Thus, the Indian Army for many years has mainly fought its own citizens. The Pakistani Army, in February and October 1992, used armed force to prevent extremists from mounting demonstrative marches into Indian territory, killing dozens. Claiming the need to protect the peace talks against those trying to disrupt them, the Israeli Army has been vainly trying to put down the Palestinian *Intifada*. Much of the terrain east of the River Jordan has been fenced off by the Jordanian Army—not to stop an Israeli invasion, but to prevent would-be Palestinian terrorists from crossing into the West Bank and carrying out acts of sabotage which would lead to retaliation. In Lebanon, organizations such as Hizbollah act under Syrian protection, yet paradoxically the Syrian Army, fearing escalation, has for several years put restraints on these operations against Israel, and has appeared likely to continue doing so in the future.

During most of the period since 1945 warfare by, between, and
against organizations other than states has been confined very
largely to various countries in the Third World; and it was expected
that, as those countries marched toward stability and prosperity,
that kind of war would largely disappear. As the eighties turned
into the nineties, however, there were abundant signs that the opposite was about to happen. Much of the Third World did not
follow the Second and First ones on the path to peace and economic
growth. Instead, parts of the Second and even the First seemed to be
following the example of developing states toward internal conflict.
All over the former Soviet bloc, countries which until a few years
ago appeared perfectly stable are being torn to pieces by savage
warfare between ill-defined, ill-organized, ill-armed militias fighting each other, house to house and even room to room. From Britain to Spain, there are clear indications that even Western states
which have been unified for centuries, and which until recently were
regarded as models of civilized life, may one day follow suit.

In a world where virtually any state which wants to should be
able to develop, acquire, or steal nuclear weapons, this kind of
conflict is almost certainly the only one with a future. The differences between it and the wars that dominated the West during the
three centuries before Hiroshima are striking. Whereas past wars
were wagged on a set of principles standing midway between politics and tactics and known as strategy, in future conflict that kind
of strategy will disappear. Whereas past wars were fought by increasingly large, regular, uniformed armies separate from governments on the one hand and civilian populations on the other, in
future conflict that kind of army will be of only very limited use.
Whereas pre-1945 wars were conducted by cohesive territorial
states numbering millions of citizens, future conflict will be the domain of much smaller, less powerful, and in many ways more primitive political entities similar to those existing before 1648. States as
we know them will have to come to terms with the *new* form of
armed conflict now developing under the very shadow of the nuclear weapons that they themselves have introduced. Either they
put an end to it or, without any doubt, it will put an end to them.

NOTES

Introduction: The Last Problem

1. See J. Keegan and A. Wheatcroft, *Zones of Conflict: An Atlas of Future Wars* (New York: Simon & Schuster, 1986).
2. E.g., International Institute of Strategic Studies, ed., *The Military Balance 1989–1990* (London: Institute of Strategic Studies, 1989), pp. 158–160 and 170–171, referring to India and Pakistan; and Jaffee Center for Strategic Studies ed., *The Middle East Military Balance 1987–88* (Tel Aviv: Jaffee Center for Strategic Studies, 1988).
3. See M. Lean-Jones, "The Future of International Security Studies," in D. Ball and D. Horner, eds., *Strategic Studies in a Changing World* (Canberra: The Australian National University Press, 1992), pp. 54–70.

Chapter I: Before Nuclear Weapons

1. See above all C. Schmitt, *The Concept of the Political* (Reading, MA: Harvard University Press, 1960).
2. On primitive "political" organization see, e.g., E. R. Service, *Origins of the State and Civilization; The Process of Cultural Evolution* (New York, W. W. Norton, 1975), pp. 47–103. Much the best single study of primitive war remains J. H. Turney-High, *Primitive War, Its Practice and Concepts* (Columbia, SC: University of South Carolina Press, 1971).
3. See M. Weber, *General Economic History* (London: Allen & Unwin, 1923), pp. 58–59. Even as late as 1600, Europeans spoke of the Ottoman Emperor as "the Grand Turk," a term by which they meant that, as a patrimonial ruler, he was free from the feudal restrictions that surrounded Western ones.
4. Though our modern "empire" comes from *imperium,* the original Latin term meant "authority" or "domination." See R. Koebner, *Empire* (Cambridge: Cambridge University Press, 1961), Ch. 1.

5. For details see, e.g., J. Barnie, *War in Medieval Society: Social Values and the Hundred Years' War* (London: Weidenfeld & Nicolson, 1974).

6. See N. Rubinstein, "Notes on the Word *Stato* in Florence Before Machiavelli," in R. G. Rowe and W. K. Ferguson. eds., *Florilegium Historiale: Essays Presented to Wallace K. Ferguson* (Toronto: University of Toronto Press, 1971), pp. 313–326; also B. Guennee, *States and Rulers in Later Medieval Europe* (Oxford: Basil Blackwell, 1985), pp. 4–6.

7. A good short summary of medieval political theory, particularly that of Thomas Aquinas, may be found in G. H. Sabine, *A History of Political Theory,* 3rd ed. (London: Harrap, 1964), pp. 224–330.

8. See, e.g., J. R. Strayer, *On the Medieval Origins of the Modern State* (Princeton, NJ: Princeton University Press, 1970), p. 77ff; also, J. W. Shennan, *The Origins of the Modern European State, 1450–1725* (London: Hutchinson, 1974), p. 24ff.

9. For the rise of political theory see G. Oestreich, *Neostoicism and the Origins of the Modern State* (London: Cambridge University Press, 1982), pp. 92–93 and 97ff. For the development of the idea that the ruler was the servant of the state, instead of the other way around, see F. Meinecke, *Machiavellism: The Doctrine of Raison d'État and Its Place in Modern History* (London: Routledge & Kegan Paul, 1957), p. 305ff.

10. For an excellent discussion of Bodin see Sabine, *op. cit.,* p. 402ff.

11. Lipsius is the subject of Oestreich's monograph (see note No. 9 above).

12. See Th. Hobbes, *Leviathan* (London: J. M. Dent, 1947 ed.), particularly Chs. 14–17. Hobbes' contemporary, Baruch Spinoza, put it even more bluntly: According to him, the object of the state is none other than peace and security of life. See *Tractatus Theologico-Politicus* (Leiden: Brill, 1979), p. 234.

13. For the elevation of the state from an instrument into an ideal see above all J. L. Talmon, *The Origins of Totalitarian Democracy* (London: Secker and Warburg, 1952), pp. 38–49; as well as E. Cassirer, *The Myth of the State* (New Haven, CT: Yale University Press, 1946), p. 254ff.; and Meinecke, *op. cit.,* p. 350ff.

14. See for example K. Marx and F. Engels, *The German Ideology* (London: Lawrence & Wishart, 1938), particularly pp. 58–62 and 68–69; also, D. McLellan, *The Thought of Karl Marx* (London: Macmillan, 1971), pp. 179–195.

15. For an impressive summary of these developments see K. Polanyi, *The Great Transformation* (London: Golancz, 1946), particularly Ch. 1.

16. For example, French authorities in 1914 had counted on a 5%–13% refusal to respond to mobilization, but found that the actual figure was only 1.5%. See M. Ferro, *The Great War* (London: Routledge, 1973), p. 8.

17. Those that come to mind most are the Hellenistic and Roman Imperial armies, which, for this reason, often served early modern ones as their model.

18. Thus, in the Book of Deutronomy, "member of the host" (*yotse tsava*) is synonymous with "adult male member of the people." The Latin term for "people, *populus,* originally could also mean "army."

19. The best modern account of the inner workings of a mercenary army remains G. Parker, *The Army of Flanders and the Spanish Road* (London: Cambridge University Press, 1972), particularly Chs. 1 and 6.

20. Quoted in Oestreich, *op. cit.,* p. 52. At that time the total forces of a first-rate power such as Spain could easily number 100,000 or more.

21. For the rise of the military commissionaries and their role in the establishment of early modern administrative structures see O. Hintze, "The Commissary and His Significance in General History; A Comparative Study," in F. Gilbert, ed., *The Historical Essays of Otto Hintze* (New York: Oxford University Press, 1975), pp. 267–302.

22. See G. Mosse, ed., *Police Forces in History* (London: Sage, 1975).

23. One is reminded of Elizabeth I's remark that, while she knew she had the weak body of a woman, she possessed the spirit of a king. For the evolution of command and its separation from government see M. van Creveld, *The Training of Officers; From Military Professionalism to Irrelevance* (New York, Free Press, 1990), pp. 7–16.

24. For the creation of the most important of these ministries see C. Rousset, *Histoire de Louvois* (Paris: Didier, 1862).

25. For the career of one famous military administrator and his work in carrying out all these different functions see H. de Nanteuil, *Daru et l'Administration militarie sous la Révolution et l'Empire* (Paris: Peyronnet & Cie, 1966).

26. C. von Clausewitz, in M. Howard and P. Paret, eds., *On War* (Princeton, NJ: Princeton University Press, 1976), pp. 585–586.

27. G. Gong, *The Standard of "Civilization" in International Society* (Oxford: Clarendon Press, 1984), pp. 74–76.

28. For a good summary of the developments in the law of war between 1864 (the St. Petersburg Conference) and 1907 (the Second Hague Conference) see G. Best, *Humanity in Warfare* (New York: Columbia University Press, 1980), Ch. 3.

29. See above all E. N. Luttwak, *Strategy: The Logic of War and Peace* (Cambridge, MA: Belknap Press, 1987), Ch 1. The meaning which Luttwak attaches to strategy is, however, more reminiscent of Thomas Schelling than of Clausewitz.

30. For a concise history of strategic terminology see Clausewitz, *On War*, pp. 133ff.; also M. van Creveld, *The Transformation of War* (New York: Free Press, 1991), pp. 95ff.

31. For Clausewitz' dismissal of the significance of pre-1648 warfare, see *On War*, pp. 173–174. Another very good example is B. H. Liddell Hart, *Strategy* (New York: Praeger, 1967) which ignores anything before Alexander, as well as the entire period from 500 to 1500 A.D.

32. Another way of putting the matter would be to say that most Greek wars were, at the same time, civil wars. On the interaction of "politics" and "strategy" in the ancient world see above all Y. Garlan, *War in the Ancient World* (London: Chatto & Windus, 1975), Ch. 1.

33. Quoted in E. Leach, S. N. Mukherjee, and J. Ward, eds., *Feudalism: Comparative Studies* (Sydney: Sydney Association for Studies in Society and Culture, 1985), p. 106.

34. See the calculations in D. Engels, *Alexander the Great and the Logistics of the Macedonian Army* (Berkeley, CA: University of California Press, 1978), p. 11ff.

35. For a modern account of the way things were done see G. Perjes, "Army Provisioning, Logistics, and Strategy in the Second Half of the Seventeenth Century," in *Acta Historica Academiae Scientarium Hungaricae,* No. 16, 1965; for a contemporary example A. Duyck in I. Mueller, ed., *Journaal* (The Hague: Nijhoff, 1886) p. 384ff.

36. A partial exception to this rule was formed by siege warfare; see M. van Creveld, *Supplying War: Logistics from Wallenstein to Patton* (London: Cambridge University Press, 1977), pp. 23–26.

37. One is reminded of Napoleon's saying that of the three obstacles facing the movements of armies (i.e., rivers, mountains, and deserts), the last-named were the worst. See *Correspondance de Napoléon I* (Paris: Plon, 1868), Vol. V, No. 3928, pp. 291–292.

38. Clausewitz, *On War*, pp. 285 and 297.

39. Fredericus Rex, in G. B. Holz, ed., *Werke*, Vol. IV, *Militaerische Schriften* (Berlin: Mittler, 1913), Ch. 18.

40. F. E. Adcock, *The Greek and Macedonian Art of War* (Berkeley, CA: University of California Press, 1957), p. 82.

41. M. van Creveld, *Command in War* (Cambridge, MA: Harvard University Press, 1985), pp. 41–55; also *idem, The Training of Officers;*

From Military Professionalism to Irrelevance (New York: Free Press, 1990) pp. 13–18.

42. See A. Gat, *Clausewitz and the Enlightenment* (Oxford: Oxford University Press, 1989), p. 41–42. The first English use, incidentally, was in 1815.

43. See W. Laqueur, *The Guerrilla Reader* (New York: Meridian, 1977), pp. 13–29. Austria was the first country to raise troops (the Pandurs) specifically for irregular warfare, and its example was followed by others.

44. *Correspondance de Napoléon I,* Vol. XI, No. 9392, p. 336.

45. A. H. Jomini, *Traité des grandes opérations militaires* (Paris: Dumaine, 1804–16).

46. On Buelow see Gat, *op. cit.,* pp. 79–94. Besides him, the most important writers of the period were Venturinus, Berenhorst, Scharnhorst, Jomini, and of course Clausewitz. In *On War,* p. 133ff., Clausewitz himself gives a good summary of the origins of the debate; for subsequent developments see above all W. Erfurt, *Der Vernichtungsssieg* (Berlin: Mittler, 1939).

47. In the American Civil War the two types of command can be seen side by side. On the side of the Union, Grant held a field command in addition to acting as Commander in Chief, which combination of duties compelled him to make use of the telegraph in order to direct operations over half a continent. On the Confederate side, since the only man responsible for the war as a whole was Jefferson Davis, field commanders such as Lee operated very much in the Napoleonic style. See E. Hagerman, *The American Civil War and the Origins of Modern Warfare; Ideas, Organization, and Field Command* (Bloomington, IN: Indiana University Press, 1989), pp. 126ff. and 264–265.

48. This study cannot trace the evolution of naval strategy. However, it should be noted that Mahan was familiar with Jomini, as befits the son of the man who reorganized West Point. Accordingly, the first thing he has to say is that lines of communication (also known as shipping lanes) play as important a role at sea as they do on land; and indeed *The Influence of Seapower on History* can be read simply as an attempt to apply Jomini's precepts to naval strategy, too.

49. Van Creveld, *Command in War,* pp.190–194. Radio, however, did reverse the trend by which commanders operated farther and farther away from the front, enabling them to locate their headquarters well up front as, e.g., Guderian, Rommel, and Patton did.

50. Van Creveld, *Supplying War,* particularly pp. 234–236.

51. For the link between the state and modernity see (most recently)

S. Toulmin, *Cosmopolis: The Hidden Agenda of Modernity* (New York: Free Press, 1990), particularly pp. 89–98, and 139–145.

Chapter II: Enter the Absolute Weapon

1. The first thing President Truman did after the war's end was to terminate lend-lease, thus effectively severing the Anglo-American alliance that formed the tightest of these coalitions. See H. S. Truman, *Memoirs,* Vol. I: *The Years of Decision* (Garden City, NY: Doubleday, 1955) pp.227–228. On the other side of the hill, the Axis powers never even achieved unified command.

2. For the planning of strategy during the last months of the war against Japan see G. Alperovitz, *Atomic Diplomacy* (Harmondsworth, Middlesex: Penguin Books, 1985).

3. On the shaping of the postwar world H. Feis, *Churchill, Roosevelt, Stalin; The War They Waged and the Peace They Sought* (Princeton, NJ: Princeton University Press, 1967) remains a standard.

4. On the origins of containment see J. L. Gaddis, "Containment: A Reassessment," in *Foreign Affairs* 55 (July 1977), pp. 873–887; also R. E. Osgood, *Limited War Revisited* (Boulder, CO: Westview Press, 1979), p. 87ff.

5. See V. I. Lenin, "Draft of Thesis on the National and Colonial Questions at the Second Congress of the Communist International" (1920), in *Selected Works* (London: Lawrence & Wishart, 1946), Vol. 10, pp. 231–238.

6. See P. Kennedy, *The Rise and Fall of the Great Powers; Economic Change and Military Conflict from 1500 to 2000* (New York: Vintage Books, 1987), particularly Ch. 7.

7. Government Publishing Bureau, *Falsificators of History* (Moscow: 1948) is a good example of a contemporary Soviet view of the events leading to World War II. Whether or not the Western powers were serious in their offer of an alliance in 1939 remains moot; see A. J. P. Taylor, *Europe, Grandeur and Decline* (Harmondsworth, Middlesex: Pelican Books, 1950), pp. 259–269.

8. One of the earliest analyses calling attention to the effect of military spending on the Soviet economy was by H. Block, "The Economic Basis of Soviet Power," Appendix I to E. Luttwak, in *The Grand Strategy of the Soviet Union* (New York: St. Martin's Press, 1983), pp. 119–175.

9. A good example is *Soviet Military Power,* an official Pentagon publication which appeared throughout the eighties.

10. On the question of a Soviet "military–industrial complex" and its ability to influence Soviet policy see D. Holloway, *The Soviet Union*

and the Arms Race (New Haven, CT: Yale University Press, 1983) pp. 156–160.

11. Speech printed in *New York Times*, 18 January 1961.

12. George Kennan, whose understanding of Stalin was second to that of no Westerner, deemed him perfectly capable of using nuclear weapons if he had thought any advantage would result therefrom: *Memoirs* (Boston, MA: Little, Brown, 1967), p. 291, quoting the famous "long telegram" of 30 September 1945.

13. N. S. Khrushchev (S. Talbot trans.), *Khrushchev Remembers* (London: Sphere Books, 1971), pp. 430–431.

14. See for example McG. Bundy, *Danger and Survival: The Political History of the Nuclear Weapon* (New York: Random House, 1988), particularly p. 584ff.

15. See W. L. O'Neill, *Coming Apart: An Informal History of America in the 1960s* (New York: Quadrangle Books, 1971), pp. 67–73.

16. A. Rhodes, *The Making of the Atomic Bomb* (New York: Simon & Schuster, 1988), p. 690.

17. See in particular Bernard Brodie, *The Absolute Weapon* (New York: Columbia University Press, 1946), pp. 22–69.

18. See L. Freedman, *The Evolution of Nuclear Strategy* (New York: St. Martin's Press, 1981), p. 22ff. During the fifties, writing articles that "proved" the continued need for conventional forces in the nuclear age was a fool-proof method for Army and Navy officers to be nominated for a prize.

19. See, e.g., the Nobel Prize-winning scientist, P. M. S. Blackett, *The Military and Political Consequences of Atomic Energy* (London: Turnstile Press, 1948), Ch. 10.

20. One list gives 2 for December 1945, 9 for June 1946, 35 for March 1948, 50 for May 1948, 150 for December 1948, and 250 for October 1949: M. Kaku and D. Axelrod, *To Win a Nuclear War: The Pentagon's Secret War Plans* (Boston, MA: South End Press, 1987), pp. x–xi. (No source for the list is given.)

21. The number of American publications that saw war in such terms is endless. See E. N. Luttwak, *Strategy: The Logic of War and Peace*, for a typical analysis.

22. See H. F. and W. F. Scott, *The Soviet Art of War: Doctrine, Strategy and Tactics* (Boulder, CO: Westview Press, 1982), pp. 134–135.

23. For a detailed comparison between the force levels on both sides as they were in 1960 see J. M. Collins, *U.S.–Soviet Military Balance: Concepts and Capabilities, 1960–1980* (New York: McGraw-Hill, 1980), pp. 25–38.

24. Bundy, *op. cit.*, p. 616.

25. For the technical details see R. I. Tammen, *MIRV and the Arms Race* (New York: Praeger, 1973); as well as R. Betts, ed., *Cruise Missiles: Technology, Strategy, Politics* (Washington, DC: Brookings Institution, 1981), pp. 31–52.

26. See *Report of Secretary of Defense James Schlesinger to the Congress on the FY 1975 Defense Budget and FY 1975–79 Defense Program* (Washington, DC: Government Printing Office, 1974); also, L. Etheridge-Davis, *Limited Nuclear Options; Deterrence and the New American Doctrine*, Adelphi Paper No. 121, Winter 1975–76 (London: International Institute of Strategic Studies, 1976).

27. See above all V. D. Sokolovsky, *Military Strategy* (New York: Praeger, 1963), pp. 183ff. Since then, Soviet nuclear doctrine has served as the subject of uncounted publications: See R. F. Laird and D. R. Herspring, *The Soviet Union and Strategic Arms* (Boulder, CO: Westview, 1984).

28. On these two crises see R. K. Betts, *Nuclear Backmail and Nuclear Balance* (Washington, DC: Brookings Institution, 1987), pp. 62–65 and 83–109.

29. For an analysis of the Soviet buildup and the reasons behind it see J. Erickson, *Soviet Military Power* (London: Royal United Services Institute, 1971); also, L. Aspin, "What Are the Russians Up To?" in *International Security* 3 (Summer 1978), pp. 30–54; and S. Carus, "The Evolution of Soviet Military Power since 1965," Appendix II to E. N. Luttwak, *The Grand Strategy of the Soviet Union*, pp. 176–230.

30. C. Gray, *The Future of Land-Based Missile Forces* (London: International Institute of Strategic Studies, 1978); also, P. Nitze, "Deterring Our Deterrent," in *Foreign Policy* 25 (Winter 1976–77), pp. 195–210.

31. See F. Chernoff, "Ending the Cold War: The Soviet Retreat and the U.S. Military Buildup," in *International Affairs* LXVII, 1 (January 1991), pp. 111–26. Chernoff shows that the cost of the response to Star Wars only represented a vanishingly small fraction of the Soviet GNP.

32. Interview with Col. Gen. Nikolai Chervov, head of the Soviet Chief of Staff Directorate, *International Defense Review*, February 1990, p. 129.

33. For a Soviet view of the arms race and its dynamics see H. Trofimenko, "The 'Theology' of Strategy," in *Orbis* 21 (Fall 1977), pp. 497–515.

34. For some terrifying anecdotes concerning the unreliability of pre-PAL nuclear controls see D. Caldwell, "Permissive Action Links,"

in *Survival* XXIX, 3 (May–June 1987), pp. 224–238. It is alleged that, until 1962, "dual control" over nuclear weapons in Europe consisted of a German pilot sitting in his aircraft at the end of the runway, and a pistol-armed American officer somewhere in the vicinity.

35. For Clausewitz' continued relevance to the contemporary world see above all A. Rappoport, ed., *On War* (Harmondsworth, Middlesex: Pelican Books, 1968), pp. 11–82; also B. Brodie, "The Continuing Relevance of *On War*," in *On War*, M. Howard and P. Paret, eds., pp. 45–60. For a fresh interpretation of Clausewitz' most celebrated phrase see van Creveld, *The Transformation of War*, p. 35ff.

36. See on this problem above all Gat, *op. cit.*, Introduction. Liddell Hart, in calling Clausewitz "the Mahdi of Mass," was making the same point; see *The Ghost of Napoleon* (New Haven, CT: Yale University Press, 1933), pp. 118–29.

37. In retrospect, Walter Millis' words ring true: "The military professional who must today preside over the design, production and employment of the giant weapons of mass destruction cannot really learn much from Napoleon, or Jackson, or Lee, or Grant—who were all managers of men in combat, not of 'weapon systems' about which one of the most salient features is that they . . . must never be allowed to come into collision." *Military History*, No. 39 (Washington, DC: Service Center for Teachers of History, 1961), pp. 16–17.

38. Kissinger, *op. cit.*, Ch. VI. The most comprehensive discussion of this entire line of thought may be found in K. Knorr and T. Read, eds., *Limited Strategic War* (Princeton, NJ: Princeton University Press, 1962).

39. For a notable contemporary criticism knocking the props from under the "limited nuclear war" theory see B. Brodie, *Escalation and the Nuclear Option* (Princeton, NJ: Princeton University Press, 1966).

40. For the technical details of these weapons see *Jane's All the World's Aircraft* and *Jane's Weapons Systems* (London: Brassey's, 1954–58).

41. The most comprehensive discussion of these theories is O. Heilbrunn, *Conventional Warfare in the Nuclear Age* (London: Allen & Unwin, 1965).

42. See above all A. J. Bacevich, *The Pentomic Era; the U.S. Army Between Korea and Vietnam* (Washington, DC: The National Defense University Press, 1986).

43. Kissinger, *op. cit.*, pp. 181–182.

44. Lt. Col. D. Lindsey, M.D., "No Time for Despair," in *Armor* 65 (May–June 1956), pp. 38–39.
45. Lt. Col. R. W. Ernst, in *Military Review* 36 (August 1956), pp. 55–62.
46. For an enthusiastic contemporary description of the most important of these tests see A. Leveiro, "Task Force Razor Shaves Big Apple 2," in *The Army Combat Forces Journal* 5 (June 1955), pp. 38–43; for a criticism of its tactical realism, The Armored School, "Final Report of Test—Armored Task Force Participation—Exercise Desert Rock VI, 1 August 1955," at the National Technical Information Service (NTIS), Springfield, Va.
47. Information supplied to me by the late Prof. M. Augursky, of The Hebrew University, Jerusalem, who claimed to have been present at some of these experiments.
48. See for example H. Scoville, "Flexible Madness?" in *Foreign Policy* 14 (Spring 1974), pp.164–177; and Senators Nunn and Barlett, 95th U.S. Congress, Senate, 1st Session, Committee on Armed Services, *NATO and the New Soviet Threat* (Washington, DC: U.S. Government Printing Office, 1977).
49. See Bacevich, *op. cit.,* pp. 43–44, for some estimates of what nuclear war in Europe would do to the unfortunate countries involved in it.
50. For the role played by nuclear weapons in the Korean War see D. Callingaert, "Nuclear Weapons and the Korean War," *Journal of Strategic Studies* 11 (June 1988), pp. 177–202.
51. See for example W. F. Kaufman, ed., *Military Policy and National Security* (Princeton, NJ: Princeton University Press, 1956); R. E. Osgood, *Limited War: The Challenge to American Strategy* (Chicago: Chicago University Press, 1957); M. D. Taylor, *The Uncertain Trumpet* (New York: Harper, 1959); and, for a short summing-up, R. Brown, "Limited War," in C. McInnes and G. D. Sheffield, eds., *Warfare in the Twentieth Century* (London: Unwin Hyman, 1988), pp. 164–193.
52. The attempt to present Vietnam as if it were a conventional war, H. Summers, *On Strategy* (New York: Dell Books, 1982), particularly pp. 106–132, is not convincing. In fact, the war was conventional only for a few very brief periods, and during some of those periods (particularly December 1972) American airpower defeated the Northern invasion hands-down.
53. The most recent discussion is D. Kinnard, "The Soldier as Ambassador: Maxwell Taylor in Saigon, 1964–1965," in *Parameters* XXI, 1 (Spring 1991), pp. 31–46.
54. For an in-depth discussion see M. Clodfelter, *The Limits of Air-*

power; The Bombing of North Vietnam (New York: Free Press, 1989), particularly Ch. 2.

55. For a criticism of the invasion of Grenada see W. S. Lind, "Report to the Congressional Reform Caucus on the Grenada Operation" (Washington, DC: Military Reform Institute, April 1985); and of the Panamian operation, E. N. Luttwak, "Just Cause—A Military Score Sheet," *Parameters* 20 (March 1990), pp. 100–101. According to *Newsweek* (5 November 1990), p. 3, fully one-quarter of all American casualties in Panama were caused either by accidents or by friendly fire.

56. At Potsdam, the Soviets set a pattern in managing to behave as if the atomic bomb did not matter or, alternatively, as if they had it, too; see Rhodes, *op. cit.*, p. 691, and the sources there quoted.

57. H. S. Dinerstein, *War and the Soviet Union* (New York: Praeger, 1959), p. 96ff.

58. See for example Marshal Malinovsky's address to the Fourth Session of the Supreme Soviet, USSR (15 January 1960), excerpted in H. F. and W. F. Scott, *op. cit.*, pp. 165–166. For Soviet criticism of "selective options" see J. Erickson, "The Soviet View of Deterrence; a General Survey," in *Survival* 26 (November–December 1982), pp. 242–251; also F. Ermath, "Contrasts in American and Soviet Strategic Thought," in *International Security* 3 (Fall 1978), p. 149.

59. See for example Marshal V. D. Sokolovsky and Maj. Gen. V. I. Zemskov, both as excerpted in Scott and Scott, *op. cit.*, pp. 174–177 and 211–215.

60. See A. H. Cordesman, *Deterrence in the 1980s: Part I, American Strategic Forces and Extended Deterrence*, Adelphi Paper No. 175 (London: International Institute of Strategic Studies, 1982), pp. 14–17 and 33–34.

61. On this episode see E. O'Ballance, *The Electronic War in the Middle East, 1968–70* (London: Faber & Faber, 1974), p. 120ff.

62. For an outline of pre-1979 Soviet activities in Afghanistan see A. Arnold, *Afghanistan; The Soviet Invasion in Perspective* (Stanford, CA: Hoover Institution Press, 1985), especially Chs. 6–8.

63. Even so, some veiled nuclear threats—though scarcely credible ones—were made by President Carter in connection with the Afghanistan crisis. See B. Blechman and D. Hart, "Dangerous Shortcuts," in *New Republic* (26 July 1980), p. 14. Betts, incidentally, includes this episode among his "Higher Risk Cases."

64. For an analysis of the war and the Soviet decision to withdraw see above all A. Saikal and W. Malley, eds., *The Soviet Withdrawal*

from Afghanistan (London: Cambridge University Press, 1989), especially Chs. 2, 6, and 9.

65.   See, e.g., C. Gray, "The Most Dangerous Decade: Historic Mission, Legitimacy and Dynamics of the Soviet Empire in the 1980s," in *Orbis* 25 (Spring 1981), pp. 13–28. This article saw the "much younger" Soviet leadership of the near future as "eager to flex" its military muscle in a foreign-policy adventure.

66.   For an attempt to quantify the impact of modern technology on military operations see T. N. Dupuy, *The Evolution of Weapons and Warfare* (Indianapolis and New York: Bobbs Merrill, 1980), Chs. 27–30; for a Soviet view, N. A. Lomov, ed., *The Revolution in Military Affairs* (Moscow: 1973; USAF trans., Washington, DC.: U.S. Government Printing Office, n.d.), especially Ch. 5, As a matter of fact, it should be argued that the predictions have proved false. In what few large-scale conventional wars were fought between 1945 and 1993, rates of advance, the depth of fronts, and the amount of destruction inflicted did *not* exceed those of World War II.

67.   See *inter alia* M. van Creveld, *Military Lessons of the Yom Kippur War,* The Washington Papers, No. 24 (Washington, DC: The Center for International and Strategic Studies, 1975). A good recent summary of these issues, as far as they pertain to the Middle East, is H. Goodman and W. S. Carus, *The Future Battlefield and the Arab–Israeli Conflict* (New Brunswick, NJ: TransAction Publishers, 1990). Ignoring nuclear weapons, it reads as if it were a hundred years out of date.

68.   At the time of writing, it remains to be seen whether cruise missiles armed with conventional warheads can alter this situation.

69.   On the Israeli side, these weapons still included American Sherman tanks, M-3 half-tracks, and 105-millimeter howitzers. The Arab arsenals still included the standard Soviet 130-millimeter field gun, the SU-85 and SU-100 tank destroyers, and even—in the case of Syria—a few Mark III ex-German Panzers. See T. N. Dupuy, *Elusive Victory* (New York: Harper & Row, 1978), p. 221ff.

70.   *Ibid.,* pp. 593 and 596. The Israeli invasion of Lebanon in 1982 *did* envisage the use of some novel systems, but in view of the IDF's massive superiority, their contribution to the outcome of the land battle was marginal.

71.   See for example Luttwak, *Strategy,* particularly pp. 101–155. Luttwak, incidentally, classifies his discussion of nuclear weapons under "nonstrategies."

72.   E.g., D. L. Maddill, "The Continuing Evolution of the Soviet Ground Forces," in *Military Review* 62 (August 1982), pp. 52–68.

73.   The best work on the cost of modern weapons and the impossibility

of sustaining them economically is F. Spinney, *Defense Facts of Life* (Boulder, CO: Westview Press, 1986).

74. Between 1976 and 1985 the USSR outproduced the U.S. by a factor of between 2.5 and 4 to 1 in most major weapons systems: See J. M. McKean, "The U.S.–Soviet Military Balance: Current and Projected Force Capabilities," in R. I. Paltzgraff and others, eds., *Emerging Doctrines and Technologies: Implications for Global and Regional Political–Military Balances* (Lexington, MA: Lexington Books, 1988), p. 296.

75. Clausewitz, *On War,* p. 79.

76. *Ibid.,* p. 77.

77. For some examples see Freedman, *op. cit.,* where almost every chapter out of twenty-five presents some new strategy.

78. Kaku and Axelrod, *op. cit.,* table on pp. x–xi. Declining enthusiasm for the plans in question is also shown by their code names: Whereas the early ones bore such colorful names as "Broiler," "Frolic," and "Sizzle," later ones were known blandly by the designated acronym SIOP (for Strategic Integrated Operations Plan) plus a number.

79. For two prominent examples see J. D. Steinbrunner, *The Cybernetic Theory of Decision: New Dimensions of Political Analysis* (Princeton, N.J., Princeton University Press, 1974); also R. Jervis, *Perception and Misperception in International Politics* (Princeton, NJ: Princeton University Press, 1976).

80. The foremost theorist of asymmetrical deterrence, also known as the doctrine of tearing out an arm, was P. Gallois; see in particular his *The Balance of Terror: Strategy for the Nuclear Age* (Boston, MA: Houghton Mifflin, 1961).

81. Freedman, *op. cit.,* p. 400.

82. Clausewitz, *On War,* p. 127.

83. T. Schelling, *Arms and Influence* (New Haven, CT: Yale University Press, 1966). The phrases entered in quotation marks are actually Schelling's chapter titles.

84. If, as has been claimed, Kennedy did not actually promise to remove the missiles, at any rate the first thing he did after the crisis was to order them removed; see D. L. Haffner, "Bureaucratic Politics and 'those Frigging Missiles'; JFK and the U.S. Missiles in Turkey," in *Orbis* 21 (June 1977), pp. 307–334.

85. For a recent account of the Soviet side of this competition for the favors of Third World states see R. A. Rubinstein, *Moscow's Third-World Strategy* (Princeton, NJ: Princeton University Press, 1988); for the American side, R. L. Rothstein, *The Third World and United States Foreign Policy* (Boulder, CO: Westview, 1981).

86. Betts, *Nuclear Blackmail and Nuclear Balance.* Some people, inci-

dentally, would put the number of threats much higher: e.g., M. H. Halperin, *Nuclear Fallacy: Dispelling the Myth of Nuclear Strategy* (Cambridge, MA: Ballinger, 1987), Ch. 2.

87.   See for example G. Golan, *Yom Kippur and After: The Soviet Union and the Middle East Crisis* (London: Cambridge University Press, 1977), pp. 122–124, which debunks the Soviet threat; also E. Karsh, *The Cautious Bear: Soviet Military Engagement in Middle East Wars in the Post 1967 Era* (Boulder, CO: Westview Press, 1985) pp. 79–80. According to Betts, *Nuclear Blackmail and Nuclear Balance,* p. 125, Kissinger later said that the DEFCON 3 maneuver was not one he would have dared repeat in the late seventies.

88.   See R. Jervis, *The Meaning of the Nuclear Revolution; Statecraft and the Prospect of Armageddon* (Ithaca, NY: Cornell University Press, 1989), p. 20ff.

Chapter III: Nuclear Weapons in Asia

1.   Already in August 1952 (i.e., long before Eisenhower took over and started brandishing nuclear weapons), Mao had made it plain to his colleagues that a truce was inevitable and that China could be proud of its achievements: Mao Tse Dong, *Selected Works* (London: Lawrence & Wishart, 1954), Vol. 5, pp. 78–80.

2.   J. S. Dulles, "Report from Asia," Department of State *Bulletin* No. 32,821 (21 March 1955); and D. D. Eisenhower, *The White House Years: Mandate for Change, 1953–1956* (Garden City, NY: Doubleday, 1963).

3.   On this episode see S. Adams, *Firsthand Report* (Westport, CT: Greenwood Press, 1974 ed.), p. 483.

4.   On the role played, or not played, by American nuclear threats in bringing the Korean War to an end see C. A. MacDonald, *Korea; The War Before Vietnam* (New York: Free Press, 1986), Ch. 10; E. C. Keefer, "President Dwight D. Eisenhower and the End of the Korean War," in *Diplomatic History* X, 3 (Summer 1986), pp. 280–281; D. Callingaert, "Nuclear Weapons and the Korean War," *Journal of Strategic Studies,* 11 (June 1988), pp. 177–201; and R. J. Foot, "Nuclear Coercion and the Ending of the Korean Conflict," in *International Security* XIII, 3 (Winter 1988–89), pp. 92–112. In the absence of Chinese documentary material, however, the evidence is inconclusive.

5.   Conveniently summed up in J. W. Lewis and X. Litai, *China Builds the Bomb* (Stanford, CA: University of California Press, 1988), p. 34ff.

6.   Khrushchev, *op. cit.,* p. 255.

7.   See various statements to this effect, dating between 1951 and 1978,

quoted in G. C. Segal, *Defending China* (Oxford: Oxford University Press, 1985), p. 56ff.

8. See M. Gurtov, *China Under Threat* (Baltimore, MD: Johns Hopkins University Press, 1980), p. 92. Mao reportedly expressed surprise that "firing a few shots" would "raise such a fuss."
9. Lewis and Litai, *op. cit.*, pp. 107–108.
10. Text printed, in *ibid.*, Appendix A.
11. Accidentally or not, this is exactly the reported range of Israel's Jericho II missile. One should always treat such figures with a pinch of salt.
12. *United States Military Posture for FY 1981* (Washington, DC: Government Printing Office, 1980), p. 76.
13. Statement by Deng Xiaoping, quoted in M. Clarcke, "Defense Modernization," in *The China Business Review* (July–August 1984), pp. 40–41.
14. See Chong Pin Lin, *China's Nuclear Weapons Strategy: Tradition Within Evolution* (Lexington, MA: Lexington Books, 1988), p. 54.
15. Printed in Lewis and Litai, *op. cit.*, p. 70. At this time, the Chinese were already speaking of their intention to develop "thermonuclear warheads with high yields and long range delivery vehicles."
16. See A. S. Whiting, *The Chinese Calculus of Deterrence* (Ann Arbor, MI: University of Michigan Press, 1975), p. 180, for the details.
17. *New York Times,* 19 August 1969; H. A. Kissinger, *The White House Years* (London: Weidenfeld & Nicolson, 1979), pp. 183–184. Interestingly, Nixon does not mention the incident in his memoirs, except to say that the possibility of a Soviet strike against China was raised by de Gaulle during a meeting between them; R. M. Nixon, *The Memoirs of Richard Nixon* (London: Sidgwick & Jackson, 1987) pp. 373–374. On the entire episode see also R. Betts, "Nuclear Peace and Conventional War," in *Journal of Strategic Studies* 11 (March 1988), pp. 79–85.
18. P. H. B. Goodwin, "Mao Zedong Revisited: Deterrence and Defense in the 1980s," in P. H. B. Goodwin, ed., *The Chinese Defense Establishment: Continuity and Change in the 1980s* (Boulder, CO: Westview Press, 1983), p. 35.
19. Segal, *Defending China*, pp. 75–76.
20. Quotation in *ibid.*, p. 57.
21. What evidence does exist is summed up in Chong Pin Lin, *op. cit.*, pp. 80–81.
22. See A. Angley-Hsieh, *Communist China's Strategy in the Nuclear Era* (Englewood Cliffs, NJ: Prentice-Hall, 1962), p. 62.
23. Lewis and Litai, *op. cit.*, p. 217.

24. See also G. C. Segal, "Strategy and Ethnic 'Chic'," in *International Affairs* 60 (Winter 1984–85), pp. 15–30.

25. Mao, *op. cit.*, Vol. 5, pp. 152–153 and 310.

26. For the evidence, which is admittedly somewhat tenuous, see Chong Pin Lin, *op. cit.*, p. 78.

27. *Ibid.*, p. 78.

28. See Segal, *Defending China*, p. 176ff.

29. Quoted in H. Gelber, "Nuclear Weapons and Chinese Policy," Adelphi Paper No. 99 (London: International Institute of Strategic Studies, 1973), p. 19.

30. Chong Pin Lin, *op. cit.*, pp. 68–73 and 134ff.

31. See M. B. Lanski, "People's War and the Soviet Threat: The Rise and Fall of a Military Doctrine," in *Journal of Contemporary History* XVII, 4 (October 1983), pp. 619–650; and H. B. Godwin, "People's War Revised: Military Doctrines, Strategy, and Operations," in C. D. Lovejoy and B. W. Watson, eds., *China's Military Reforms: International and Domestic Implications* (Boulder, CO: Westview Press, (1986), pp. 1–14.

32. See Chong Pin Lin, *op. cit.*, p. 84.

33. See on this question an undated quotation in *ibid.*, p. 85, from which it may perhaps be learned that the Chinese have no more been able to solve this problem than anybody else.

34. See Y. I. Verzberger, *China's Southwestern Strategy: Encirclement and Counterencirclement* (New York: Praeger, 1985), particularly Ch. 1. It is important to note that, as far as matters Indian are concerned, China's nuclear arsenal is hardly ever mentioned—though, needless to say, it is always there.

35. See A. J. Gregor and M. Hsia Chang, *The Iron Triangle: U.S. Security Policy for Northeastern Asia* (Stanford, CA: Hoover Institution Press, 1984), p. 125ff., for an analysis.

36. See P. Karniol, "Taiwan's Space and Missile Program," in *International Defense Review* (August 1989), pp. 1077–1078.

37. E. Snow, *The Long Revolution* (New York: Random House, 1972 ed.), pp. 175–176.

38. Concerning Nehru's thoughts on the nuclear question see W. Crocker, *Nehru: A Contemporary's Estimate* (London: Allen & Unwin, 1966), p. 116; also G. Sarvepalli, *Jawaharlal Nehru—A Biography* (Cambridge, MA: Harvard University Press, 1984), p. 189.

39. For the father–son relationship that existed between Bhaba and Nehru see R. S. Anderson, *Building Scientific Institutions in India: Saha and Bhaba*, Occasional Paper No. 11 (Montreal: Centre for Developing-Areas Studies, McGill University, 1975).

40. For a short summary see L. S. Spector, "New Players in the Nuclear

Game," in *Bulletin of the Atomic Scientists* (January–February 1989), pp. 29–32. India's nuclear establishment comprises several research reactors as well as electricity-generating plants, a plutonium breeder reactor, and no fewer than three different plutonium separation plants.

41. See R. G. C. Thomas, "India's Nuclear and Space Programs: Defense or Development? in *World Politics* XXXVIII, 2 (January 1986), pp. 315–344, for a discussion of this problem.

42. See O. Brosh, "Perceptions and Public Attitudes Towards the Nuclear Dimension in Multilateral Conflicts," Ph.D. thesis (Jerusalem: The Hebrew University, 1990), pp. 223–224; also Y. I. Verzberger, "Bureaucratic–Organizational Politics and Information Processing in a Developing State," in *International Studies Quarterly* XXVIII, 1 (March 1984), p. 87ff.

43. See R. Krishna, "India and the Bomb," in *India Quarterly* XXI, 2 (April–June 1965), pp. 119–137, for the details.

44. For the background see L. Kavic, *India's Quest for Security: Defence Policies, 1947–1965* (Berkeley, CA: University of California Press, 1967), p. 169ff; also Y. I. Verzberger, *Misperceptions in Foreign Policy Making: The Sino–Indian Conflict, 1956–1962* (Boulder, CO: Westview Press, 1984).

45. A. Lall, *The Emergence of Modern India* (New York: Columbia University Press, 1981), p. 167.

46. As an example of Indian equanimity see V. R. C. Rao, "China's Missile Capability," in *Mainstream* (May 24, 1980), pp. 5–6; and for a discussion of the China factor in India's strategy, see Brosh, *op. cit.*, p. 270ff., and G. G. Mirchandani, *India's Nuclear Dilemma* (New Delhi: Popular Books Service, 1968), p. 91ff.

47. See L. E. Rose, "Pakistan's Role and Interests in South and Southwest Asia," in *Asian Affairs* IX, 1 (September–October 1981), p. 56.

48. For a discussion of Indian "hegemonial" aspirations and their impact on other regional powers see L. E. Rose, "India's Regional Policy: Nonmilitary Dimensions," in S. P. Cohen, ed., *The Security of South Asia; American and Asian Perspectives* (Urbana, Il: University of Illinois Press, 1978), pp. 3–21.

49. For a summary of Pakistani perceptions of the problem see B. Naqvi, "The Peace Option for Pakistan," in *ibid.*, pp. 106–118.

50. See Kavic, *op. cit.*, pp. 8–28, for the origins of India's foreign policy.

51. On the background see P. K. S. Namboodiri, "Perceptions and Policies in India and Pakistan," in K. Subrahmanyam, ed., *India and the Nuclear Challenge* (New Delhi: Lancer International, 1986), p. 222; and on the Pakistani reaction to the statement Brosh, *op. cit.*, p. 283.

52. See Mirchandani, *op. cit.*, pp. 56–57; also R. L. M. Patil, *India— Nuclear Weapons and International Politics* (New Delhi: National 1969), p. 24. The most important factor that prevented an Indian nuclear weapon from being built was the fear that Pakistan would follow suit—or so the government claimed.

53. For the origins and development of the Indian–Soviet connection see N. A. Husain, "India's Regional Policy: Strategic and Security Dimensions," in S. P. Cohen, ed., *The Security of South Asia: American and Asian Perspectives*, p. 29ff.

54. The best account of the events that led to the war remains G. W. Choodhury, *The Last Days of United Pakistan* (Bloomington, IN: Indiana University Press, 1974). The author is an ex-official of the Pakistani Foreign Ministry.

55. Nixon, *The Memoirs of Richard Nixon,* pp. 527–528.

56. See P. S. Jayaramu, *India's National Security and Foreign Policy* (New Delhi: ABC, 1987), p. 83ff., for a semiofficial Indian assessment of the episode and its implications.

57. See C. K. Ebinger, *Pakistan: Energy Planning in a Strategic Vortex* (Bloomington, IN: Indiana University Press, 1981), p. 80.

58. P. K. S. Namboodiri, "Perceptions and Policies in India and Pakistan," in K. Subrahmanyam, ed., *India and the Nuclear Challenge,* p. 226ff., gives the most coherent Indian view of Pakistan's nuclear development. For Bhutto's own accounts of his efforts see Z. A. Bhutto, *If I Am Assassinated* (New Delhi, Vikas, 1979), p. 137ff.

59. Brosh, *op. cit.,* p. 224ff., sums up the statements made by India's various Prime Ministers over the years.

60. As of 1991, India had eight commercial power reactors on line, seven under construction, and another ten in the planning stages, making its peaceful nuclear program the world's second largest after Japan. B. Challeney, "South Asia's Passage to Nuclear Power," in *International Security* XVI, 1 (Summer 1991), p. 30.

61. L. S. Spector, "If India and Pakistan Go to War," in *International Herald Tribune* (8 June 1990), p. 6.

62. For India's missile program see Y. Pahl, "Focus—Specificities of India's Space Program," in *Mainstream* 29 (February 1985), pp. 7–10 and 34; *International Herald Tribune* (26 February 1986); G. Milhollin, *loc. cit.,* pp. 31–35; and Brosh, *op. cit.,* p. 263ff., which is the most complete and up-to-date survey of all.

63. India's attempts to purchase a supercomputer may be understood against this background; see *The Hindu* (Madras), 24 November 1984, p. 1; *The Telegraph* (Calcutta), 11 March 1985, p. 4; and *The Hindustan Times* (New Delhi), 16 October 1986. On the assumption that one accuses others of trying to do what one has already

done oneself, a hint concerning Indian tactical nuclear capabilities may be contained in R. G. Sawherry, "Pakistan's Military Capability," in *Journal of Institute for Defense Studies and Analysis* XVI, 3 (January–March 1984), pp. 205–206.

64. For a convenient summary see J. Singh, "The Challenge of Our Time," in K. Subrahmanyam, ed., *India and the Nuclear Challenge,* Ch. 1; and *idem,* "The Threat of Nuclear Weapons," *ibid,* Ch. 2. The two articles together present the best available rationale behind India's nuclear policy; they also bear a semiofficial character in that, at the time of writing, Subrahmanyam was director of the Institute for Defense Studies and Analysis and Singh his Deputy.

65. See A. R. Khan Abbasi, "Thirty-Five Years of Pakistan–China Relations," *in Strategic Studies* IX, 4 (Summer 1986), pp. 22–43, for details.

66. See, e.g., *New York Times,* 21 September 1982; *Hindustan Times* (New Delhi), 21 October 1985, p. 3; Delhi Domestic Service in English, 21 October 1985, DRSA, 21 November 1985, E-1; *The Statesman* (Calcutta), 26 July 1986, p. 8; and *Times of India* (New Delhi), 1 April 1986, p. 1. The Chinese have consistently denied the allegations: *News from China* (Bulletin of the Chinese Embassy in New Delhi), 5 November 1985; and Delhi Domestic Service in English, 21 November 1985, DRSA, 21 November 1985.

67. See S. Johal, "America's Arming of Pakistan; Indian Views in the 1950s and 1980s," in *Strategic Studies* IX, 2 (Winter 1986), pp. 68–79, for an Indian interpretation of this question.

68. See in particular K. Subrahmanyam, "Implications of Nuclear Assymetry," in *idem,* ed., *Nuclear Myths and Realities: India's Dilemna,* p. 215ff.

69. See K. Subrahmanyam, "Pakistani Credibility Gap," in *Journal of the Institute for Defense Studies and Analysis* XIV, 1 (July–September 1981), pp. 116–117; S. Rashid Naim, "Asia's Day After: Nuclear War between India and Pakistan?" in S. P. Cohen, ed., *The Security of South Asia,* Appendix 1, pp. 243–250; S. P. Cohen, "Conclusions," in *ibid.,* p. 236; and A. R. Siddiqi, "Nuclear Non-Proliferation in South Asia; Problems and Prospects," in *Strategic Studies* X, 4 (Summer–Autumn 1987), p. 115. Mirchandani, *op. cit.,* p. 153, claims that Nehru was actually one of the first to worry about the effects of nuclear weapons on the environment; already in 1954 he set up an expert committee to study the problem, and had its findings published.

70. For the background see R. G. Wirsing, "The Siachen Glacier Dispute," Parts 1, 2, and 3 of *Strategic Studies* X,1 (Autumn 1987), pp. 49–66; XI, 3 (Spring 1988), pp. 75–94; and XII, 1 (Autumn 1988),

pp. 38–54; and, for a ground view of the hostilities, see "War on the High Ground," *Time* (17 July 1989), pp. 19–25.

71. *Dawn* (Karachi), 2 March 1983, p. 1; *Jang* (Karachi, Urdu), 6 August 1983, p. 3; *Mashriq* (Karachi, Urdu), 25 May 1984, p. 3; *The Muslim* (Islamabad), 16 September 1984, p. 4; 2 October 1985, p. 4; 5 November 1985, p. 4. The Pakistanis have also published Indian denials: *Jang* (Karachi, Urdu), 18 January 1986, p. 3.

72. *The Telegraph* (English, Calcutta), 7 March 1987.

73. For a Pakistani view of the origins of the conflict see A. Samad Khan, "The Indo–Pakistani Rivalry and the Sub-Continental Security Calculus," in *Strategic Studies* IX, 1 (Autumn 1985), pp. 15–45.

74. See R. B. Rais, "Pakistan's Nuclear Program; Prospects for Proliferation," in *Asian Survey* 25 (April 1985), pp. 458–472, for details.

75. In fact, there are some signs of rivalry between the two parts of Pakistan's program, the civilian and the military. See Brosh, *op. cit.*, p. 135.

76. R. R. Subrahmanian and K. Subrahmanyam, "Mutual Inspection and Verification," in K. Subrahmanyam, ed., *India and the Nuclear Challenge*, pp. 168–169; and J. C. Snyder, "The Non-Proliferation Regime: Managing the Impending Crisis," in N. Joeck, ed., *Strategic Consequences of Nuclear Proliferation in South Asia* (London: F. Cass, 1986), p. 24. However, the International Atomic Energy Commission, which visited KANUPP in 1989, found no plutonium missing from it: See Spector, *The Undeclared Bomb*, p. 152, Note D.

77. Rais, *loc. cit.*, p. 467.

78. In 1979 the government at the Hague published the results of its investigation into this affair with the objective of minimizing its significance and reestablishing Dutch reliability. It appears that Qadir Khan was able to get specifications of centrifuges, as well as manuals for their operation, and the addresses of German companies which manufacture them. See Subrahmanyam, ed., *Nuclear Myths and Realities*, Appendix I, pp. 165–189.

79. *The Washington Post*, 10 February 1984, p. 34-A.

80. *New York Times*, 5 May 1987, p. 1; 15 July 1987, p. 1; and Brosh, *op. cit.*, p. 313.

81. See *India Today* (New Delhi), 31 March 1987, pp. 72–80.

82. L. S. Spector in *International Herald Tribune*, 8 June 1990.

83. *Dawn* (Karachi), quoted by Delhi Domestic Service in English, 29 January 1989; Foreign Broadcasting Intelligence Service (FBIS), NES-89-018, 77. The best source on the entire question is Brosh, *op. cit.*, pp. 315–316.

84. See for example Mohammed Ayub Khan, "The Pakistan–America Alliance: Stresses and Strains," in *Foreign Affairs* 42 (January 1964), p. 196; and Z. A. Bhutto's appropriately titled book *The Myth of Independence* (London: Oxford University Press, 1969). Zia Ul Haq is said to have repeated the claim: *The Telegraph* (Calcutta), 22 February 1987, p. 6.

85. See S. Ganguly, "Avoiding War in Kashmir," in *Foreign Affairs* LXIX, 5 (Winter 1990–91), p. 67ff., for an analysis.

86. For a very good exposition of way the Pakistanis see the entire tangle cf. Lt. Gen. A. I. Akram, "Security and Stability in South Asia," in Cohen, ed., *op. cit.*, pp. 163–180.

87. "The army is still visibly and substantially more British than Mughal"; Cohen, *The Pakistani Army,* pp. 8 and 42.

88. P. Iqbal Cheema, "American Policy in South Asia: Interests and Objectives," in Cohen, ed., *The Security of South Asia,* pp. 124–125.

89. See T. Kheli, "New Pakistan's Foreign Policy," in *Orbis* (Fall 1976), p. 753, for Bhutto's reaction to India's PNE.

90. Bhutto, *op. cit.,* p. 137.

91. See Brosh, *op. cit.,* pp. 289–290, for various high-ranking Pakistani statements to this effect.

92. *Mashriq* (Karachi, Urdu), 25 February 1986, pp. 1 and 7.

93. *Pakistan Times* (Lahore), 8 December 1986, Supplement, p. iii; and *Dawn* (Karachi), 7 June 1983, Supplement, p. vi. See also S. Tahir-Kheli and W. O. Staudemeier, "The Saudi–Pakistani Military Relationship; Implications for U.S. Policy," in *Orbis* XXVI, 1 (Spring 1982), pp. 155–172.

94. *Washington Post,* 8 April 1990.

95. Much the best account of this entire issue is Brosh, *op. cit.,* p. 316ff.

96. Rais, *loc. cit.,* pp. 463–465; J. S. Metha, "India and Pakistan: We Know the Past. Must We Live in It?" in Cohen, ed., *The Security of South Asia,* p. 198; and A. Samad Khan, *loc. cit.,* p. 19ff.

97. See Rashid Naim, *loc. cit.,* especially pp. 287 and 280–281; also A. R. Siddiqi, "Nuclear Non-Proliferation in South Asia; Problems and Prospects," *Strategic Studies* X, 4 (Summer–Autumn 1987), p. 115. Siddiqi, incidentally, is editor of the Karachi *Defense Journal,* which is closely tied to the Pakistani Army.

98. See M. Ayoob, ed., *Regional Security in the Third World,* pp. 3–26, for an excellent analysis of these problems.

99. See Hong Shi, "China's Political Development After Tiananmen; Tranquility by Default," in *Asian Survey* XXX, 12 (December 1990), pp. 1206–1217.

100. On these problems see D. Goodman and G. Segal, eds., *China at Forty: Mid-Life Crisis?* (Oxford: Clarendon Press, 1989).

101. See Wang Xiaoquiang and Bai Nanfeng, *The Poverty of Plenty* (London: Macmillan, 1991).

102. See K. Forster and O-K Tam, "Chinese Fiscal Reform," in *Chinese Economic Studies* XXIV 1 (Fall 1990), p. 12.

103. A. Waldon, "The Warlord: Twentieth Century Chinese Understanding of Violence, Militarism, and Imperialism," in *American Historical Review* XCVI, 4 (October 1991), pp. 1073–1100. On the problems of central government versus regional resistance in China see K. Liebenthal and M. Oksenberg, *Policy Making in China: Leaders, Structures, and Pressures* (Princeton, NJ: Princeton University Press, 1989), p. 340ff. Decentralization and regionalism also have strong roots in Chinese history; see Min Tiku, *National Policy and Local Power; The Transformation of Late Imperial China* (Cambridge, MA: Harvard University Press, 1989), especially Ch. 4.

104. See V. Louis, *The Coming Decline of the Chinese Empire* (New York: Salisbury, 1984 ed.). The common fear of insurrection among peoples straddling the common border may be one reason behind the *détente* in Soviet–Chinese relations that took place in 1991: See L. Homes, "Afghanistan and Sino–Soviet Relations," in Saikal and Malley, eds., *op. cit.,* pp. 135–136.

105. For a good discussion of these problems see R. L. Hardgrave, *India Under Pressure: Prospect for Political Stability* (Boulder, CO: Westview Press, 1984).

106. See Ganguly, *loc. cit.,* p. 62ff., for the background.

107. See *Economist,* 22 September 1991, p. 22, for an analysis.

108. For the general background see L. Ziring, *Pakistan: The Enigma of Political Development* (Boulder, CO: Westview Press, 1980).

109. See S. J. Burki, *Pakistan: A Nation in the Making* (Boulder, CO: Westview Press, 1986), particularly p. 199ff., for a sophisticated discussion of this problem.

110. See M. P. Singh, "The Crisis of the Indian State," *Asian Survey* XXX, 8 (August 1990), especially p. 817.

111. See for example M. Ziauddin, "Islamizing the Economy: Process Seen as Ineffective," in *Dawn* (Karachi, English), 20 November 1983, Business Supplement, pp. i and iv.

112. See Cohen, *The Pakistan Army,* particularly Chs. 2 and 5; also Ziring, *op. cit.,* Ch. 12.

113. See W. Barton, *India's Northwestern Frontier* (London: J. Murray, 1939), p. 286ff., for the origins of this problem.

Chapter IV: Nuclear Weapons in the Middle East

1. See M. Bar Zohar, *Ben Gurion* (Tel Aviv: Am Oved, 1975), p. 1345 [Hebrew]; Bar Zohar, a journalist and Labor MK, was close to Ben Gurion and also did extensive work on the Ben Gurion archives at Sdeh Boker.
2. Interestingly, one of the best short appreciations is to be found in C. S. Raj, "Israel and Nuclear Weapons: A Case of Clandestine Proliferation,"; in Subrahmanyam, ed., *Nuclear Myths and Realities,* pp. 87–118. See also S. Aronson, *Conflict and Bargaining in the Middle East; An Israeli Perspective* (Baltimore, MD: Johns Hopkins University Press, 1978), p. 15ff.
3. See the account of a 1962 meeting in which the issue was thrashed out in Y. Evron, *Israel's Nuclear Dilemma* (Tel Aviv: Hakibutz Hamehuhad, 1987), p. 17ff. [Hebrew]
4. See above all the following series of articles in the left-wing periodical *New Outlook:* IV, 5 (March–April 1962), pp. 18–21; V, 4 (May 1962), pp. 13–20; V, 9 (November–December 1962); VII, 2 (February 1964), pp. 34–38; VIII, 2 (March 1965), p. 21 (an appeal for nuclear disarmament, signed by some of Israel's leading academics and scientists); IX, 3 (March–April 1966), pp. 3–6; and IX, 5 (June 1966), pp. 44–47.
5. Brosh, *op. cit.,* 59ff. and the vast literature there quoted.
6. See *New York Times,* 7 March 1966 (report of Israeli newspaper editors asking for a relaxation of the ban on discussing nuclear weapons).
7. Eshkol's decision to slow down the development of surface to surface missiles led to the resignation of Professor Yuval Ne'eman, the eminent Israeli nuclear scientist, from the Ministry of Defense; see Ne'eman's own account in *Ha'aretz* (Tel Aviv, Hebrew), 6 February 1976.
8. The evidence for the Johnson administration's attempts to restrain Eshkol, and its results, are available in the Lyndon Johnson Library. See Brosh, *op cit.,* p. 66ff.
9. Bundy, *op. cit.,* p. 510; S. M. Hersch, *The Samson Option: Israel's Nuclear Arsenal and American Foreign Policy* (New York: Random House, 1991), Ch. 12, has many details on the Israeli attempts to mislead the U.S. inspection teams.
10. Brosh, *op. cit.,* p. 80ff.
11. See the next section," "The Arab States."
12. See Y. Allon, *The Making of Israel's Army* (London: Sphere Books, 1971), pp. 78–79.

13. Aronson, *op. cit.*, pp. 95–96; also *Time*, 12, April 1976, p. 19.

14. P. Pean, *Les deux bombes* (Paris: Fayard, 1982), p. 113–121; H. Krossney and S. Weissmann, *The Islamic Bomb* (Jerusalem: Adam & Kastel, 1982) p. 11 [Hebrew]; *Sunday Times* (London, 5 and 12 October 1986; and Brosh, *op. cit.*, p. 78.

15. The best indication that the Bomb had actually become available in the Summer of 1969 may be found in the fact that the U.S. put an end to its attempt to make Israel sign the Non-Proliferation Treaty (NPT); see Brosh, *op. cit.*, p. 84.

16. See *ibid.*, p. 82ff., for a detailed discussion of this period.

17. For example, the raids launched by the IDF against targets west of Suez in the Autumn of 1969; also the start of "strategic" bombing in the winter of 1970. The best English-language account of the war remains E. O'Ballance, *The Electronic War in the Middle East, 1968–1970* (London: Faber & Faber,1974).

18. See, e.g., speech to officer cadets reported in *Ha'aretz*, 24 July 1972.

19. See A. Kahalani, *A Warrior's Story* (Tel Aviv: Steimatzky, 1989), p. 15 [Hebrew], for the early assessment of the war by Israeli Military Intelligence. For what happened in Washington, A. Dowty, *Middle East Crisis: U.S. Decision-Making in 1958, 1970, and 1973* (Berkeley, CA: University of California Press, 1984), p. 229, reporting on the reaction of the Watch Committee Middle East, to the outbreak of the war.

20. Information about this meeting was published for the first time by *Time* magazine, 24 April 1976, p. 19. Hersch, *op. cit.*, pp. 225–227, places it in the evening of 8 October.

21. Herzog's works are *The War of Atonement* (London: Futura, 1975), pp. 112–113; and *The Arab–Israeli Wars; War and Peace in the Middle East* (New York: Random House, 1982). See also Dupuy, *op. cit.*, pp. 458–459; M. Dayan, *Story of My Life* (London: Sphere, 1976), p. 488; A. Kahalani, *Oz 77* (Tel Aviv: Schocken, 1976), p. 104ff. [Hebrew]; and, above all, the specialized study by E. Hecht, "The Yom Kippur War on the Golan Heights—6 to 10 October 1973" (unpublished paper, Tel Aviv: 1987) [Hebrew]. None of these mentions nuclear weapons in any way; yet none offers a convincing explanation as to why the Syrians suddenly withdrew after having achieved what was effectively a breakthrough.

22. See C. Wakebridge, "The Syrian Side of the Hill," in *Military Review* (February 1976), p. 29.

23. *New York Times*, 19 May 1966.

24. *Ma'ariv* (Tel Aviv, Hebrew), 12 December 1974. This warning was duly noted in the Arab world: S. Shazly, *The Arab Military Option* (San Francisco, CA: American Mideast Publications, 1986), p. 39.

25.   See statements by Prime Minister Rabin, Minister of Defense Peres, and Foreign Minister Alon: *Ma'ariv,* 8 April 1976; *Davar* (Tel Aviv, Hebrew), 30 April 1976; and *Ha'aretz,* 9 September 1976.

26.   To this day, there are many who are convinced that Vanunu, a technician at Dimona, was either working for Israeli Intelligence or unwittingly used by them. See on this entire affair F. Barnaby, *The Invisible Bomb* (London: Tauris, 1989), particularly the Introduction.

27.   R. W. Tucker, "Israel and the United States: From Dependence to Nuclear Weapons?" *Commentary* (November 1975), pp. 29–43.

28.   See A. Dowty, "Israel and Nuclear Weapons," in *Midstream* XXII, 7 (November 1976), pp. 7–22, for the most sophisticated discussion as well as an extensive list of sources. Other prominent authors involved in the debate include S. Rosen, "Nuclearization and Stability in the Middle East," in *The Jerusalem Journal of International Relations* I, 3 (Spring 1976), pp. 1–38; and Y. Evron, "Some Effects of the Introduction of Nuclear Weapons in the Middle East," in A. Arian, ed., *Israel; A Developing Society* (Tel Aviv: Sapir Center, 1980), pp. 105–126. The highest ranking Israeli to take this line of thought in public was none other than Moshe Dayan: See his comments as reported in *Ma'ariv,* 20 February 1976.

29.   See above all S. Feldman, *Israeli Nuclear Deterrence: A Strategy for the 1980s* (New York: Columbia University Press, 1982).

30.   The leading Israeli advocate of this approach is Y. Evron, "Israel and the Atom; The Uses and Misuses of Ambiguity," in *Orbis* 17 (Winter 1974), pp. 1326–1343.

31.   Feldman, *op. cit.,* p. 55. Here it is pointed out that, whereas 30 percent of Israel's population live in three large cities, the corresponding figures for Egypt, Syria, Jordan, Saudi Arabia, and Libya respectively are 25, 28, 38, 21 and 41 percent. Feldman's analysis is not altogether convincing, since it excludes the people living in what are effectively the suburbs of Tel Aviv. On the other hand, it does point out the vulnerability of the other side; to say nothing of the fact that both Egypt and Iraq have dams that could be destroyed by nuclear weapons with absolutely disastrous results.

32.   Here it is not out of place to point out that many of the academics in question also serve in the IDF, particularly in the Planning and Intelligence Branches. Also, in Israeli academic circles, Hebrew-language publications hardly count; it is writings appearing in the "international" arena that matter with regard to prestige and advancement.

33.   Barnaby, *op. cit.,* Ch. 3; see also Hersch, *op. cit.,* Ch. 21—which, however, adds little not already known.

34. *Jerusalem Post,* 8 January 1991.
35. *Ha'aretz,* 2 June 1989. Using veiled language, Peres—then serving as Minister of Finance—concluded that the time had come to base Israel's defense on its nuclear deterrent, incidentally making the return of the territories possible.
36. See, e.g., A. Yaniv, *Ha'aretz,* 29 May 1990, p. B6.
37. *Ibid.*
38. Israel TV, 22 August 1990, "Mabat."
39. See Brosh, *op. cit.,* p. 102ff. and 135ff., for all the quotations one could wish for on this subject.
40. A. Shukeiri, Chairman of the Palestinian Council speaking to students in Cairo; Palestinian Liberation Organization (PLO) Radio, 27 December 1965.
41. *Al-Usbu Al-Arabi* (Beirut, Arabic), 11 October 1965; and *Al-Achbar* (Cairo, Arabic), 20 October 1965.
42. Telegrams, Deputy Secretary of State Ball of AmEmbassy (Cairo), 28 and 30 May 1964; Lyndon B. Johnson Library, quoted in Brosh, *op. cit.,* p. 68.
43. Radio Baghdad, 20 February 1966; *Al-Hawviya* (Beirut, Arabic), 21 February 1966; and *New York Times,* 21 February and 18 April 1966.
44. Deputy Secretary of State Ball to AmEmbassy (Cairo), 19 March 1966, No. 2379, Lyndon Baines Johnson (LBJ) Library, Country File UAR, Box 159–161, item 20; quoted in *ibid.,* pp. 204–205.
45. *Al-Dif'a* (Amman, Arabic), 12 May 1966; and *New York Times,* 4 February 1966. The story was confirmed in retrospect by Isma'il Fahmi in *Al-Sha'b* (Cairo, Arabic), 17 February 1971, and in *Al-Ahram* (Cairo, Arabic), 26 February 1981.
46. In standard accounts of the origins of the war, e.g., W. Laqueur's *The Road to Jerusalem* (London: Weidenfeld & Nicolson, 1968), nuclear issues are not even mentioned.
47. Telegrams, Ambassador Battle (Cairo) to Secstate, 21 February 1966, LBJ Library; compare this with the Egyptian version as it appeared in *Al-Yawm* (Beirut, Arabic), 1 May 1966, from which it appears that Sadat refused to take Johnson's assurances at face value.
48. Telegram, American Ambassador, Cairo, to State Department, 11 April 1964, No. A 737, LBJ Library, NSF Country File UAR, Box 158, item 39; quoted in S. Aronson, *The Politics and Strategy of Nuclear Weapons in the Middle East,* Unpublished Manuscript (Jerusalem: The Hebrew University, 1991), pp. 198–199.
49. *Al-Achbar* (Cairo, Arabic), 5 February 1965; *Al-Thwara Al-Arabia* (Baghdad, Arabic), February 1966; Radio Baghdad, 6, 19 May

1966; and *Al-Manar* (Amman, Arabic), 14 February 1967. All these made explicit references to the need to fight a "preventive war" before Israel built the Bomb.

50. See on this episode Brosh, *op. cit.*, pp. 79–80.

51. E.g., *Al-Ahram*, which on 14 June 1967 informed its readers that Israel's "next step" would be to build the Bomb; also *Roz Al-Joussuf* (Cairo, Arabic), 27 May 1968, and Aronson, *Conflict and Bargaining*, p. 150.

52. Shazley, *The Arab Military Option*, p. 39; and *Newsweek*, 2 February 1969. According to Nasser, "Egyptian experts" did not believe Israel capable of developing nuclear weapons in short order; coming from him, this was news indeed.

53. *Al-Ahram*, 11 November 1969. This statement, interestingly enough, came one day before the *New York Times* declared that Israel had built the Bomb.

54. *New York Times*, 21 November 1968.

55. Radio Cairo, 11 January 1969.

56. Among other episodes, Nasser used the problem of nuclear weapons to explain to Ghadafi as to why no "war of destruction" against Israel was possible; yet on the other hand he carefully skirted the question of whether Israel itself possessed those weapons. See M. Heikal, *The Road to Ramadan* (London: Sphere, 1974), pp. 74–75.

57. See *Israel and Nuclear Weapons: Present Options and Future Strategies* (London: Chatto & Windus, 1971). This book, incidentally, was immediately translated into Arabic.

58. *Al-Ahram*, 19 October 1973; *Al-Anuar* (Beirut, Arabic), 16 February 1976; *ibid.*, 12, 15, and 19 June 1977; *Al-Achbar*, 23 November 1977; and *Al-Ahali* (Alexandria, Arabic), 15 December 1982. Heikal's own views are analyzed at length in S. Aronson, "The Nuclear Dimension of the Arab–Israeli Conflict," in *Jerusalem Journal of International Relations* VII, 1–2 (1984), p. 134ff.

59. Fahmi in *Al Sha'b* (Cairo, Arabic), 17 February 1981; Muhi a Din in *Al-Watan Al-Arabi* (Beirut, Arabic), 24 July 1981; Shazly in Al-Mukaf Al-Arabi (Beirut, Arabic), 3 January 1983; also Shazly *op. cit.*, pp. 39–40, where he is concerned to show that the Arab world might take on Israel even without the Bomb.

60. *Al-Ahali*, 22 October 1986.

61. Former Foreign Minister Ismail, at the December 1987 Nuclear Disarmament Conference, Cairo, quoted in *Hazab* (Daily Report, Israeli Intelligence Service), No. 843/23, 27 January 1988. See also *Al-Dustur* (Amman, Arabic), 7 and 13 October 1986, where the Vanunu revelations are said to be part of a deterrence-campaign launched by Prime Minister Shimon Peres.

62. *Al-Sha'b* (Cairo, Arabic), 14 October 1986; *Al-Mukaf Al-Arabi* (Beirut, Arabic), December 1986, p. 32; *Al-Anba'a* (Cairo, Arabic), 7 January 1987, p. 23.
63. For the details see Brosh, *op. cit.*, p. 122ff.; on Egypt's sensitivity to ecological problems resulting out of nuclear waste see also M. Heikal, *Autumn of Fury* (New York: Random House, 1983), p. 180. More recently, the head of Egypt's Atomic Energy Committee has reaffirmed this position: *Al-Anba'a*, 15 March 1987.
64. Sadat interview with *Ittela At* (Teheran, Farsee), 17 December 1974; Sadat on French television, 27 February 1975; Minister of Defense Gamassy in *Al-Mandia* (Ri'ad, Arabic), 7 December 1975; Sadat interview with *Al-Ziad* (Beirut, Arabic), 12 January 1976; Sadat press conference in Rome, reported in *Ha'aretz*, 9 April 1976; and *Washington Post*, 1 May 1976. All have in common that the Egyptians claimed "not to know" whether Israel had the Bomb but added that, if she did, Egypt was in a position to get it, too. For a list of such statements see Y. Evron, "The Relevance and Irrelevance of Nuclear Options in Conventional War: The 1973 October War," in *Jerusalem Journal of International Relations* VII, 1–2 (1984), p. 155.
65. *Al-Ahram*, Friday Supplement, 1 May 1976.
66. *Al-Musawwar* (Cairo, Arabic), 8 May 1987; Cairo Domestic Service, Arabic, 8 May 1987; *Al-Sharq Al-Aswat* (London, Arabic), 18 August 1987; and *Mena* (Cairo, Arabic), 8 November 1987.
67. BBC World Service, "Radio Newsreel," 2 October 1988.
68. Though the performance of the armed forces, and their failure to liberate the whole of the Sinai, have been subject to growing criticism in Egypt, strangely the debate contains no reference to nuclear weapons. See Ch. Raviv, "The Failure: An Egyptian Version,"*Bamachaneh*, 22 October 1986, pp. 9–10. [Hebrew]
69. *Al-Atchad* (Cairo, Arabic), 12 January 1989; see also *Roz Al-Joussuf*, 28 November and 5 and 12 December 1988, where the rationale behind Cairo's ostrich-like strategy, as well as its reasons for not wanting nuclear weapons, are explained in some detail.
70. During eighteen months' research, I only have been able to locate one source wherein an Egyptian explicitly admits the impact of nuclear weapons on the peace between Egypt and Israel, and even that one is contained in an English-language publication—and buried in a footnote. See A. M. Said Aly Abdel Aal, "The Superpowers and Regional Security in the Middle East," in Ayoob, ed., *Regional Security in the Third World*, p. 212, footnote 15.
71. See Feldman, *op. cit.*, pp. 78–82, for the details.
72. Damascus Radio, 7 July 1966; *Al-Musawwar*, 16 December 1966; and *Al-Thwara* (Damascus, Arabic), 11 July 1967.

73. *Al-Usbu Al-Arabi* (Beirut, Arabic), 1 July 1974. The author was reportedly a Col. Ayubi of the Syrian Military Intelligence Service.

74. *Ibid.*, 4 July 1974, by the same author.

75. *Al-Thwara,* 13 November 1976. Much later, Asad claimed that the same factors would make Israel think twice before using nuclear weapons against Syria; Radio Damascus, 1 August 1986.

76. *Al-Manar* (London, Arabic), 10 December 1977; and *Tishrin* (Damascus, Arabic), 2 August 1980, 18 November 1980, and 24 November 1980.

77. Quoted in *Ma'ariv,* 2 June 1985.

78. For an analysis of Soviet–Syrian relationships during this period and Asad's persistent attempts to get more out of Moscow than the latter was prepared to grant see E. Karsh, "A Marriage of Convenience: The Soviet Union and Asad's Syria," in *Jerusalem Journal of International Relations* XI, 4 (December 1989), p. 9ff.

79. See also Mu'amar Ghadafi's attempts to get nuclear weapons first from China and then from Pakistan: Heikal, *The Road to Ramadan,* pp. 74–75; Feldman, *op. cit.,* pp. 79–81; and Brosh, *op. cit.,* pp. 178–179.

80. Hafez Asad in speech on Armed Forces Day, Radio Damascus, 1 August 1986. For an analysis of the Syrian concept of "strategic parity" see Brosh, *op. cit.,* pp. 186–187.

81. *Tishrin,* 3 November 1982; and *Al-Thwara,* 24 November 1982.

82. *Al-Thwara,* 24 November 1982; and *Tishrin,* 5 June 1986. The author explicitly says that it is not part of the Ba'ath Party ideology to commit suicide. Given the possibility that Israel may resort to nuclear weapons/and or bombardment with radioactive materials in another war, the liberation of Palestine will have to be achieved by other means.

83. Radio Damascus, 24 January 1987. See also M. Ma'oz, *Asad: The Sphinx of Damascus* (New York: Grove Weidenfeld, 1988), p. 179ff.

84. On 13 June 1990 the Israeli newspaper *Ha'aretz* reported another speech by Asad in which, while very carefully skirting the question of nuclear weapons, he said in effect that there would *not* be another major war against Israel.

85. See A. Ben Tzur, "The Arabs and the Israeli Reactor," in *New Outlook* (April 1961), pp. 18–21.

86. For the latest on Iran's nuclear status see Task Force on Terrorism and Unconventional Warfare, House Republican Research Committee, U.S. House of Representatives, "Iran Strategy and Nuclear Capabilities," 20 January 1992.

87. See A. Bar'am, "Saddam Hussein: A Political Profile," in *The Jeru-*

salem Quarterly, 17 (Fall 1980), pp. 129 and 137. In November Saddam Hussein, the perfect opportunist, even said he would cooperate with Israel if that's what it took to get the Syrians out of Lebanon: See E. Karsh and I Raufsi, *Saddam Hussein: A Political Biography* (New York: Free Press, 1991), p. 201.

88. Much the best account of Iraq's *Ba'ath* regime and its goals in life is A. Bar'am, "Particularism and Integration in Iraqi Thought and Action under Ba'ath Rule," Ph.D Thesis (The Hebrew University Jerusalem, 1986) [Hebrew], particularly p. 301ff.

89. *Ibid.,* pp. 266–267.

90. See undated conversation between A. Tamir, Director General of the Israeli Foreign Ministry under Begin, and Iraqi Vice President Tareg Abdel Aziz; reported in *Yedi'ot Acharonot* (Tel Aviv, Hebrew), 15 February 1991.

91. See Brosh, *op. cit.,* p. 165, and the evidence there adduced.

92. See *ibid.,* p. 166ff., for the most detailed account.

93. See, however, M. J. Brenner, "The Iran–Iraq War: Speculations About a Nuclear Re-Run," in *Journal of Strategic Studies* VIII (1 March 1985), pp. 22–37.

94. Brosh, *op. cit.,* p. 172ff.

95. Iraqi memo to the Arab League, undated (Spring 1977[?]), reported in *Al Usbu Al Arabi,* 17 October 1977.

96. See *International Herald Tribune,* 9 September and 28 November, 1990. As far as anyone can make out, Iraq was attempting to follow the Pakistani road toward the Bomb by employing centrifuges for uranium enrichment, while at the same time adopting an "ambiguous" declaratory policy. Iraq, however, also had—and may still have—approximately 13 kilograms of highly enriched uranium, salvaged from Osiraq. In November 1990, Baghdad permitted IAEC access to this uranium, thus simultaneously proving that it had not used the material to build the Bomb and that it *could* do so if it really wanted to.

97. See *Washington Times,* 14 December 1989; *Ma'ariv,* 15 December 1989; *Newsweek,* 9 April 1990, p. 8; *New York Times,* 28 April 1991; *Yedi'ot Acharonot,* 25 October 1992, all reporting on Iraq's nuclear potential before and after the Gulf War.

98. *Ha'aretz,* 4, 5, 6 April 1990. *Al-Ahali,* 16 May 1990, even claimed Iraq had "tips" concerning an imminent Israeli attack. Following Saddam's threats against Israel, the Israeli government reportedly gave assurances it had no intention of attacking him.

99. Quoted in the *Jerusalem Post,* 12 July 1990; see also Bar'am's comments, *ibid.*

100. *Al-Jumhuriya* (Baghdad, Arabic), 21, July 1991. Thanks are due

to Dr. Norman Cigar of the Marine Corps University, Quantico, VA, for drawing my attention to this article.

101. *Yedi'ot Acharonot,* 15 March 1991. This may have been Saddam Hussein's way of making sure that if, by any remote chance, a missile *did* hit the reactor, the result would not be a Jordanian Chernobyl.

102. *Al-Ra'y* (Amman, Arabic), 20, 22, 24, and 26 January 1976.

103. The best single work on the Palestinian uprising so far is Z. Schiff and E. Ya'ari, *Intifada* (London: Weidenfeld & Nicolson, 1989).

LIST OF NEWSPAPERS QUOTED (BY LANGUAGE)

ARABIC

Al-Achbar (Cairo)
Al-Ahali (Alexandria)
Al-Ahram (Cairo)
Al-Anba'a (Cairo)
Al-Anuar (Beirut)
Al-Atchad (Cairo)
Al-Di'fa (Amman)
Al-Dustur (Amman)
Al-Hawviya (Beirut)
Al-Jumhuriya (Baghdad)
Al-Manar (Amman)
Al-Manar (London)
Al-Mandia (Ri'ad)
Al-Mukaf Al-Arabi (Beirut)

Al-Musawwar (Cairo)
Al-Ra'y (Amman)
Al-Sha'b (Cairo)
Al-Sharq Al-Aswat (London)
Al-Thwara (Damascus)
Al-Thwara Al-Arabia (Baghdad)
Al-Usbu Al-Arabi (Beirut)
Al-Wattan Al-Arabi (Beirut)
Al-Yawm (Beirut)
Al-Ziad (Beirut)
Mena (Cairo)
Roz Al-Joussuf (Cairo)
Tishrin (Damascus)

ENGLISH

Dawn (Karachi)
The Hindu (Madras)
Hindustan Times (New Delhi)
International Herald Tribune
(New York)
Jerusalem Post (Jerusalem)
The Muslim (Islamabad)
Newsweek (New York)
New York Times (New York)

Sunday Times (London)
The Telegraph (Calcutta)
Time (New York)
Times of India (New Delhi)
Wall Street Journal (New York)
Washington Post (Washington,
DC)
Washington Times (Washington,
DC)

HEBREW

Al Hamishmar (Tel Aviv)

Davar (Tel Aviv)

Ha'aretz (Tel Aviv)

Ma'ariv (Tel Aviv)

Yedi'ot Acharonot (Tel Aviv)

URDU

Jang (Karachi)

Mashriq (Karachi)

BIBLIOGRAPHY

Abbasi, A. R. Khan. "Thirty-Five Years of Pakistan–China Relations." *Strategic Studies* IX, 4 (Summer 1986), pp. 22–43.

Adams, S. *Firsthand Report* (Westport, CT: Greenwood Press, 1974 ed.).

Adcock, F. E. *The Greek and Macedonian Art of War* (Berkeley: University of California Press, 1957).

Allon, Y. *The Making of Israel's Army* (London: Sphere Books, 1971).

Alperovitz, G. *Atomic Diplomacy* (Harmondsworth, Middlesex: Penguin Books, 1985).

Anderson, R. S. *Building Scientific Institutions in India; Saha and Bhaba,* Occasional Paper No. 11 (Montreal: Centre for Developing-Areas Studies, McGill University, 1975).

Angley-Hsieh, A. *Communist China's Strategy in the Nuclear Era* (Englewood Cliffs, NJ: Prentice-Hall, 1962).

Armored School, The. "Final Report of Test—Armored Task Force Participation—Exercise Desert Rock VI, 1 August 1955," at the National Technical Information Service (NTIS), Springfield, VA.

Arnold, A. *Afghanistan: the Soviet Invasion in Perspective* (Stanford, CA: Hoover Institution Press, 1985).

Aronson, S. "The Nuclear Dimension of the Arab–Israeli Conflict." *Jerusalem Journal of International Relations* VII, 1–2 (1984), pp. 107–142.

Idem. *The Politics and Strategy of Nuclear Weapons in the Middle East,* Unpublished Manuscript (Jerusalem: The Hebrew University, 1991).

Idem. *Conflict and Bargaining in the Middle East: An Israeli Perspective* (Baltimore, Md: Johns Hopkins University Press, 1978).

Aspin, L. "What Are the Russians Up To?" *International Security* 3 (Summer 1978), pp. 30–54.

Ayoob, M. "Dateline India: the Deepening Crisis." *Foreign Policy* 85 (Winter 1991–92), pp. 166–184.

Idem, ed. *Regional Security in the Third World* (London: Croom Helm, 1986).

Ayub Khan, M. "The Pakistan–America Alliance: Stresses and Strains." *Foreign Affairs* 42 (January 1964), pp. 195–209.

Bacevich, A. J. *The Pentomic Era: The U.S. Army Between Korea and Vietnam* (Washington, DC: The National Defense University Press, 1986).

Bar'am, A. "Particularism and Integration in Iraqi Thought and Action under Ba'ath Rule." Ph.D Thesis (Jerusalem: The Hebrew University, 1986). [Hebrew]

Idem. "Saddam Hussein; A Political Profile." *The Jerusalem Quarterly* 17 (Fall 1980), pp. 115–144.

Barnaby, F. *The Invisible Bomb: The Nuclear Arms Race in the Middle East* (London: Tauris, 1989).

Barnie, J. *War in Medieval Society: Social Values and the Hundred Years' War* (London: Weidenfeld & Nicolson,1974).

Barton, W. *India's Northwestern Frontier* (London: J. Murray, 1939).

Bar Zohar, M. *Ben-Gurion* (Tel Aviv: Am Oved, 1975). [Hebrew]

Ben Tzur, A. "The Arabs and the Israeli Reactor." *New Outlook* (April 1961), pp. 18–21.

Bertram, C., ed. *Strategic Deterrence in a Changing Environment* (London: International Institute for Strategic Studies, 1981), pp. 5–41.

Best, G. *Humanity in Warfare* (New York: Columbia University Press, 1980).

Betts, R., ed.*Cruise Missiles: Technology, Strategy, Politics* (Washington, DC: Brookings Institution, 1981).

Idem. Nuclear Blackmail and Nuclear Balance (Washington, DC: Brookings Institution, 1987).

Bhutto, Z. A. *If I Am Assassinated* (New Delhi: Vikas, 1979).

Idem. The Myth of Independence (London: Oxford University Press, 1969).

Blackett, P. M. S. *The Military and Political Consequences of Atomic Energy* (London: Turnstile Press, 1948).

Blainey, G. *The Causes of War* (Melbourne: Sun Books, 1976).

Blechman, B. *Nuclear Blackmail and Nuclear Balance* (Washington, DC: Brookings Institution, 1987).

Idem, and D. Hart. "Dangerous Shortcuts," *New Republic* (26 July 1980), p. 14.

Brenner, M. J. "The Iran–Iraq War: Speculations About a Nuclear Re-Run." *Journal of Strategic Studies* VIII, 1 (March 1985), pp. 22–37.

Brodie, B. *The Absolute Weapon* (New York: Columbia University Press, 1946).

Idem. Escalation and the Nuclear Option (Princeton, NJ: Princeton University Press, 1966).

Brosh, O. "Perceptions and Public Attitudes Towards the Nuclear Dimension in Multilateral Conflicts." Ph.D Thesis (Jerusalem: The Hebrew University, 1990). [Hebrew]

Brown, R. "Limited War." In C. McInnes and G. D. Sheffield, eds. *Warfare in the Twentieth Century* (London: Unwin Hyman, 1988) pp. 164–193.

Bundy, McG. *Danger and Survival: The Political History of the Nuclear Weapon* (New York: Random House, 1988).

Caldwell, D. "Permissive Action Links," *Survival* XXIX, 3 (May–June 1987), pp. 224–238.

Callingaert, D. "Nuclear Weapons and the Korean War." *Journal of Strategic Studies* 11 (June 1988), pp. 177–202.

Cassirer, E. *The Myth of the State* (New Haven, CT: Yale University Press, 1946).

Challeney, B. "South Asia's Passage to Nuclear Power." *International Security* XVI, 1 (Summer 1991), pp. 43–72.

Chari, P. R. "China's Nuclear Posture: An Evaluation." *Asian Survey* 18 (August 1978), pp. 151–178.

Chernoff, F. "Ending the Cold War: The Soviet Retreat and the U.S. Military Buildup." *International Affairs* LXVII, 1 (January 1991), pp. 111–126.

Chong Pin Lin. *China's Nuclear Weapons Strategy: Tradition Within Evolution* (Lexington, MA: Lexington Books, 1988).

Choodhury, G. W. *The Last Days of United Pakistan* (Bloomington, IN: Indiana University Press, 1974).

Clarcke, M. "Defense Modernization." *The China Business Review* (July–August 1984), pp. 40–41.

Clausewitz, C. von. (M. Howard and P. Paret, eds.) *On War* (Princeton, NJ: Princeton University Press, 1976).

Clodfelter, M. *The Limits of Airpower: The American Bombing of North Vietnam* (New York: Free Press, 1989).

Cohen, S. P. *The Pakistani Army* (Berkeley: University of California Press, 1982).

Idem, ed. *The Security of South Asia: American and Asian Perspectives* (Urbana, IL: University of Illinois Press, 1978).

Collins, J. M. *U.S.–Soviet Military Balance, Concepts and Capabilities, 1960–1980* (New York, McGraw-Hill, 1980).

Cordesman, A. H. *Deterrence in the 1980s: Part I, America's Strategic Forces and Extended Deterrence*, Adelphi Paper No. 175 (London: International Institute for Strategic Studies, 1982).

Correspondance de Napoléon I, Vols. III, V, and XI (Paris: Plon, 1868).

Creveld, M. van. *Command in War* (Cambridge, MA: Harvard University Press, 1985).

Idem. *Military Lessons of the Yom Kippur War*, The Washington Papers, No. 24 (Washington, DC: The Center for International and Strategic Studies, 1975).

Idem. Supplying War; Logistics from Wallenstein to Patton (London: Cambridge University Press, 1977).

Idem. Technology and War; From 2000 B.C. to the Present (New York: Free Press, 1989).

Idem. The Training of Officers; From Military Professionalism to Irrelevance (New York: Free Press, 1990).

Idem. The Transformation of War (New York: Free Press, 1991).

Crocker, W. *Nehru: A Contemporary's Estimate* (London: Allen & Unwin, 1966).

Dayan, M. *Story of My Life* (London: Sphere, 1976).

Dinerstein, H. S. *War and the Soviet Union* (New York: Praeger, 1959).

Dowty, A. "Israel and Nuclear Weapons." *Midstream* XXII, 7 (November 1976), pp. 7–22.

Idem. Middle East Crisis: U.S. Decision-Making in 1958, 1970 and 1973 (Berkeley, CA: University of California Press, 1984).

Ducci, R. "The World Order in the Sixties." *Foreign Affairs* XLII, 3 (April 1964), pp. 379–390).

Dupuy, T. N. *Elusive Victory* (New York: Harper & Row, 1978).

Idem. The Evolution of Weapons and Warfare (Indianapolis and New York: Bobbs Merill, 1980).

Duyck, A. (I. Mueller, ed.) *Journaal* (The Hague: Nijhoff, 1886).

Ebinger, C. K. *Pakistan: Energy Planning in a Strategic Vortex* (Bloomington, IN: Indiana University Press, 1981).

Eisenhower, D. D. *The White House Years: Mandate for Change, 1953–1956* (Garden City, NY: Doubleday, 1963).

Engels, D. *Alexander the Great and the Logistics of the Macedonian Army* (Berkeley, CA: University of California Press, 1978).

Erfurt, W. *Der Vernichtungssieg* (Berlin: Mittler, 1939).

Erickson, J. *Soviet Military Power* (London: Royal United Services Institute, 1971).

Idem. "The Soviet View of Deterrence: A General Survey." *Survival* 26 (November–December 1982), pp. 242–251.

Ermath, F. "Contrasts in American and Soviet Strategic Thought." *International Security* 3 (Fall 1978), pp. 138–155.

Ernst, R. W. "Atomic Impact on G-1's Functions." *Military Review* 36 (August 1956), pp. 55–62.

Etheridge-Davis, L. *Limited Nuclear Options: Deterrence and the New American Doctrine,* Adelphi Paper No. 121 (Winter 1975–76) (London: International Institute for Strategic Studies, 1976).

Evron, Y. "Israel and the Atom; The Uses and Misuses of Ambiguity." *Orbis,* 17 (Winter 1974), pp. 1326–1343.

Idem. Israel's Nuclear Dilemma (Tel Aviv: Hakibbutz Hameuhad, 1987). [Hebrew]

Idem. "Some Effects of the Introduction of Nuclear Weapons in the Middle East." In A. Arian, ed. *Israel; A Developing Society* (Tel Aviv: Sapir Center, 1980), pp. 105–126.

Feis, H. *Churchill, Roosevelt, Stalin: The War They Waged and the Peace They Sought* (Princeton, NJ: Princeton University Press, 1967).

Feldman, S. *Israeli Nuclear Deterrence: A Strategy for the 1980s* (New York: Columbia University Press, 1982).

Ferro, M. *The Great War* (London: Routledge, 1973).

Foot, R. J. "Nuclear Coercion and the Ending of the Korean Conflict." *International Security* XIII, 3 (Winter 1988–89), pp. 92–112.

Forster, K., and O-K Tam. "Chinese Fiscal Reform."*Chinese Economic Studies* XXIV, 1 (Fall 1990), pp. 5–14.

Fredericus Rex. (G. B. Holz, ed.) *Werke,* Vol. IV, *Militaerische Schriften* (Berlin: Mittler, 1913).

Freedman, L. *The Evolution of Nuclear Strategy* (New York: St. Martin's Press, 1981).

Gaddis, J. L. "Containment: A Reassessment." *Foreign Affairs* 55 (July 1977), pp. 873–887.

Gallois, P. *The Balance of Terror; Strategy for the Nuclear Age* (Boston, MA: Houghton Mifflin, 1961).

Ganguly, S. "Avoiding War in Kashmir." *Foreign Affairs* LXIX, 5 (Winter 1990–91), pp. 57–73.

Garlan, Y. *War in the Ancient World* (London: Chatto & Windus, 1975).

Gat, A. *Clausewitz and the Enlightenment* (Oxford: Oxford University Press, 1989).

Gelber, H. *Nuclear Weapons and Chinese Policy,* Adelphi Paper No. 99 (London: International Institute for Strategic Studies, 1973).

Ghaus, A. S. *The Fall of Afghanistan, an Insider's Account* (London: Pergamon-Brassey's, 1988).

Godwin, P. H. B., ed.*The Chinese Defense Establishment: Continuity and Change in the 1980s* (Boulder, CO: Westview Press, 1983).

Golan, G. *Yom Kippur and After: The Soviet Union and the Middle East Crisis* (London: Cambridge University Press, 1977).

Gong, G.*The Standard of "Civilization" in International Society* (Oxford: Clarendon Press, 1984).

Goodman, D., and G. C. Segal, eds. *China at Forty: Mid-Life Crisis?* (Oxford: Clarendon Press, 1989).

Goodman, H., and W. S. Carus. *The Future Battlefield and the Arab–Israeli Conflict* (New Brunswick, NJ: TransAction Publishers, 1990).

Government Publishing House, *Falsificators of History* (Moscow: 1948).

Gray, C. *The Future of Land-Based Missile Forces* (London: International Institute for Strategic Studies, 1978).

Idem. "The Most Dangerous Decade: Historic Mission, Legitimacy and

Dynamics of the Soviet Empire in the 1980s." *Orbis* XXV, (Spring 1981), pp. 13–28.

Gregor, A. J., and M. Hsia Cheng. *The Iron Triangle: U.S. Security Policy for Northeastern Asia* (Stanford, CA: Hoover Institution Press, 1984).

Guennee, B. *State and Rulers in Later Medieval Europe* (Oxford: Basil Blackwell, 1985).

Gupta, A. "The Indian Arms Industry; A Lumbering Giant?" *Asian Survey* XXX, 9 (September 1990), pp. 846–861.

Gurtov, M. *China Under Threat* (Baltimore, MD: Johns Hopkins University Press, 1980).

Haffner, D. L. "Bureaucratic Politics and 'Those Frigging Missiles'; JFK and the U.S. Missiles in Turkey." *Orbis* XXI (June 1977), pp. 307–334.

Hagerman, E. *The American Civil War and the Origins of Modern Warfare: Ideas, Organization, and Field Command* (Bloomington, IN: Indiana University Press, 1989).

Halperin, M. H. *Nuclear Fallacy: Dispelling the Myth of Nuclear Strategy* (Cambridge, MA: Ballinger, 1987).

Hardgrave, R. L. *India Under Pressure; Prospects for Political Stability* (Boulder, CO: Westview Press, 1984).

Harrison, S. S. *In Afghanistan: Baluchi Nationalism and Soviet Temptations* (New York: Carnegie Endowment, 1981).

Hect, E. "The Yom Kippur War on the Golan Heights—6 to 10 October 1973," Unpublished Paper (Tel Aviv, 1987). [Hebrew]

Heikal, M. *Autumn of Fury* (New York: Random House, 1983).

Idem. The Road to Ramadan (London: Sphere, 1974).

Heilbrunn, O. *Conventional Warfare in the Nuclear Age* (London: Allen & Unwin, 1965).

Hersch, S. M. *The Samson Option: Israel's Nuclear Arsenal and American Foreign Policy* (New York: Random House, 1991).

Herzog, H. *The War of Atonement* (London: Futura, 1975).

Hintze, O. "The Commissary and His Significance in General History; A Comparative Study." In F. Gilbert, ed. *The Historical Essays of Otto Hintze* (New York: Oxford University Press, 1975), pp. 267–302.

Hobbes, Th. *Leviathan* (London: J. M. Dent, 1947 ed.).

Holloway, D. *The Soviet Union and the Arms Race* (New Haven, CT: Yale University Press, 1983).

Jayaramu, P. S. *India's National Security and Foreign Policy* (New Delhi: ABC Publishing, 1987).

Jervis, R. *The Meaning of the Nuclear Revolution: Statecraft and the Prospect of Armageddon* (Ithaca, NY: Cornell University Press, 1989).

Idem. Perception and Misperception in International Politics (Princeton, NJ.: Princeton University Press, 1976).

Joffe, E. *The Chinese Army After Mao* (London: Weidenfeld & Nicolson, 1987).

Johal, S. "America's Arming of Pakistan; Indian Views in the 1950s and 1980s." *Strategic Studies* IX, 2, (Winter 1986), pp. 68–79.

Jomini, A. H. de *Traité des grandes opérations militaires* (Paris: Dumaine, 1804–1816).

Kahalani, A. *Oz 77* (Tel Aviv: Schocken, 1976). [Hebrew]

Idem. A Warriors's Story (Tel Aviv: Steimatzky, 1989). [Hebrew]

Kaku, M., and D. Axelrod. *To Win a Nuclear War; The Pentagon's Secret War Plans* (Boston, MA: South End Press, 1987).

Karniol, P. "Taiwan's Space and Missile Program." *International Defense Review* (August 1989), pp. 1077–1078.

Karsh, E.*The Cautious Bear: Soviet Military Engagement in Middle East Wars in the Post–1967 Era* (Boulder, CO: Westview Press, 1985).

Idem, and I. Raufsi. *Saddam Hussein: A Political Biography* (New York: Free Press, 1991).

Kaufmann, W. F., ed. *Military Policy and National Security* (Princeton, NJ: Princeton University Press, 1956).

Kavic, L. *India's Quest for Security: Defence Policies, 1947–1965* (Berkeley, CA: University of California Press, 1967).

Keefer, E. C. "President Dwight D. Eisenhower and the End of the Korean War." *Diplomatic History* X, 3 (Summer 1986), pp. 275–289.

Keegan, J., and A. Wheatcroft. *Zones of Conflict: An Atlas of Future Wars* (New York: Simon & Schuster, 1986).

Kennan, G. *Memoirs* (Boston, MA: Little Brown, 1967).

Kennedy, P. *The Rise and Fall of the Great Powers: Economic Change and Military Conflict from 1500 to 2000* (New York: Vintage Books, 1987).

Khrushchev, N. S. (S. Talbot, trans.) *Khrushchev Remembers* (London: Sphere Books, 1971).

Kinnard, D. "The Soldier as Ambassador: Maxwell Taylor in Saigon, 1964–65." *Parameters* XXI, 1 (Spring 1991), pp. 31–46.

Kissinger, H. A. *The White House Years* (London: Weidenfeld & Nicolson, 1979).

Knorr, K., and T. Read, eds. *Limited Strategic War* (Princeton, NJ: Princeton University Press, 1962).

Koebner, R. *Empire* (Cambridge: Cambridge University Press, 1961).

Krishna, R."India and the Bomb." *India Quarterly* XXI, 2 (April–June 1965), pp.119–137.

Krossney, H., and S. Weissman. *The Islamic Bomb* (Jerusalem: Adam & Kastel, 1982). [Hebrew]

Laird, R. F., and D. R. Herspring. *The Soviet Union and Strategic Arms* (Boulder, CO: Westview, 1984).

Lall, A. *The Emergence of Modern India* (New York: Columbia University Press, 1981).

Lambeth, B. S. "Selective Nuclear Options and Soviet Strategy." In J. J. Holst and U. Nerlich, eds. *Beyond Deterrence* (New York: Crane, Russak & Co., 1977).

Lanski, M. B. "People's War and the Soviet Threat: The Rise and Fall of a Military Doctrine." *Journal of Contemporary History* XVIII, 4 (October 1983), pp. 619–650.

Laqueur, W. *The Guerrilla Reader* (New York: Meridian, 1977).

Idem. The Road to Jerusalem (London: Weidenfeld & Nicolson, 1968).

Leach, E., S. N. Mukherjee, and J. Ward, eds. *Feudalism: Comparative Studies* (Sydney: Sydney Association for Studies in Society and Culture, 1985).

Lee, N. *China's Defence Modernisation and Military Leadership* (Sydney: Australian National University Press, 1989).

Lenin, V. I. "Draft of Thesis on the National and Colonial Questions at the Second Congress of the Communist International" (1920). In *Selected Works* (London: Lawrence & Wishart, 1946), Vol. 10, pp. 231–238.

Leshem, D. "Surface to Surface Missiles in Iraq." Study No. 33 (Tel Aviv: Jaffee Center, 1990). [Hebrew]

Leveiro, A. "Task Force Razor Shaves Big Apple 2." *The Army Combat Forces Journal* 5 (June 1955), pp. 38–43.

Lewis, J. W., and X. Litai. *China Builds the Bomb* (Stanford, CA: University of California Press, 1988).

Liddell Hart, B. H. *The Ghost of Napoleon* (New Haven, CT: Yale University Press, 1933).

Idem. Strategy (New York: Praeger, 1967).

Liebenthal, K., and M. Oksenberg. *Policy Making in China; Leaders, Structures and Pressures* (Princeton, NJ: Princeton University Press, 1988).

Lind, W. S. "Report to the Congressional Reform Caucus on the Grenada Operation." (Washington, DC: Military Reform Institute, April 1985).

Lomov, N. A., ed. *The Revolution in Military Affairs* (Moscow: 1973; USAF trans., Washington, DC: U.S. Government Printing Office, n.d.)

Louis, V. *The Coming Decline of the Chinese Empire* (New York: Salisbury, 1984 ed.).

Lovejoy, C. D., and B. W. Watson, eds. *China's Military Reforms: International and Domestic Implications* (Boulder, CO: Westview Press, 1986), pp. 1–14.

Luttwak, E. N. *The Grand Strategy of the Soviet Union* (New York: St. Martin's, 1983).

Idem. "Just Cause—A Military Score Sheet." *Parameters* 20 (March 1990), pp. 100–101.

Idem. Strategy: The Logic of War and Peace (Cambridge, MA: Belknap Press, 1987).

MacDonald, C. A. *Korea: The War Before Vietnam* (New York: Free Press, 1986).

Maddil, D. L. "The Continuing Evolution of the Soviet Ground Forces." *Military Review* 62 (August 1982), pp. 52–68.

Mao, Tse Dong. *Selected Works* (London: Lawrence & Wishart, 1954).

Ma'oz, M. *Asad: The Sphinx of Damascus* (New York: Grove Weiden-feld, 1988).

Marx, K., and F. Engels. *The German Ideology* (London: Lawrence & Wishart, 1938).

McLellan, D. *The Thought of Karl Max* (London: Macmillan, 1971).

Meinecke, F. *Machiavellism; The Doctrine of Raison d'État and Its Place in Modern History* (London: Routledge & Kegan Paul, 1957).

Milhollin, G. "India's Missiles—with a Little Help from Our Friends." *Bulletin of the Atomic Scientists* (November 1989), pp. 31–35.

Millis, W. *Military History,* No. 39 (Washington, DC: Service Center for Teachers of History, 1961).

Mirchandani, G. G. *India's Nuclear Dilemma* (New Delhi: Popular Books Service, 1968).

Mosse, G., ed. *Police Forces in History* (London: Sage, 1975).

Nanteuil, H. de. *Daru et l'Administration militarie sous la Révolution et l'Empire* (Paris: Peyronnet & Cie, 1966).

Nee, V., and S. Sijiri. "Institutional Change and Economic Growth in China: The View from the Villages." *The Journal of Asian Studies* 49 (February 1990), pp. 3–25.

Nitze, P. "Deterring Our Deterrent." *Foreign Policy* 25 (Winter 1976–77), pp. 195–210.

Nixon, R. M. *The Memoirs of Richard Nixon* (London: Sidgwick and Jackson, 1987).

O'Ballance, E. *The Electronic War in the Middle East, 1968–70* (London: Faber & Faber, 1974).

Oestreich, G. *Neostoicism and the Origins of the Modern State* (London: Cambridge University Press, 1982).

O'Neill, W. L. *Coming Apart; An Informal History of America in the 1960s* (New York: Quadrangle Books, 1971).

Osgood, R. E. *Limited War; The Challenge to American Strategy* (Chicago: Chicago University Press, 1957).

Idem. Limited War Revisited (Boulder, CO: Westview Press, 1979).

Paltzgraff, R. I, *et al.,* eds. *Emerging Doctrines and Technologies: Impli-*

cations for Global and Regional Political–Military Balances (Lexington, MA: Lexington Books, 1988).

Parker, G. *The Army of Flanders and the Spanish Road* (London: Cambridge University Press, 1972).

Patil, R. L. M. *India—Nuclear Weapons and International Politics* (New Delhi: National, 1969).

Pean, P. *Les deux bombes* (Paris: Fayard, 1982).

Perjes, G. "Army Provisioning, Logistics and Strategy in the Second Half of the Seventeenth Century." *Acta Historica Academiae Scientarium Hungaricae*, No. 16, 1965.

Polanyi, K. *The Great Transformation* (London: Golancz, 1946).

Rais, R. B. "Pakistan's Nuclear Program: Prospects for Proliferation." *Asian Survey* XXV (April 1985), pp. 458–472.

Rao, V. R. C. "China's Missile Capability." *Mainstream* 24 (May 1980), pp. 5–6.

Raviv, Ch. "The Failure: an Egyptian Version." *Bamachaneh* (22 October 1986), pp. 9–10. [Hebrew]

Rhodes, A. *The Making of the Atomic Bomb* (New York: Simon & Schuster, 1988).

Rose, L. E. "Pakistan's Role and Interests in South and Southwest Asia." *Asian Affairs* IX, 1 (September–October 1981), pp. 50–65.

Rosen, S. "Nuclearization and Stability in the Middle East." *The Jerusalem Journal of International Relations* I, 3 (Spring 1976), pp. 1–32.

Rothstein, R. L. *The Third World and United States Foreign Policy* (Boulder, CO: Westview, 1981).

Rousset, C. *Histoire de Louvois* (Paris: Didier, 1862).

Royal United Services Institute (RUSI), ed., *Defence Yearbook 1984* (Oxford: Brassey's, 1984).

Rubinstein, N. "Notes on the Word *Stato* in Florence Before Machiavelli." In R. G. Rowe and W. K. Ferguson, eds. *Florilegium Historiale, Essays Presented to Wallace K. Ferguson* (Toronto: University of Toronto Press, 1971), pp. 313–326.

Rubinstein, R. A. *Moscow's Third World Strategy* (Princeton, NJ: Princeton University Press, 1988).

Sabine, G. H. *A History of Political Theory,* 3rd ed. (London: Harrap, 1964).

Saikal, A., and W. Malley, eds. *The Soviet Withdrawal from Afghanistan* (London: Cambridge University Press, 1989).

Samad Khan, A. "The Indo-Pakistani Rivalry and the Sub-Continental Security Calculus." *Strategic Studies* IX, 1 (Autumn 1985), pp. 15–45.

Sarvepalli, G. *Jawaharlal Nehru—A Biography* (Cambridge, MA: Harvard University Press, 1984).

Sawherry, R. G. "Pakistan's Military Capability." *Journal of the Institute for Defense Studies and Analysis* XVI, 3 (January–March 1984), pp. 195–214.

Schelling, T. *Arms and Influence* (New Haven, CT: Yale University Press, 1966).

Schiff, Z., and E. Ya'ari. *Intifada* (London: Weidenfeld & Nicolson, 1989).

Schmitt, C. *The Concept of the Political* (Reading, MA: Harvard University Press, 1960).

Scott, H. F., and W. F. Scott. *The Soviet Art of War: Doctrine, Strategy and Tactics* (Boulder, CO: Westview Press, 1982).

Scoville, H. "Flexible Madness?" *Foreign Policy* 14 (Spring 1974), pp. 164–177.

Segal, G. C. "China's Nuclear Posture for the 1980s." *Survival* XXIII, 1 (January–February 1981), pp. 11–18.

Idem. Defending China (Oxford: Oxford University Press, 1985).

Idem. "Strategy and Ethnic 'Chic.' " *International Affairs* 60 (Winter 1984–85), pp. 15–30.

Service, E. R. *Origins of the State and Civilization: The Process of Cultural Evolution* (New York: W. W. Norton, 1975).

Shao, Chen Leng, ed. *Change in China: Party, State and Society* (Lanham, MD: University Press of America, 1987).

Shazly, S. *The Arab Military Option* (San Francisco: American Mideast Publications, 1986).

Shennan, J. W. *The Origins of the Modern European State, 1450–1725* (London: Hutchinson, 1974).

Shi, Hong. "China's Political Development After Tiananmen: Tranquility by Default." *Asian Survey* XXX, 12 (December 1990), pp. 1206–1217.

Siddiqi, A. R. "Nuclear Non-Proliferation in South Asia; Problems and Prospects." *Strategic Studies* X, 4 (Summer–Autumn 1987), pp. 109–124.

Singh, M. P. "The Crisis of the Indian State." *Asian Survey* XXX, 8 (August 1990), pp. 809–819.

Snow, E. *The Long Revolution* (New York: Random House, 1972 ed.).

Sokolovsky, V. D. *Military Strategy* (New York: Praeger, 1963).

Spector, L. S. "New Players in the Nuclear Game." *Bulletin of the Atomic Scientists* (January/February 1989), pp. 29–32.

Spinney, F. *Defense Facts of Live* (Boulder, CO: Westview Press, 1986).

Spinoza, B. *Tractatus Theologico–Politicus* (Leiden: Brill, 1979).

Steinbrunner, J. D. *The Cybernetic Theory of Decision: New Dimensions of Political Analysis* (Princeton, NJ: Princeton University Press, 1974).

Strayer, J. R. *On the Medieval Origins of the Modern State* (Princeton, NJ: Princeton University Press, 1970).

Subrahmanyam, K., ed. *Nuclear Myths and Realities: India's Dilemma* (New Delhi: ABC Publishing, 1981).

Idem., ed. *India and the Nuclear Challenge* (New Delhi: Lancer International, 1986).

Idem. "Pakistani Credibility Gap." *Journal of the Institute for Defense Studies and Analysis* XIV, 1 (July–September 1981), pp. 105–127.

Subramahnian, R. R. *India, Pakistan, China: Defense and Nuclear Tangle in South Asia* (New Delhi: ABC Publishing, 1989).

Summers, H. *On Strategy* (New York: Del Books, 1982).

Talmon, J. L. *The Origins of Totalitarian Democracy* (London: Secker & Warburg, 1952).

Tammen, R. I. *MIRV and the Arms Race* (New York: Praeger, 1973).

Taylor, A. J. P. *Europe, Grandeur and Decline* (Harmondsworth, Middlesex: Pelican Books, 1950).

Taylor, M. D. *The Uncertain Trumpet* (New York: Harper, 1959).

Thomas, R. G. C. "India's Nuclear and Space Programs: Defense or Development?" *World Politics* XXXVIII, 2 (January 1986), pp. 315–344.

Toulmin, S. *Cosmopolis: The Hidden Agenda of Modernity* (New York: Free Press, 1990.

Trofimenko, H. "The 'Theology' of Strategy." *Orbis* 21 (Fall 1977), pp. 497–515.

Truman, H. S. *Memoirs,* Vol. I: *The Years of Decision* (Garden City, NY: Doubleday, 1955).

Tucker, R. W. "Israel and the United States: From Dependence to Nuclear Weapons?" *Commentary* (November 1975), pp. 29–43.

Turney-High, J. H. *Primitive War: Its Practice and Concepts* (Columbia, SC: University of South Carolina Press, 1971).

U.S. 95th Congress, Senate, 1st Session, Committee on Armed Services. *NATO and the New Soviet Threat* (Washington, DC: U.S. Government Printing Office, 1977).

Verzberger, Y. I. "Bureaucratic–Organizational Politics and Information Processing in a Developing State." *International Studies Quarterly* XXVIII, 1 (March 1984), pp. 86–101.

Idem. *China's Southwestern Strategy: Encirclement and Counterencirclement* (New York: Praeger, 1985).

Idem. *Misperceptions in Foreign Policy Making: The Sino–Indian Conflict, 1959–1962* (Boulder, CO: Westview Press, 1984).

Waldon, A. "The Warlord; Twentieth-Century Chinese Understanding of Violence, Militarism, and Imperialism." *American Historical Review* XCVI, 4 (October 1991), pp. 1073–1100.

Weber, M. *General Economic History* (London: Allen & Unwin, 1923).

Whiting, A. S. *The Chinese Calculus of Deterrence* (Ann Arbor, MI: University of Michigan Press, 1975).

Wirsing, R. G. "The Siachen Glacier Dispute." Parts 1, 2, and 3. *Strategic Studies* X, 1 (Autumn 1987), pp. 49–66; XI, 3 (Spring 1988), pp. 75–94; and XII, 1 (Autumn 1988), pp. 38–54.

Yaniv, A. *Dilemmas of Security: Politics, Strategy, and the Israeli Experience in Lebanon* (Oxford: Oxford University Press, 1987).

Ziring, L. *Pakistan: The Enigma of Political Development* (Boulder, CO: Westview Press, 1980).

INDEX